INTERPLAY

Some books by the same author:

Collected Poems 1987
Selected Poems 1990
Under the Circumstances
Old Men and Comets

*

Memoirs of a Mendicant Professor
The Alluring Problem: An Essay on Irony
Fields of Vision

*

The Oxford Book of Death
The Oxford Book of the Supernatural

INTERPLAY

a kind of commonplace book

D. J. Enright

Oxford   New York

OXFORD UNIVERSITY PRESS

1995

Oxford University Press, Walton Street, Oxford OX2 6DP

Oxford New York
Athens Auckland Bangkok Bombay
Calcutta Cape Town Dar es Salaam Delhi
Florence Hong Kong Istanbul Karachi
Kuala Lumpur Madras Madrid Melbourne
Mexico City Nairobi Paris Singapore
Taipei Tokyo Toronto
and associated companies in
Berlin Ibadan

Oxford is a trade mark of Oxford University Press

British Library Cataloguing in Publication Data
Data available

Library of Congress Cataloging in Publication Data
Enright, D. J. (Dennis Joseph), 1920–
Interplay : a kind of commonplace book / D. J. Enright.
p. cm.
1. Enright, D. J. (Dennis Joseph), 1920–
—Notebooks, sketchbooks, etc. 2. Commonplace-books.
I. Title.
PR6009.N6I53 1995 821'.914—dc20 94-48447

ISBN 0-19-282493-7

1 3 5 7 9 10 8 6 4 2

Typeset by Graphicraft Typesetters Ltd., Hong Kong
Printed in Great Britain
on acid-free paper by
Bookcraft (Bath) Ltd
Midsomer Norton, Avon

Contents

Title explained   xi

Family rules — Improper study of mankind —
Childhood and schooldays — What my father told me —
Unearned moral capital — *Poètes maudits* — An amatory
dilemma — Self-sacrifice to one's self   1

Children — Young murderers — Sex education — The
age of innocence — Original sin — A scholar in the
making   9

Frankenstein's 'monster' and the wife he almost had —
Paradise lost and retrieved — Freud and the Impartial
Person — The Superman/woman   19

A degree of order — 'Good writing' — Dementia in
reviewers — A 'dying literary landscape' — Effects of
reading   23

'The guardianship of the Muses', and of bridges —
Švejk in an asylum — Wilde as reviewer   28

Linguistic mayhem and 'mute points' — Literally speaking
— All too human, humorous — An antiquary — Japanese
inventions — 'Night words'   30

Tradition, its eternal recurrence — ''Tis Lilith!' 'Who?' —
Faust, parts and preferences   35

Definitions and perversions — The man who ate a
dictionary — Mysterious expressions — What's in a title?

— 'We all quote' — The trials of the translator —
Grammatical permissiveness: 'The Queen may have
married several suitors'   39

Canetti on 'China' — The defining and self-defining of
nations — 'A grand night' — *Ars erotica*   49

Universal history — God as a sphere — And as a
metaphor — Aphorisms: miniature jewels or performing
fleas?   54

Anecdotiana — Young George Eliot's favourite reading
— No surprise in Eden — Wanted, a more earthly
relationship — A pillow book — A talk on Modern
Verse Drama — 'Horrid operations'   58

Professors, profaners — Biography as the slayer of
literature — 'Areas soiled by poets' — Warning to writers
— Admonitory instances   68

Good and evil, uncloistered virtue and censorship —
'Some clapped-out judge' — The philosophy of horror
films — Horrible images easily conceived   73

Affectionate exhortations to the young — Grub Street
still new — To achieve fame it is advisable to be famous
— The truth about an author — From a genuine
commonplace book — Trollope as a preacher —
Philistinism and political continence — The Wimsatt
Law — Touching little stories — Nietzsche on television
— An inheritance   76

'Time corrupts all' — How to encourage the purchase of
books — Sorrows of a Publisher — Sorrows of an
Author — Conspirators in retirement — On being
overqualified — The impudence of computers   90

Realism and fantasy — An unexpectedly happy marriage
— Sad fate of a children's novel — A true fairy tale   97

The deaths of others — 'Clever talk disrupts virtue':
Confucius in brief — Dreams, cruel and consolatory, 'not
planted for nothing' — A Proustian dream — Freud on
the subject — 'An uninterpreted dream is like an unread
letter'   102

J'accuse — Genius allied to moral insanity — Irony and
sentimentality — Scribbling cats   111

Shifty bosses — Government, art of the impossible? —
Bribe v. bonus — The nasty name 'moralist' — Exciting
job prospects — Communicators and talent consultants
— The Royal Family — Honours won and lost   117

Divine philosophy — 'Not just a new car, a new life-
style' — Inverted romanticism — Writers who put us
down — 'The news is always blood and dead'   127

'The game goes on briskly' — Mencius tackles a vexed
question — Coleridge on Ireland — A dream of the IRA
— Touched by Allah — Samizdats and diacritical marks
— Babylon as a tourist centre — A thank-you letter   132

Nietzsche as aphorist — 'A god who begets children on a
mortal woman' — The greatest German tragic idea —
'Yes and No are lies'   142

Schopenhauer read as literature — Flowers, and their
essence — Immortality — Religion's bad conscience —
Legends, allegories, and truths   146

Sayings of Lichtenberg — A good metaphor: 'something
even the police should keep an eye on' — Books, those

strange wares — The forests are getting smaller — A
horse who preferred Horace to Pope 151

Where do babies come from? — Body and soul —
Ecumenicalism in translation, and elsewhere — Kafka on
stealing the devil's thunder — Swift on the Lord's Day —
Natural law — Charitable appeals — Doubts, desires and
devices — Jesus's last words — And the Bishop of
Durham's 155

Reading between the lines — Beware the common touch!
— English literature in foreign parts — The British
Empire in disgrace — The stitching together of nations
— De Quincey on English 'eating up all other languages'
— The Leavises at home and abroad 165

Brilliant French academics in Egypt and their beautiful
pupils — Compared with British teachers and their
students — Barthes on beefsteak, *le catch, sinité,* and
striptease 176

Men and women — Wives and husbands — Socrates and
his high-spirited beast — Political corrections — Is rape a
civil offence? — Demise of the maternal instinct — Plato's
objection to poetry as nurturing sex and violence 179

Superstitious fear of writing things down — Horrible
imaginings — Yet writing is a means of getting rid of one's
thoughts — How to make the best use of your mind 188

Brave words — Vernon Lee on adjectives — Iris
Murdoch on art enabling us 'to look without sin upon a
sinful world' — The 'immense expense of art' —
Television adaptations of the classics — On nothing
being intrinsically superior to anything else 190

The best tunes — The noise of parties, the poetry of
earth — On not being shocked any more — The haiku:
no time for a rhyme?   195

Literary theories and proclamations of purpose — A
deconstruction — A ludic critic — Signs without
wonders — Research topics — Wittgenstein on good
will and vanity   198

A saga of sickness — 'Best before end of . . .' — Elderly
person in the underground — Not an inn but a hospital
— Toilet training   208

Doomed boys in Mann, Emerson, and others — Before
the Fall, Adam's inability to understand the words 'good',
'evil', and 'die' — The child compared with Adam   215

The art of living, and of dying — Well-meant
commonplaces — A Jewish joke? — An elementary form
of decency — Word without end — Small mercies and
large — 'To the bed's-foot life is shrunk' — Heaven at
hand — Night visitors — Cantankerous thoughts —
Rights of ways — Love as a subject — Satire is easier —
An epitaph — A neurosis — An epigraph   218

Acknowledgements   237

INTERPLAY

One always had misgivings about oneself. Now it appears that other people are no better, and some of them worse. This is embarrassing.

—Tao Tschung Yu

In fine, it is our being. It is our all in all. Things that have a nobler and richer being may accuse ours, but it is against nature that we should despise and carelessly set ourselves at naught. It is a particular infirmity, which is not seen in any other creature, to hate and disdain himself.

—Montaigne

'INTERPLAY', for reasons that are obvious, even if 'play' isn't always. 'A kind of', admitting to hesitancy, hinting at hope. 'Commonplace', as concerns some places, in its common meaning. 'Book', because printed pages bound together are called a book.

❦

Family rules, old-style

Keep your head down where it belongs.

Remember you are not common, you are like everybody else.

Being polite doesn't mean you have to smile at policemen.

Remember that medicine costs money. Make sure you empty your bowels or vomit promptly after taking.

One day they will invent special paper for it. In the meanwhile cut the newspaper into neat squares.

Play with the boys at school, don't bring them home, you don't know what it might lead to. Cousins are enough.

They say it takes all sorts but liquorice sweets are safer, except when offered by strangers.

If your dad is called Mick as like as not he is Irish. But don't dwell on it.

Don't dwell on anything.

Think how lucky we are. There's a depression and it makes no difference.

You may not have pocket money but you have pockets.

The coalhole is where the coal is kept. The bath is where we would wash if we had one.

Rice pudding is for every day. Senna is for Fridays. Vimto is for Christmas.

If you've been at the vinegar again it will dry up your blood, but don't imagine it will make you drunk.

Think of the workhouse as a hospital for old people, but don't speak of it.

Once They have noticed you They won't leave you alone.

Politics, cocktails and concubines are for Them, not you, and don't keep asking questions.

If little pitchers have big ears they'll get clipped round them.

Go to church regularly while they pay you to sing in the choir, or why did we send you to Sunday school?

Don't forget to ask God to bless the Co-op too.

Pay as you buy. If you can't pay, don't buy.

Count the change, even in Piper's Penny Bazaar.

Books are all right but don't let them give you ideas.

Don't write down the rules. As a rule, don't write anything down.

Our folk—not disenchanted because never enchanted. Hardly disappointed since barely appointed. Not given to disowning, nor much to owning. No marked disesteem since not too much esteem. Disgrace where little grace? Discomforted, after what great comfort? Or dispossessed? Scarcely in disarray, seeing how arrayed. After such little content, what great discontent? Yet disengaged? No, somehow still engaged, for ever it seems.

Identity crisis? Searching for it. Hoping to be helped to find it. Succouring it. Good gracious! Far more a question of hiding it, disowning it, letting chosen (or sometimes hapless) bits be glimpsed now and again, as and when . . . No offence intended ever. Only defence—and the sole arms those Stephen Dedalus allowed himself: silence, exile (but to just round the corner), and cunning.

The improper study of mankind is man . . . Anaïs Nin, a case in point. Diaries, biographies, autobiographies . . . they make one realize how egregiously stolid, unenterprising, faint-hearted and insensitive one is. One neglected to sleep with one's mother or father, one omitted to seduce one's psychoanalyst (one omitted to acquire a psychoanalyst), one failed to engage in love-triangles or quadrangles with famous figures (perhaps one knew no famous figures), one shirked having an abortion in a backstreet, one never came into money suddenly, one never found oneself literally penniless (only metaphorically). Can one belong to the same species, one asks oneself. One doesn't even keep a diary.

When I was a kid the local newspaper was full of births, marriages, and an occasional death, fêtes, school sports and speech days, new flower-beds in the Jephson Gardens, the benign doings of the town council, and the odd petty larceny. Now my local paper is packed with muggings, murders, rapes, drugs, hit-and-run accidents, and the closing of public baths and lavatories. Is this the result of improved communications?

Next you'll be wittering on about the days when you didn't think of locking the front door. True, you didn't own anything worth stealing.

3

'Time was when, in the pastoral retreat,
Th'unguarded door was safe; men did not watch
T'invade another's right, or guard their own.
Then sleep was undisturb'd by fear, unscar'd
By drunken howlings; and the chilling tale
Of midnight murder was a wonder heard
With doubtful credit, told to frighten babes.
But farewell now to unsuspicious nights,
And slumbers unalarm'd! Now, ere you sleep,
See that your polish'd arms be prim'd with care,
And drop the night-bolt . . .'

—William Cowper, *The Task*, 1785

You would be more certain of the smallness of the life you gave up
if you were more certain of the largeness of the life you took up.
And vice versa. (This assumes that you are really concerned to be
sure in matters of this nature.)

When I was a youngster . . . The sister of a friend, she was six or
seven years older, had a baby, though she wasn't married. This
was awful, just about the ultimate in unspeakable shame. And
you might actually bump into her in the street. Then she had
another, whether by the same man or not I can't recall and
probably never knew. This—for she wasn't the local idiot girl,
she was an intelligent woman—was something else, it had to
be. There must have been a reason. But what? No one ever told
us.

The school caretaker was 'living with' a woman. For some reason
unknown to us—we knew there *was* a reason—they couldn't get
married. They were obviously very much in love; it was clear even
to us insensitive schoolboys. You could tell when you saw them
together, from time to time, in the school grounds. They shone
with tenderness and devotion. None of us ever called out a bad

word, or whispered it, or made a rude sign. So what was so special about marriage, then, what was it for?

In *The True Paradise*, his posthumously published memoir of growing up in Ceylon (as it then was), Gāmini Salgādo tells how he was stopped by a policeman for crossing a main road against a red light. He said that his mother had just died, and the embarrassed policeman waved him on with a caution. Young Gāmini felt ashamed of himself.

This reminded me of how at school I got myself excused from writing a poem, an occasional homework task, when I told the teacher that my father had just died. I didn't feel ashamed in the least. There was nothing I hated so much at fourteen as writing poems to order.

Perhaps when something bad happens—something which is likely to bring dimly envisaged but miserable consequences—a child will try to gain what he or she can out of it, to turn it to some small immediate advantage. Perhaps not only a child.

Had it been my mother who died, I would have asked for a whole week off school.

One thing my father told me I have never forgotten. (Mostly what he talked of had to do with remote unlikely matters like Gallipoli and Brian Boru.) It seemed enormously significant. 'You can always be sure who your mother is, but you can never be sure of your father.' It didn't strike me for a moment that this was a slur on women, on my mother. Nor, I'm certain, did my father intend it as such, or know that he was echoing Aristotle. He may have been hinting, via an elementary biological joke beyond me, that he himself had no very grandiose conception of fatherhood and its responsibilities as touted in England. Indeed, I supposed that this indubitable though dark pearl of wisdom meant that you could rely on your mother, she was always there, whereas your father only turned up in the evenings, and wasn't always entirely himself. And soon died anyway—which clinched it.

5

Saving up

Whatever the fate might be of
whatever it was that wasn't the body,
and to which, engaging yourself in the
good of others, you never paid heed,
the question was always beyond you
(beyond us all, though some don't deem it)—
the object, in one so little inclined
to save for herself, was to set aside
enough for the body's lodging, no pauper's,
but 'laid to rest', for the final time
(virtually the first), this comprising
the only care you showed for your own—
and more truly a care still for others,
for their amour propre, and their purses.

Wilfrid Mellers's mother, nicknamed 'Beetle', was a great woman. Once, when some early affection had met with a setback, she told me (it was the first time I had heard it, at any rate the first time it meant anything), 'When one door shuts, another opens.' The dictionary, I now see, describes it as a Spanish proverb.

She and her husband, 'Stol', seemed to have an amicable arrangement, never remarked on, whereby she was romantic and (up to a point) fanciful, and he was rational and realistic. (A fruitful parentage for a future musician.) Stol was a dedicated pipe-smoker. When they were first married, Beetle took it into her head that his pipes were a filthy, smelly old lot, what you would expect of a bachelor, so she stewed them for hours in a cauldron of soapy water. Notwithstanding this fearful vandalism, they stayed married. People were hardier plants in those days.

One good thing about not going to a public school was that you didn't get recruited to spy for the Soviet Union. I was at Cambridge, but nobody approached me. Scholarship boys didn't have a guilty conscience (or not the right sort).

6

Reminded of him by a reference in a poem by another civil servant, C. H. Sisson: 'the poet with his floppy hair' who 'courted ladies who were not his wife'. Humbert Wolfe! I recall an intense, brief enthusiasm for him. An unlikely introduction to modern poetry? But you don't choose, these things just happen, they work in hidden ways.

Do I dare go back to him? I think I'll choose not to revisit that bit of the past.

People who admire the great working class, which they barely know. You did your best to get out of it. Don't expect them to admire you.

People who carry with them a large sum of unearned moral capital. You grope in your pocket for a groat's-worth. How sure they are! How unprincipled they make you feel. How shabby. Maybe you are rather shabby.

'Don't send your children to a private school!' You don't, perforce. You notice that they send all theirs to private schools.

'Of course you *must* use the National Health Service!' You do, perforce. You discover that their families go private.

> 'The class whose vices
> he pilloried was his own,
> now extinct, except
> for lone survivors like him
> who remember its virtues.'
>
> (Auden: 'Marginalia')

It was great, being finely decadent when everybody else was stuffily respectable. But now that everybody's degenerate, and in some cases depraved to a degree you could never have imagined, what remains to be? A eulogist of the good old respectable days, when you knew what you were.

What happened to the *poètes maudits* of yesteryear? These days you are more likely to hear of a businessman *maudit*, or a broker, an estate agent, an MP, or even a bishop.

'You can't make a Hamlet/without breaking eggs,' Michael Foley writes mockingly. The last *poète maudit* I knew personally (*not* the Rimbaud of Cwmdonkin Drive) had a hard time living up to specifications. Poets ought to suffer, and he courted suffering to the point of virtually forcing his wife into infidelities of a recherché kind—in order to ensure a steady supply of misery, of accursedness, on which to nourish his art. It drove him to drink, and a premature end.

Once, in a rare moment of *bonhomie*, he presented me with one of his early books, crossing out the previous inscription, which was to his wife.

Trapped in an amatory dilemma, the young man cries out in anguish, 'Oh this post-modern sex!' Those within earshot catch their breath. Can they help? But what exactly does he mean?

Perhaps the scholars will throw light. One of them defines post-modern as 'characterized by a superabundance of disconnected images and styles'. Doesn't seem to fit. Or, 'a culture of fragmentary sensations, eclectic nostalgia, disposable simulacra'—pardon?—'and promiscuous superficiality, a random swirl of empty signals'. And recently someone else summed it up as 'battles without a war'. All that, and him so young?

More likely his dilemma has to do with superabundance of free speech, intellection it's called, or even thrashing things out. First you sleep with girls, then the arguments set in. For us pre-moderns it was contrariwise, fragmentary sensations maybe, but war all the way, without much in the shape of arguments. 'Please', 'No', 'Yes', 'Oi!' Tongue-tied is what we were; though our signals couldn't be called empty.

Post-modernism must be terribly exhausting. The lad will have to keep his strength up. All we can do is advise him to eat well and sleep (preferably alone) as much as he can.

'To say that each man should sacrifice himself to the good of all is in my view a false principle,' said Goethe. 'Each man should sacrifice himself to his own conviction.'

> 'I was of delicate mind, I stepped aside for my needs,
> Disdaining the common office. I was seen from afar and
>   killed . . .
> How is this matter for mirth? Let each man be judged by
>   his deeds.
> *I have paid my price to live with myself on the terms that I*
>   *willed.'*

Kipling's ignoble, slightly comical occurrence—a soldier prefers not to urinate in company—issues in a weighty conclusion. So much packed into that last line, just one line. All that's needed is a further line, speaking for those, less happy, who weren't free to will the terms they would live on, and still paid a price.

Children. Three snippets from Clarice Lispector's *Discovering the World*:

'One of my sons when he was very little announced with great excitement: —People say we're in the twentieth century, is that true? —Yes, I replied, watching his anxious expression. —Gosh, Mummy, we are behind the times!'

'The little boy: —Mummy, I saw a baby hurricane, but so small and feeble that all it could do was to send three tiny leaves swirling gently round on the pavement.'

'When the hour of parting comes: —You do understand, don't you, Mummy, that I can't love you like this for ever and ever.'

Our grandson, then four years old, was told to amuse himself while lunch was being prepared. 'I shall sit by myself,' he said obligingly, 'and think of all the things I know.'

Children aren't *quaint*. Nor *cute*, though often disconcertingly acute. Their senses are fresh, their responses undimmed by custom, and they say the things we would like to say but are too old to. When we were of the right age, we must have lacked the necessary genius; or else no one was listening.

Given the depravity of adults, we can only hope that children are not as innocent as probably most of them are. Hence the soothing charm of books, from *A High Wind in Jamaica* to *Lord of the Flies*, that represent them as callous, cruel, malign, 'the bad seed', possessed by the devil (as in the *Exorcist* and *Omen* films, lurid successors to *Rosemary's Baby*), at very least 'little egoists' (Freud), and the curious thrill derived from, say, B. M. Gill's *Nursery Crimes*, described by the blurb as 'a deliciously wicked black comedy'. A judge helpfully opines that an eight-year-old victim of sexual abuse is herself 'not entirely an angel'—as if some fictional character called Lolita were in the dock. Hence the shabby relief we feel on hearing of a thirteen-year-old in America who is on a murder charge and has sixty-five previous convictions, or the Leeds boy, also thirteen, arrested between fifty and sixty times and dubbed by the police 'a crime wave all on his own'. That couldn't possibly have been *our* fault, could it?

The abduction and killing in 1993 of two-year-old James Bulger by two boys aged ten can have given few people any sort of relief. Being, as the press commented, 'incredible', 'inexplicable', 'unimaginable', the event probably hasn't lacerated many consciences either.

How young murderers happen. In 1956 we—my wife, our daughter, and I—returned to England from Japan by P & O. We had flown out there by Comet; we came back by sea simply because we had no home or job to go to, and the voyage took around five weeks during which we were fed and housed.

At Hong Kong a horde of unruly British children joined the *Chusan*. Their fathers, businessmen or officials, weren't due for leave; their mothers passed the time playing bridge in a first-class lounge. The children seemed barely to know them; they had been given over to the care of amahs, and some spoke Cantonese more readily than English.

One of them, a girl of eight or nine years, attached herself to us; more particularly, and fiercely, to my wife. She hung around us most of the day; at night she did her utmost to stay in our cabin. Me she saw as a nuisance, surplus to requirements, and went for me one bedtime with her nails. Our daughter, then five and a half, posed a greater threat. She had plans for her.

One morning our daughter had gone off to join other children in the play area. We were walking along the deck when we saw the girl methodically pushing her between the rails; being the bigger and stronger, she had got her halfway through. A few seconds later, and there would have been another juvenile murderer, another nursery crime.

We tracked down the mother at her bridge and told her what had happened. Chastened, if barely surprised, she promised to keep the girl by her, and did so for the rest of the voyage.

Simple lack of affection . . .

A mixed-race couple—the wife a Guyana-born Indian—apply to adopt a child of mixed race. Questioned by the local adoption council, they state they are happy where they live, in Norfolk, and have suffered no discrimination, though the wife admits to having experienced a small amount of verbal abuse while at school. This, the husband says, was 'not the answer the official wanted to hear'. The application is turned down, on the grounds that they haven't suffered racial abuse and therefore are 'too racially naïve' to be trusted with a child of mixed race. The couple don't mind what kind of child they adopt, but the catch is, because of their 'background' they are restricted to a child of mixed race.

('If I tell you you've suffered from racism, then you've suffered. If you disagree, you must be bloody dim!')

You can't stop people giving birth to babies. You can't stop them neglecting or ill-treating them. But when a decent loving couple want to *adopt* a child—watch out, they could be perverts, at best simpletons! Let's make it as difficult as we can!

Are adoptable children so rare, then? The world, you would think, is full of orphans.

Another area in which our grudging or jealous attitude towards children manifests itself is sex education. From a Family Planning Association workbook for primary schools: 'Exercise for 4–7 years. Materials: large pieces of paper, felt tips, Sellotape, labels with names of body parts including sexual and reproductive organs (e.g. nipples, penis, vagina, testicles, pubic hair) . . .' ('What we want is, Facts': *mutatis mutandis*, it sounds like Mr Gradgrind.) It appears from a newspaper report that the Association insists on the need for under-11s to be informed about heterosexual AIDS, which means explaining homosexuality, about lesbianism, the sensitivity of the clitoris, and the whereabouts of the labia. (This brings to mind the well-meaning demand for multi-religious teaching, equally likely to leave children confused.) The idea is to 'try to help', in that children as young as four are exposed to television programmes about various and often violent forms of sexual behaviour (easier to ban such television programmes, I'd have thought), and because they are vulnerable to sexual abuse.

It may be that after all this is a sphere in which self-help, though devious, scrappy, often failing ludicrously, is the best we can hope for. But yes—and with abuse, that fashionable evil, in mind—it is painfully difficult to know what to do, or whether. Our world isn't made for innocents. Yet the more we tamper with innocence, the more guilt we engender. And who is to do this teaching, who are to be the engineers of young souls? People endowed with uncommon sense and sensibility, not necessarily people who show themselves eager for such employment. Almost as hard to track down as Milton's ideal censors.

Do we have the right to impoverish human life, its diversity, by taking away that unique time, that experience, of sexlessness?

An association should be formed to provide classes for us adults, to show us what we might have been. I imagine the 'materials' would consist largely of music, though not what the BBC offers as 'Music in Our Time'.

The Chinese, it might appear, had no illusions about the innocence of babes or their need for sex education. In *Things Chinese* (1892) J. Dyer Ball mentioned the towers of northern China, provided to house the bodies of dead infants. Separate orifices, on opposing sides of the structure, served to keep the sexes apart and thus obviate any temptation to immorality among the baby ghosts. Yet this, it could be argued, was no more than a bizarre manifestation of a general and exquisite sense of propriety. The same chronicler related that it was bad form to ask a man to repay what he had borrowed from you; instead, you would request a loan from him equivalent to the amount owed.

The age of innocence. Given that neither parent was a happy example to youth and innocence, the court might be expected to nominate some respectable third person *in loco parentis*, except that no such person was known to those involved. Hence Maisie is bundled back and forth between her divorced parents, and then between succeeding spouses and lovers; a pawn, a pretext, a means of scoring points or getting even. By her absence she enables the permutated couples to play their game of musical beds; by her presence she keeps them 'perfectly proper'.

For Maisie 'concealment had never necessarily seemed deception; she had grown up among things as to which her foremost knowledge was that she was never to ask about them . . . Everything had something behind it: life was like a long, long corridor with rows of closed doors.' She has a doll, Lisette, to whom on one occasion she behaves as adults behave towards her. She is convulsed by the doll's innocence precisely as adults go into shrieks of laughter at her naïve questioning. There are 'things she really couldn't tell even a French doll'. 'Find out for yourself!' she tells Lisette, mimicking her mother. Corruption, you might reckon, is well under way.

But children must be allowed to play their games too. And Maisie's intentions are ingenuously good, as when, hearing that some girls are taught by masters, she proposes that the gentleman now living with her mother might become her tutor, for that would make it 'right', just as having for her governess the mistress of her father makes it right for them. She wants to bring people together; she wants, as children do, domestic stability. When her remarks are gratifying, she is a sweet little thing; when they are not, she is a heartless little beast; when her percipience is neutral in tendency, she is a 'funny old man'. In defence she learns the 'pacific art of stupidity', but isn't very good at it. That we are not positively invited to laugh at her must have required immense literary skill! It would have taken much less to make us cry.

'Oh I know more than you think!' She knows all about 'bolting', and that it's an ugly word. She knows what 'compromised' means: a condition rather like being left alone in the dark or slapped with a hairbrush, and neither of these ordeals is held to have as much effect as it ought. But what does she know? In the end everything, except . . .

In his preface James alludes with laboured scorn to the old charge that faces observers of manners, conveyed in such terms as 'painful', 'unpleasant', 'disgusting'. He has himself been lectured for 'mixing up' a child with unseemly goings-on. One half expects him to declare that he cannot praise a cloistered virtue. But *What Maisie Knew* truly is a painful book, and one effect of its devilish cleverness is the desire to wipe the knowing look off James's face. The reader is cast in the role of multiple voyeur, spying on the child and, through her sketchy intimations, on the adults. But granted, the reader will be less embarrassed on this head than simply anxious for Maisie. Her people are such monkeys that it would be better for her—though of course out of the question, for hasn't she at very least two fathers, two mothers, and two homes, 'six protections in all'?—to be taken 'into care' by the local council.

The author makes no bones about exploiting the child: 'so handsomely fitted out, yet not in a manner too grossly to affront probability, she might well see me through the whole course of my design', as he horribly puts it in the preface. Without her mediation how could he have told, how could he have got away with, so shocking, so squalid a story?

But then, it has to be admitted, Maisie was lucky. She had Henry James for a godfather. She was not a real little girl.

In our time, Leon Edel has suggested, James would be profoundly concerned with 'what the cinema and the television communicate to the impressionable and plastic receiving consciousness of childhood'. He would watch television? He would go to the cinema? He would write letters to *The Times*? But Edel has made a good point on the side.

On the other hand . . . The manager insists they returned your credit card to you, oh most certainly. You can't find it. You have looked upon the wine when it was red (white, actually), you may have put the card in your socks, up your sleeves, anywhere. They don't have it. You can't locate it. They want to close. 'What can we do?' you mumble feebly. Your five-year-old grandson, apparently snoozing after his chicken baguette and apple tart, shouts out: 'Call for the police!' And the card is promptly discovered, tucked between two plates at the rear of the restaurant. Out of the mouth of . . .

Passing a lenient sentence on a man charged with killing his baby by dropping it on its head from a height, the judge informed the prisoner that he had a good record and that the affair had 'had an impact' on him. One might have thought it was the baby who suffered the impact. Can it be held that worrying over the misuse or infelicitous use of language is nothing more than aesthetic quibbling?

(According to an account of wartime atrocities fairly distant in time and place, the employment of prisoners as targets in bayonet practice was a means of helping raw recruits to 'acquire guts'.)

Another judge told a man who had killed his baby by shaking it violently: 'Your wife has forgiven you. So I forgive you too.' A hard sentence: condemned to live with the Christlike forgiveness of the judiciary.

In the paper: the story of an eighteen-month-old boy whose parents are both dying from AIDS-related diseases. When he reaches the age of two, he will be tested for the virus himself. The mother became pregnant by accident, and didn't realize the fact until she was seven months gone and it was too late for an abortion. She is quoted as saying that if the test on the little boy should prove positive, she will never believe in God again. 'Why did God let me get pregnant when he knew I was HIV positive?'

Why did God let her get to be HIV positive? Why did God allow AIDS to come into the world? Why . . .? Once we start this questioning, where will it end? But at least where children are concerned— 'he who offends one of these little ones . . .'—we can hardly refrain. This is our Lisbon earthquake.

The rot set in with Lewis Carroll's Alice, who, 'though slightly too passive to qualify as one of the new breed of naughty children, has great trouble trying to remember the improving poems she has been made to learn, and instead recites inspired nonsensical parodies' (Peter Keating), and with such authors of books for children as S. R. Crockett, whose *The Surprising Adventures of Sir Toady Lion* (1897) bore the provocative subtitle, 'An Improving History for Old Boys, Young Boys, Good Boys, Bad Boys, Big Boys, Little Boys, Cow-Boys, and Tom-Boys'. 1897 also saw the publication of *What Maisie Knew*. Henry James didn't go in for subtitles.

18 February 1994: 'A boy aged 16 yesterday admitted a plot to extort £100,000 from two wealthy women by threatening to kill their children. The boy appeared at Winchester Crown Court, where he admitted three charges of blackmail. The case was adjourned for the preparation of psychiatric reports.'

But why psychiatric reports? This is simply part of the enterprise culture: the boy is obviously well up in current affairs and has followed, to the best of his youthful abilities, the lead of his elders and equivalents. Money is the root of all good. The laudable end justifies the unorthodox means. You may never be found out.

If you are, hire a psychiatrist of your own.

'Imagine a number of men in chains, all condemned to death, some of whom each day have their throats cut in full view of the others, those who remain seeing their own condition in that of their fellows and, looking at one another with grief and without hope, await their turn. This is the image of the human condition.'

Even Pascal, who could bring himself to accept anything so long as it was allowed that man was 'made for thinking' and his weakness was his greatness, granted that the transmission of sin was the mystery furthest removed from our understanding. 'Without doubt nothing shocks our reason more than to say that the sin of the first man has rendered guilty those who are so distant from that source as to seem incapable of sharing in it.' The flow of guilt from that source strikes us as not only impossible but most unjust. 'What could be more contrary to the rules of our miserable [*sic*] justice than to damn eternally a child incapable of will, because of a sin in which he seems to have played so little part that it was committed 6,000 years before the child came into being?'

The answer, substantially the old one ('God moves in a mysterious way'), is that without this mystery, the most incomprehensible of all mysteries, we should be incomprehensible to ourselves. So this is an instance in which reason ought to submit, for 'there is nothing so consistent with reason as this denial of reason'. Submit to what? To 'the heart', which has its reasons that reason knows nothing of? That would entail a definition of 'heart' curious by any standard.

Thomas à Kempis, not given to cleverness of this kind, simply remarked that if the works of God were readily understandable by human reason, they wouldn't be wonderful. All this reasoning makes one sick at heart.

Oh that these autumnal browsings could bring a spring to one's heels!

Bad baby

The baby cries without reason
This is original sin
The baby declines to sleep at night
For no discernible reason
Which is original sin
The baby sicks up perfectly good food
It messes its nappy
The moment the nappy is changed
This is original sin
The baby bites its mammy
Which is original
The baby does not trust its daddy
Or whatever the male person is
This is unreasonable
The baby is thrown against the wall
It is dropped on its head
This is not original at all
For this there are reasons.

A scholar in the making. Showing his primary-school project on electricity, how it is made and what it does. The last page is headed 'BIBLIOGRAPHY'. You ask him if he knows what the word means. 'It's . . . it's a sort of shopping list.'

'Make me happy, and I shall again be virtuous.' A common story by now, but we gave the claim more credence when it issued from the mouth of Dr Frankenstein's 'monster'. 'My virtues will necessarily arise when I live in communion with an equal . . . and become linked to the chain of existence and events from which I am now excluded.' The monster displays a deeper knowledge of human nature than his creator possessed, and at least as good a prose style. He was asking for a companion, a female (in this following his favourite reading, *Paradise Lost*, which perhaps he never finished), one with whom he could live 'in the interchange of those sympathies necessary for my being'.

This is sound Christian doctrine. 'It is not good that the man should be alone,' the Lord said: 'I will make him an help meet for him.' The thought may have occurred to Dr Frankenstein that vices can arise equally well—or, his mind running more on vices than on virtues, better—when one lives in communion. He knew what the interchange of sympathies could lead to, what the events to be participated in were; the only chain the monster deserved to be linked to was a strong iron one. The solitary may not be especially virtuous, but nor is he likely to be conspicuously vicious. Hence, having begun to fashion a help meet for the monster, the Doctor had second thoughts, and destroyed her.

The new Eve might have given birth to a race of devils. Unless she was to have been unnaturally prolific, this may not strike us as a serious threat: Adam and Eve had two sons (one of whom died young), then another when Adam was 130 years of age, and (we are told) an unspecified number of sons and daughters during the next 800 years, the rest of his days. Not a great score for so long a life. (And where, one wonders, did Cain's wife come from: another rib-delivery? Some scholars have proposed that she was of a pre-Adamite race about which nothing else is known, albeit a seventeenth-century Jewish writer contended that Gentiles are descendants of that race.) Moreover, Frankenstein reflected, Mrs Monster might desert her mate for the 'superior beauty of man'. (We presume this beauty is of the skin-deep variety.) If handsome men recoiled from her—she was to be created 'equal', no more alluring physically than her

Adam—then she would simply rape them. Ah, the sexual jealousy of the other, the alien race, overgrown, oversexed, and over here in Switzerland!

As it is, we shall never know whether the couple could have achieved respectable domesticity, virtuous and happy, a Philemon and Baucis, he farming Frankenstein's land, she cooking and cleaning at the big house.

Here today. Talmudists say that Adam spent only twelve hours in Eden, presumably from the misty morning till the cool of the day. They spell out what occurred hour by hour: thus, during the sixth hour Adam gave the animals their names, during the seventh Eve became Adam's mate, during the eighth they ascended to bed as two and descended as four, i.e. Cain and his twin sister were born, or perhaps just conceived. (This may answer the question posed above: Cain's wife was not rib-delivered but his normally engendered sister.) In the twelfth hour they were expelled.

Hardly time to unpack the gardening tools, let alone get to know your bride. We hear it took 311 years to complete the Talmud. But God moves swiftly, on occasion. Why should he waste time, his or theirs, why prolong the agony (or, which comes to the same thing, the enjoyment)? He knew how it would end. Best if they didn't settle in. And there was a world waiting elsewhere.

Digital technology, we are told, can produce and promulgate an adapted, mutilated or parodied text. This portends the death of the author, but also promises the birth of any number of authors. You are dissatisfied with the conclusion of *Paradise Lost*? Then simply rewrite it.

The Archangel Michael is handed a last-minute stay of execution, the Lord in his mercy having decided that the guilty pair were not entirely responsible for their actions. Michael makes sure the serpent hasn't crept back into the garden. He orders the border guards, an élite body of cherubim, to stand at ease, except for those detailed to chop the tree down. This done, he invites the two humans to return.

> They hand in hand, with forthright steps and fast,
> Retrace through Eden their familiar way.

Freud submitted that the Bible story had reversed the original myth, some 'apprentice priest' having got it wrong. Eve was Adam's mother, the *man* gave the *woman* a fruit to eat (ancient marriage ritual), and what was at issue was the motif of mother-incest, 'the punishment for which, etc.'.

Outside the confines of psychoanalysis, the Bible story is a good deal more germane.

The Socrates of Our Time

The Impartial Person has heard that the analyst fixes an appointment with the patient, listens to him, talks to him in turn, and gets him to listen.

'So it's a kind of magic,' the Impartial Person says. 'You talk, and blow away his ailments.'

'Quite true,' Freud replies. That's to say, it would be magic if it worked rather faster. But analytic treatments take months, even years. All the same, the *word*, and many words will be spoken and listened to during those months or years, can be regarded as a sort of magical act.

Later on the Impartial Person (who is not to be supposed an utter fool or a sitting duck: he is 'trying to understand') remarks that it all seems 'a strange anatomy of the soul—a thing which, after all, no longer exists at all for the scientists'.

'What do you expect?' It is a hypothesis. Freud feels it unnecessary to appeal to the 'as if' which has become so popular, to Vaihinger and his *Als Ob*. (But he does.) The usefulness of such 'fictions' depends on how useful they are.

Unwisely, the Impartial Person uses the word 'pure' in connection with traditional psychology, and Freud asks him what he means by it. In an embarrassed, would-be tactful manner, the Impartial Person mentions reports which have it that 'the most intimate—and the nastiest—events in sexual life' come up for discussion during analyses, in every detail, so wouldn't it be better if such treatments were restricted to proper doctors, MDs, since they are recognized as people of discretion and good character?

It is true, Freud grants, that doctors enjoy certain privileges in the sphere of sex. 'They are even allowed to inspect people's genitals'—but not invariably, for they were prohibited from doing so in the East (no authority given), and some idealistic reformers in the West dispute the privilege (Tolstoy, James Strachey's footnote says). Moreover, sex isn't the only thing discussed with candour: financial circumstances are aired with equal openness and in equal detail. And furthermore, the analyst 'never entices his patient on to the ground of sex'; he merely allows him to say what he has to say, and before long what he has to say concerns sex. Why, he himself, Freud, always used to warn his pupils: their opponents contend that analysts will come upon cases in which the factor of sex plays no part, so they must be careful not to introduce the subject into analyses and spoil the chances of finding such a case. 'But so far none of us has had that good fortune.'

Then Freud suggests, somewhat ungratefully, that his interrogator's dislike of the stress placed on sexuality in the causation of neurosis is hardly consistent with his role as an Impartial Person. The Impartial Person apologizes for letting him down, and asks why he didn't choose someone else to fill the role. Because that someone else wouldn't have thought any differently, Freud explains. Or if he did, everyone would have exclaimed: 'Why, that is no Impartial Person, that is one of Freud's disciples!'

The dialogue ends with the Impartial Person—who hasn't been given much leeway, but has just made a vulgar crack in likening psychoanalysts to 'a new kind of Salvation Army'—being told that it doesn't really matter what he thinks. He has become a Non-Person. (See *The Question of Lay Analysis*, 1926.)

The Superman (including woman) is—the one who has gained starred firsts in a dozen different disciplines. Or, has made a fortune in some ecologically irreproachable industry and donated half of it to charity. Or, has written an epic poem quite as long as *Paradise Lost* but more relevant and in immediately intelligible language. Or, has led the nation through a number of victorious wars. Or, has remained married to the same woman/man all his/her long life in perfect and undivided amity. Or, has climbed Everest dressed in pyjamas and without oxygen or ice-axe . . .

No, Nietzsche got it right. The Superman/woman has to be the one who can actually endure, no, positively welcome, eternal recurrence, whose love of life is so powerful that he/she can knowingly live his/her own life over and over again, world without end. He or she will need to be a good, sweet person, albeit spiritually muscular, whose goodness and sweetness are fully approved by others who will preferably respond in similar terms. Or, since this sounds too undemanding for one so elevated, a person cheerfully capable of following Yeats's lines, 'I am content to live it all again and yet again . . .', even though it embraces all that folly, frog-spawn, and foulness, and . . .

This and this alone defines the Superman/woman. And in effect eliminates him/her from our inquiries.

THE CAREFUL connecting of phrases, the discipline (too martial a word) of syntax, and hence of thought, however modest, the arrival at a degree of order (order can be more than it sounds) in a world increasingly random and gratuitous, more abundant in assertion than in sense . . . Thus a rudimentary account of the continuing function of literature, or rather—for who can be sure what weight of responsibility it can still bear, what earnest expectation it can meet?—the mitigating intimations it holds out.

One pleasure in reading almost anything: focusing on a word or sentence and asking oneself how one would have put it. Gratifying if one's rephrasing seems an improvement. Pleasing if, seeing why it is how it is, one concludes that the writer got it right, righter than one would have oneself.

Clarity begins at home. Knowledge puffeth up, but clarity edifieth. Clarity suffereth long. It should stay at home.

Clarity became an object of scorn and pity in my youth. That none the less I kept up a jittery association with it stemmed from the sheepish feeling that obscurity was fine so long as you were clear about it in your own mind.

Am tempted to misquote a remark of Catherine Morland in *Northanger Abbey*: 'I cannot write well enough to be unintelligible.'

Curious, how the notion of 'good writing' has practically disappeared. Because 'good writing' is élitist? ('He/she writes well': it usually means there's nothing else to be said about him or her.) But more likely because it's just difficult to spot and be sure of.

I remember, in a past life, striving to get a young lecturer's contract renewed, on the grounds that, while he hadn't published, he was a good teacher. 'Ah,' said the Vice-Chancellor. 'But we are all good teachers. What we need is something more—objective.'

The Booker Prize, 1993. Possibly the chairman of the judges didn't see why he should have to explain the absence from the short list of Vikram Seth's *A Suitable Boy*. He did however let slip the opinion that the book should have been edited down (yes, it could with advantage have been reduced to some seven-eighths of its size), and that, despite the presence of private grief and public violence, it was 'bland'. The epithet must hint at the novel's innocence of cannibalism, serial killings, sexual psychopaths or shenanigans of any very extraordinary kind.

Blandness hasn't been a bar in the past, any more than a lack of stylistic innovation. (The 'experimental' is something we yearn to see, until we see it.) So perhaps the Prize committee ought in future to lay down a maximum length as a condition of entry.

True, *A Suitable Boy* is as long as five normal novels. But what are those normal novels you would have read instead?

Reviewing . . . The fly in the ointment (sometimes more fly than ointment), the grub in Grub Street, is that reviewers can't go on for long slating the books they are sent, nor can they too often decline a commission. Consequently—reviewers of fiction in particular— they are driven to extremes of ingenuity, not to say duplicity. And even, torn between what they actually feel and what they are ex- pected to say, they are plunged into a species of dementia.

Thus: 'I would have killed anyone who wrested this novel from my hands', a melodramatic protestation which begins with the word 'Nevertheless', conceding the reviewer's inability to admire the book. More frantic is another reviewer's verdict on another book: 'X's novel is the most loathsome novel I have read. I have read it twice to make sure and I am oppressed by a sickening, fatalistic feeling that I may soon read it again.' This abject confession was seized on by the publishers, who reproduced it in other papers with key-phrases in large print: 'most loathsome', 'read it twice', 'fatalistic feeling', 'read it again'. I thought I'd better check for myself, but couldn't get through the book once, it was so tedious.

In a quality Sunday paper: 'It should be impossible for a book to be almost unreadable yet still make compulsive reading.' A subtle point, worthy of the medieval schoolmen. The book in question concerns a brilliant academic with a taste for sado-masochism who dies of AIDS. It juxtaposes, we hear, an 'inimitably donnish style with situ- ations in which men are variously chained, tortured, urinated on and gang-banged'. Which is to say (a) the book is inimitable, (b) it has variety, and (c) the reviewer goes on to credit it with a moral:

'life without loving is nullity'. So that's all right then. Like *Fanny Hill*, whose author explained that if he had decked vice with flowers it was solely in order 'to make the worthier, the solemner sacrifice of it to virtue'.

To which, in the graceful poeticism of that bygone age, the answer is: 'oval reservoirs of the genial emulsion'.

In comparison the following simple encomia are barely up to scratch: '. . . readers of course will be better for knowing that Etonians masturbate, even if they had already guessed'; 'lashings of buggery and philosophy . . . He may shock but he will never bore'; and 'a tiny gem: 61 breathy depictions of masturbation which read like haikus tossed off by a mad mathematician. We learn how, where, sometimes why and usually to what effect in as little as two lines and never more than 21.'

After which, the hyping of another book as 'the ultimate reading machine' is positively homely. 'Where did you put the reading machine, dear?' 'It's under the stairs, with the vacuum cleaner.'

The authors' photographs on the jackets of such books have grown saturnine, menacing, sinister, 'Mephistophelian'. This has nothing to do with what (in 1966) Lionel Trilling called the adversary or subversive intention characterizing modern writing or 'the free creative spirit at war with the bourgeoisie'. The less we believe in 'evil', the more we like to play with it.

Otherwise, some 300 pages of high-grade paper, clearly printed, handsomely cased, maybe with ribbon bookmark . . . And we used to smile at the Japanese for their exquisite packaging of valueless trifles.

Easy to see the point of Umberto Eco's spoof review of a 'new' book entitled *Lady Chatterley's Lover*: 'Here, at last, is a clean, straightforward love story, absolutely unsophisticated, the sort of read our grandmothers used to enjoy . . . a book the younger generation should read. It would help them form a cleaner, more modest view of life, entertain genuine feelings, not adulterated, and develop a taste for simple, honest things, like the smell of new-mown hay or baking bread . . .'

An article in one of the Sunday supplements claims that England is virtually finished as a subject for novelists, nothing's going on, it's 'a dying literary landscape', and the brightest British novelists now turn to foreign parts for sustenance. The USA is *where it's all at*, exciting, virile, meaningful, throbbing with multifarious life . . .

But what does it matter that Julian Barnes, say, has occupied himself with a French fellow, Flaubert, so long as what he writes has general application and interest? (As Flaubert's writings do, perhaps despite himself.) And as for Bret Easton Ellis's *American Psycho* and its 'huge, ambitious subject', packed with real-life symbols—I'd say it was throbbing with multifarious death and packed with huge, ambitious boredom, and—a commodity to be found worldwide— with ordure. If the Americans do this kind of thing with greater brio and conviction than we do, so much the worse for them. (For all of us, alas.)

The writer of the article has it both ways, which must be a comfort to him. The best people don't write about England because it is dying. England is dying because the best people don't write about it.

There are those who insist that reading books about violence, serial killers and so forth, actually discourages the committing of violent acts. I wonder what they say about the books on sex.

They might claim that there is nothing more suggestive, more titillating, than reading what those old novelists didn't write about sex.

The belief that bad books can have a palpably bad effect doesn't require the seemingly associated belief that good books can have a palpably good effect. Logic is a fine thing, but it doesn't always operate in human affairs. On the whole we worsen more readily than we improve.

A LITERARY editor hesitates to send me books to review on the grounds that I am 'against criticism'. The characterization surprises me somewhat since I'd thought that what I was 'against' was specific kinds of criticism, notably that which preens itself at the expense of literature.

Coleridge wrote lots of criticism. Yet he remarked on how the critic rose as the author sank, noting the 'curious fact' that if the critic finds a passage or poem which he considers particularly worthless, he is sure to reproduce it in his review, thus wasting far more paper than the author did, since the print run of most periodicals is far larger than that of a book of poetry, 'in some, and those the most prominent instances, as ten thousand to five hundred'. The intellectual claims of the individuals he had in mind to 'the guardianship of the Muses' struck Coleridge as 'analogous to the physical qualifications which adapt their oriental brethren for the superintendence of the Harem'. In a less cutting analogy he added: 'Thus it is said, that St Nepomuc was installed the guardian of bridges, because he had fallen over one, and sunk out of sight.'

It takes rather longer for the critics to sink out of sight. Moreover, the saint in question was an upright priest, drowned—for refusing to tell the king what the queen had divulged during confession—by the bad King Wenceslaus IV, not to be confused with the good one.

Jaroslav Hašek was a great hoaxer, and once pretended to commit suicide by jumping off the Charles Bridge in Prague, at the spot where St John of Nepomuk was thrown in. Unfortunately the police arrived, and Hašek was removed to a mental hospital. But this paid off, for it enabled him to gather material for the chapter in

The Good Soldier Švejk relating the hero's adventures in a lunatic asylum. It was like being in paradise, Švejk thought; you could do or say whatever you liked and nobody reproached you; even the socialists hadn't conceived of such freedom. People could pass themselves off as God Almighty, the Virgin Mary, the Pope, the King of England, or St Wenceslaus—though the reckless fellow who claimed to be the good St Wenceslaus was stripped naked, tied up, and flung into solitary confinement.

You are commissioned to write a 3,000-word piece. Four words would suffice: 'The author is mad', or 'This work is bad.' But you write 3,000 words, and tell less of the truth. Indeed, by the sheer space you take over it, you tell a lie.

The trouble with him (or her), you would say, is that he (or she) can't write. Except that this doesn't matter. If publishers depended on authors who can *write*, their seasonal lists would be thin. Publishers admit, or proclaim, that too many books are being published (though not by the one who is speaking). True, no doubt. But if publishers are to cut back, you can be sure that the first authors to be dropped will be the ones who can *write*. So perhaps after all there is safety in numbers.

'. . . is about the inhabitants of a decaying cheese who speculate about the origin of their species and hold learned discussions upon the meaning of evolution and the Gospel according to Darwin. This cheese-epic is a rather unsavoury production and the style is at times so monstrous and so realistic that the author should be called the Gorgon-Zola of literature.' Why don't we get reviews like this nowadays? We do get publications comparable to *The Chronicle of Mites*.

For further examples of Oscar Wilde's reviewing—e.g., of a drama in blank verse: 'It may be said to possess all the fatal originality of inexperience'—see *Aristotle at Afternoon Tea*, edited by John Wyse Jackson.

The painful feeling as one looks at a book one is to review, a book of a more than commonly serious nature—that one doesn't *know* enough, not even for 600 carefully chosen words. The slight, sad, attendant surprise, for one had thought one knew a *bit* more at least on the subject. The nagging suspicion (or hope)—that once one *did* know more, and one has forgotten it. (One's memory, one remembers, is not what it was.)

Or can it be that these days you are quite properly, i.e. maturely, less *sure* of yourself, conscious that things are sometimes more complicated than careless youth and confident middle age assumed, and that there is more to be said (more than 600 words)? A kindly notion—but isn't it more likely that, out with it, that your mental powers are simply in decline. As it happens, in the book you are failing to review, it says rather germanely . . . Good, you are well into the 600 words requested.

(The editor observed of the above as originally phrased that the word 'one' occurred fourteen times in a single paragraph. So now there are two paragraphs, the word 'one' occurring nine times in the first and the word 'you' five times in the second. This makes for variety. The word 'I' does not appear at all, however.)

CLIVE JAMES's spoof, far from far-fetched, of an experienced journalist at work:

'X has finally flaunted one rule too many . . . Already cursed with chronic unemployment in the arts field, X was always one more Aussie expatriot than Britain needed. Do we need *any* of them? Its been a mute point up to now.'

Don't miss that (debatable) dangling participle. A curious variation on flaunt/flout occurs in a recent book subtitled 'In the Steps of J. B. Priestley': in Newcastle, 'when you are not disappointed your expectations are flounced'.

Ubiquitous is 'émigré' docked of its first accent; along with its fellow-sufferer, 'résumé', it can always be blamed on the typesetter, willing under duress to allow a word one accent but jibbing at two. It must have been a dogged compositor who was responsible for an advert in a Seychelles paper for a film starring Dennis Price. The name appeared as Dennis Prick. This was corrected in the next issue, which assured the public that the star was actually Penis Price.

'Deprecate' used instead of 'depreciate'—as if the person in question is positively deploring himself—is so common that *Collins English Dictionary* lists it as a synonym without a word of deprecation, albeit the *Concise Oxford Dictionary* still considers it a confusion. Not uncommonly one meets 'mitigate' where 'militate' is intended, and vice versa; there may still be a chance of restoring order here, but generally speaking usage mitigates abuse and militates against correctness. As Horace said, 'Many a word long dead will be born again, and others/which now enjoy prestige will fade, if Usage requires it./ She controls the laws and rules and standards of language' (Niall Rudd's translation). Why is a dog's breakfast a dreadful mess while a dog's dinner signifies flashy dressing? (Except when it means the same as dog's breakfast.) Reason not the reason.

An entry in the *Times Diary* referred to '. . . nine more stanzas, easily knocked off by a man of A. P. Herbert's felicity': what Clive James's journalist would term a mute point in that Herbert, who rhymed with facility, was indeed a felicitous rhymer. A local councillor interviewed on television asserted that some situation had been 'perpetrated', where the context suggested that 'perpetuated' was meant. On the morning of the 1994 France v. England match, in connection with England's inability to score tries, a *Times* sports reporter made mention of the country which only two years before had 'lauded it' over the others: a homophonic scuffle in the scrum. (The élite who went to listen to Emerson's lectures in 1856 were proclaimed 'the effete of Boston'.) In 1803 the amiable antiquary, Samuel Pegge, included among cockney peculiarities the deformation of 'scholar' into 'scholard', which he described as pretty general everywhere among the lower orders, and fashioned after such familiar words as 'coward', 'drunkard', etc. More recently I heard an ITN presenter announcing that a poor old person had died of pneumonia caused by emancipation; and an item on BBC News revealed that councils would be taken to court 'if they don't keep the streets clean, and the people too'. We expect so much from local government.

Curious, how people use the word 'literally' when they mean the opposite. Clarice Lispector writes (or her translator does) that 'between the ages of thirteen and fifteen . . . I literally devoured every book I could lay my hands on'. 'Devour' derives from *vorare*, to swallow, so you could be a voracious reader (simple metaphor) and devour books *tout court*. But literally devour? Chomp, chomp? 'This book made me literally throw up' might be fair enough.

'The crowd has literally gone mad,' the commentator cried when a goal was scored at last. (Had he said, 'The crowd has gone mad', we might think he intended it literally.) 'He literally took his head off,' another commentator said as one wrestler caught the other across the throat with a stiff arm. In a serious-minded piece in *The Times* we read that in the trade a certain BBC producer is 'a name— literally—to conjure with'; and on the morning of the Derby we heard that breeders were 'literally living from hand to mouth'. (Since the speaker was the BBC racing correspondent, the statement might be thought to have come straight from the horse's mouth.) 'I was literally burning with rage,' someone declared on television recently. Alas, we didn't see it, nor did we see the man who literally split his sides laughing or the woman who was literally frightened out of her skin by an intruder.

So 'literally' is now a stress mark, an emphaticism, signifying 'I am not joking', 'I really mean what I say' (or almost). Thus 'The government has literally thrown the baby out with the bath-water' is a *very* severe rebuke. 'I was literally in hell' and Prince Charles's description of life at Gordonstoun as 'literally hell' just about get by since hell survives chiefly as a much shrunken metaphor. No one is going to say, 'I was metaphorically burning with rage' or 'I devoured books, figuratively speaking'. All that, like the superannuated simile, is too mild for our vehement, assertive, apocalyptic times, when we live literally at the end of our tether.

A example of impeccable usage: when someone contended that poverty was a virtue, a bystander remarked, 'That is literally making a virtue of necessity.'

But tread warily, for it will not do to flout our superiority in these matters. It is only humane to er.

Erring humanly, sometimes humorously. An Englishman in Goethe's time is said to have expressed surprise that the father in the 'Erlking' ballad should be so agitated over his threatened child seeing that he had lots of offspring. Asked what evidence there was for this, he recited the line, 'Er hält in Armen das achtzehnte Kind' ('He holds in his arms his eighteenth child'). It was pointed out to him that the word was not 'achtzehnte' but 'ächzende' ('moaning'). And last week, in a London bus, when a child was struggling to decipher a BT ad, 'Jemand zu Hause möchte gern von Ihnen hören', her mother comforted her: 'You see, it's basically French.'

Samuel Pegge, the antiquary quoted above, tells a pleasant story, illustrative of the lengths scholars will go to, in his *Anecdotes of the English Language*. The name *Chiswick* is corrupted, 'as most others are', and should properly be written *Cheesewick*, the Saxon *wic* denoting a little harbour on the banks of a river. Chiswick was therefore 'the great emporium for cream-cheeses, made upon the Meads of Twickenham', which name itself contains a *wic* (here meaning a village or farm, in particular a dairy farm), a *ham* (hamlet), and an *en* ('being the termination of the Saxon Genitive Case'): 'So that the name is, as plain as can be, The *Wic's*, or *The Wicken Ham*, corrupted into *Thwickenham*, and thence to *Twickenham*. This appears from a Saxon Chronicle, once the property of Venerable Bede, and now in the Library of the Emperor of Morocco. This, among some other extracts of a like kind, was made by Humphry Llhuyd, who, when he was abroad, turned Mahometan for about a fortnight, on purpose to have a sight of this MS. from whence I am enabled to give several other extracts, as occasion may require. To remove all doubts, my informant, who received this account from Mr. Llhuyd, assured me, on the same authority, that any Christian might have the privilege of seeing the MS. on the same terms.'

A recent researcher tells us that the word *roricon* (portmanteau for 'Lolita complex') has now entered the Japanese language, along with *YMCA*, denoting call-girl organizations. And a news item reports the invention of a bra that plays Mozart, though when is not mentioned, nor what—perhaps 'Martern aller Arten'. Further signs of how far perversion has gone in the country . . . Not that the Japanese are necessarily more perverted than other people, for all that one might have supposed from the fiction of Tanizaki, Kawabata, Mishima *et al.* Western novelists have long since overtaken these unworldly aesthetes. No, they are merely more ingenious. As confirmed by the artificial hymen, intended to give the long-married husband an unexpected kick, reminding him (if the wife deems this tactful) of his wedding night. Thus not merely a consummation devoutly to be wished, but an incitement to marital fidelity and the stability of family life. Rumour has it that one husband grew so confused that he had a heart attack; he didn't know where he was.

In fact an Italian, twenty-six years old, has gone one better by patenting (May 1994) 'a condom with a microchip that warns of a break in the condom during sex by playing a theme from Beethoven'. 'Muss es sein? Es muss sein'?

The 'night words', George Steiner has said, the words once used only on the most private and intimate occasions (if then), are now 'the jargon of morning and noon'. What implications might this have? That after the incessant blaring of day and its 'carnal exactitudes', we shall lapse (or rise) into the new-found purity—at least inexplicitness—of night, into wordless dreams of spiritual love, spiritual lust even, sensations intense and yet curiously delicate and poignant? There must be some gain to be had somewhere, in this redistribution of discourse.

ONE form, or one recognition, of 'tradition' consists in 'modernizing' (crude term) the writings of the past, changing their outward apparel, relating them to current situations: by these interactions both showing respect and gratitude and reaffirming continuity. Parasitism? No: 'Why should the poet shrink from picking flowers where he finds them?' (Goethe). Nothing brings a bit of life into the present so much as a remembrance of the past. Mann's *The Magic Mountain* is a case in point.

During the Walpurgis Night scene in Goethe's *Faust*, the witches' carnival, Mephistopheles turns to his companion (victim, pupil), saying, ' 'Tis Lilith, see!' Faust, more ignorant in the matter than befits a former student of theology, asks, 'Who?' And Mephistopheles tells him, 'Adam's first wife is she', and—rather oddly, one might feel, but no doubt the devil knows his business, and commerce with a witch ranks lower in iniquity than the ruination of an innocent maiden—warns him to beware of her beautiful tresses: once a young man is caught in them he won't get away easily.

Carnival, in this case Fasching, is celebrated at Mann's International Sanatorium Berghof too, in a chapter entitled 'Walpurgis Night', on another mountain, magic in its own way. As Clavdia Chauchat swirls past, the temptress, the *femme fatale* who evokes the link between *l'amour* and *la mort*, Settembrini quotes, 'Look at her well . . . The fair one, see! 'Tis Lilith!' Whereupon his young

35

companion (and pupil), Hans Castorp, asks, 'Who?' (His ignorance of the national poet is more forgivable since he has trained as an engineer.) 'What Lily do you mean? Did Adam marry more than once? I didn't know.' So Settembrini explains that according to the Hebraic story, 'Lilith became a night-tripping fairy, a *belle dame sans merci*, dangerous to young men especially, on account of her beautiful tresses.'

Not that Settembrini, though he is battling with the Jesuit, Naphta, for Castorp's soul, is any sort of Mephistopheles. Each of these eloquent debaters, the radical and the reactionary, sees the other as a corrupter, a disciple of the devil in one shape or another. To have quoted so imprudently, the austere and determinedly rational Settembrini must have been temporarily disarmed by the spirit of carnival.

Clavdia, a Russian and therefore exotic, given to fingering the braids of her reddish-blond hair, has some kinship with Lilith: she provides Castorp with his sentimental education, a service which we suppose Lilith rendered for Adam. We might remember that it was not she who brought about Adam's downfall.

In any case Mann kept the Faust legend proper for later and more dreadful use. Among other things, *The Magic Mountain* is a *Bildungsroman*, and Hans Castorp, a direct successor to Goethe's Wilhelm Meister, the conventional 'still unwritten page': here an amiable, unremarkable young man who enters an Alpine sanatorium as a casual visitor, stays on, begins to question and speculate, and, while remaining amiable, becomes remarkable and representative. He is discharged into neither hell nor heaven, but into a world at war.

But Lilith, what a fascinating story hers would make! If only we knew more about her. But this shouldn't deter researchers. I see that someone, stating his sources with scholarly propriety (to wit, Isaiah, chapter 34), has already broached the question: 'The evidence suggests she was as much sinned against as sinning, and we must hope that, as a usually reliable source has envisaged, she will "find for herself a place of rest".' For instance in a memoir.

Assuming that verse 27 of the first chapter of Genesis, 'male and female created he them', refers to Lilith—it is not until verse 22 of the second chapter that Eve appears, fashioned out of Adam's rib, not simply 'created'—then what went wrong? Did Adam cast Lilith off for some reason? Did she grow bored with him and decamp? Why was she called a 'screech owl'? Was she a feminist *avant la lettre*? What part did God play in the breakup of the marriage? Could it be he had a 'soft spot' for her? What was the relationship between her and Satan? Did she introduce the art of snake-charming into the world? What truth is there in the charge that she subsequently abused children? What colour was her hair? What *made her tick*? It's all bound to come out one day.

Stop press. According to a character of Alice Thomas Ellis's—Lili (note the name), the narrator of *The Fly in the Ointment* (surely a reference to Beelzebub, Lord of Flies)—Lilith left Adam because she reckoned it was her turn to lie on top, but Adam dissented, he wanted to preserve his dominance, so she grew vast black wings and flew away in a rage, to live in desert places. Then Adam married Eve. Second wives, Lili says, are all the same, 'a push-over for door-to-door salesmen', and tell their husbands: 'Oh, darling, such a charming serpent called today and he sold me this apple. *Such* a bargain.' Which the husband, second time round and his confidence damaged, puts up with. Stupid Eve had betrayed the cause—to the point of having children; Lilith just couldn't stand children.

One function of literature in the mass: fitting things together, no matter how disparate or discrepant they appear. This doesn't make them all look alike.

'As the glittering wealth of lyric cascades past him, the reader of Part Two can only grit his teeth to think how little of it can be changed into the human currency of Part One' (*Commentary on Goethe's Faust*, 1949). My, what youthful imprudence, or impudence!

No doubt it is a sign of a continuing vulgarity, an inveterate sensation-seeking, still to smile with relief when the old Mephistopheles crops up in Part Two. For instance, when he intrudes on the labours of Wagner, erstwhile famulus, now a fully fledged experimental scientist with a laboratory of his own. Wagner is engaged in creating life through alchemical processes: 'A man is being made'; and Mephistopheles cracks a typically low joke: 'A man? So you have locked an amorous pair/Up in your chimney-stack somehow?' Wagner replies indignantly:

> 'Why, God forbid! That method's out of fashion now:
> Procreation's sheer nonsense, we declare! . . .
> By animals, no doubt, it's still enjoyed,
> But man henceforth, being so highly gifted,
> Must have an origin much more uplifted!'
>
> (David Luke's translation)

Mephistopheles' customary reductiveness elicits a risible exaltation of man.

The lively outcome, the Homunculus, addresses Wagner as 'dad' (*Väterchen*) and Mephistopheles as 'my mocking cousin' (*Herr Vetter*: 'a sort of kinship,' Goethe informed Eckermann). Briefly he sounds like Faust in those far-off beginnings:

> 'Since I exist, I must find things to do:
> I'd like to set to work this very day,
> And you know how to set me on my way.'

Unlike the others present, he can read the sleeping Faust's 'prophetic' dream of Leda bathing and the Swan approaching with some alacrity—a preparation for the Helena Act and, immediately, a motivation for the journey to Pharsalus, it being, as he 'recalls', Classical Walpurgis Night.

Mephistopheles ought to be pleased with the Homunculus, another demonstration of man's arrogance, here in usurping God's role as creator. Though perhaps the thought assumes a more direct reference back to the distant Prologue in Heaven and Mephistopheles' allusion to man as 'the little earth-god' than Goethe had in mind. (When a man has worked on the same subject over a period of some sixty years it won't be easy to tell what is in his mind, or what isn't.) Arriving so opportunely, Mephistopheles may have had some hand in the success of Wagner's endeavours; this is uncertain, but Goethe told Eckermann that he would try to think of inserting a few lines to make the point clearer. (Which in the event he didn't do.) During the ensuing fly-past of classical myths Mephistopheles does his best to retain his old identity, to keep his end up in the strange surroundings in which, he is told, he has no place: 'Dark ages are your proper habitat'—though Thessalian witches might hold some appeal for him.

Wrong-headed?—but not altogether unforgivable to want to make *Faust* more of a whole than it encourages you to do. It pains me to confess that I wish the work had stayed Gothic, dark-aged, or Romantic ('Romantic ghosts are all you lot know,' is the Homunculus's caustic remark to Mephistopheles). 'I call the Classical *healthy*, the Romantic *sickly*': Goethe to Eckermann, 1829. But the health is so remote, the sickliness so intimate. Better the devil you know than the one you don't—even if they tell you the latter doesn't exist.

THE WORDS contain the thoughts, they carry them lightly wrapped, wriggling slightly. Sometimes silly thoughts, it must be admitted, even nasty ones. The mind, though it likes to think otherwise, is just a channel for the words, words not invariably flooding in, but trickling steadily, with a minor overflow every now and then. Not merely the daughters of earth, virtually the sons of heaven as well. Can't pride oneself on intelligence or taste, when so much—can it be all?—is being done for one. (Don't fret too much over simple ignorance: one of the sources of poetry, says Wallace Stevens. But one isn't always writing poetry.) At most one resembles the humble worker who stands at a conveyor belt throwing aside the occasional spoiled fruit or lopsided matchbox. Yes, we are the People of the Book, the dictionary.

And the drow was dog . . . Dialectical, antithetical, and binary processes working in this sphere as in others, and books having already bred antibooks full of antimatter, there are bound to be compilations, discordances as it were, like the one reported by Christopher Reid: Dr Spillaine's *Contradictionary*, 'that vast rebuttal/of all established/lexicographical lore', in which 'there was hardly a word/whose accepted meaning/he had not contested', and which rested on 'his glorious disdain/for so-called alphabetical order'.

How marvellously useful it is, Marcus Aurelius reflected, to see things as they really are, their true nature laid open. For example (in Meric Casaubon's translation, 1634, of the *Meditations*), 'Coitus is but the attrition of an ordinary base entrail, and the excretion of a little vile snivel, with a certain kind of convulsion.' Ah, so that's what our word 'bonking' means?

'I see in the Bible a prophet whom God orders to eat a book. I don't know in what world Victor Hugo ate beforehand the dictionary of the language he would be called to speak; but I see that the French lexicon, issuing from his mouth, has become a world, a colourful, melodious and mobile universe': Baudelaire, reflecting on his contemporaries.

The word *maudlin*, 'weakly or tearfully sentimental, especially in a tearful and effusive stage of drunkenness', comes from 'Mary Magdalene', with reference, the *Concise Oxford Dictionary* adds, to pictures of her weeping. No matter whether you see the penitent sinner washing Christ's feet with her tears—Crashaw compared her eyes to 'two walking baths . . . portable and compendious oceans'— or the woman weeping at the empty tomb 'because they have taken away my Lord'.

You might think that such powerful associations would have forbidden so disrespectful, so contemptuous a usage. Surely people have been burnt at the stake for lesser offences. But *vox populi* has proved louder and more sustained than *vox Dei*. Ambrose Bierce commented in *The Devil's Dictionary*: 'With their Maudlin for Magdalen, and their Bedlam for Bethlehem, the English may justly boast themselves the greatest of revisers.'

Not too dissimilar is the current use of *gay*; and falling back on the colloquial and rare sense of 'immoral' doesn't improve matters. Eric Partridge has '*gay*: (Of women) leading an immoral, or a harlot's life: 1825'—as the penitent sinner once did. Inapt, for positively, peculiarly gay gays are rare in my experience, but unstoppable. *Collins English Dictionary* even gives 'homosexual' as the word's primary meaning, with 'carefree and merry' as its second.

Opening a dictionary at random and stumbling on a beautiful alternative to the grim word 'gerontology'—*nostology*, from the Greek, 'a return home'; related to 'nostalgia', where 'algia', also from the Greek, denotes a painful condition, though maybe nothing worse than wistfulness. *Nostologic* (adj.): to do with finding one's way back, perhaps by a lengthy, roundabout route. 'Go home now,' the poet wrote poignantly, 'you have fed your fill, the evening star is coming.'

Alas, the dictionary adds: 'with reference to second childhood', an expression defined in turn as 'dotage, senility'. Ignore it: dictionaries are not novels or poetry, not books of life; they bark abruptly and pass on. Like the goats to whom, as it happens, Virgil was addressing himself.

Short list of mysterious, seductive, fearful expressions

Agapemone	Lente, lente currite, noctis equi
Animula vagula blandula	Man is an onion
Ayenbite of inwit	Masculine ending
Couvade	Mastication of corpses
Criminal conversation	Nintendo
Defenestration	Odalisque
Entropy	Phantom aesthetic state
Extreme prejudice	Pig in the middle
Fumarole	Poor perdu
Ghost in the machine	Principalities and powers
Hibakusha	Psychopomp
Hidden agenda	Quantum of the sin
Hutch of tasty lust	Son of the morning
Incunabula	The star is called Wormwood
Ite missa est	They flee roaring to and fro
Ka	Turn down an empty glass
Laidly worm	Venusberg

But Ivan Morris remarked of Sei Shōnagon's catalogues of place-names, temples, poetic subjects, things that make the heart beat faster, and so forth, that however meaningful to the compiler, they might well be of no more interest to readers 'than arcane laundry lists'. An ever-present consideration.

'Literature as a profession is destructive; one should *fear* words more' (Canetti). Thrilling words, those! Some people write such very long books. To keep their spirits up? To show how fearless they are? They certainly scare me.

In length of days, understanding. Browsing through a not especially large English dictionary, and discovering that you don't know what 20 per cent of the words mean or how 30 per cent of them are pronounced.

It won't do to hold words responsible for one's difficulties, to blame them for their tendency to 'strain, crack and sometimes break, under the burden', their absence when needed, their presence when not . . . More ridiculous than cursing one's screwdriver or saw. As carpenters say, it's a bad writer who quarrels with his tools. Still, words can be exhausting. The common expression, 'going all round the houses', cropped up in a television comedy. Unthinkingly I began to explore it, I accompanied it step by step, round only too many houses. A long walk, an arduous circumlocution, for an imagination which isn't as young as it used to be.

And then that tricky expression, 'not half'. 'It isn't half bad' means 'not bad at all', i.e. 'good'. So I'm told. But 'you ain't 'alf awful', as we used to say in my childhood, means 'awful to an extreme degree'. The first usage is described by the *Concise Oxford Dictionary* as colloquial, the second as slang. This duality of sense appears to be a class indicator, the first form found among the middle classes, the second among the lower classes. Presumably the upper classes avoid the expressions altogether. So do I, because by now I'm hopelessly befuddled.

What's in a word? Quite a lot. The original title, *Alice's Adventures Underground* was not quite the thing: 'underground' is dull, and would come to have unsuitable associations, and everybody has adventures in books. At one point the author thought of *Alice's Hour in Elfland*, nicely alliterative but limiting. Then *Alice's Adventures in Wonderland*, whereupon the public dropped 'Adventures' and fondly made Alice more central. (You can just about discount the consideration that what you have long been used to seems only right, and the idea that a rose by absolutely any other name would smell exactly as sweet.)

Hypothetically speaking, how inferior *Alice Through the Mirror* would have been, though in its place 'Mirror, mirror on the wall . . .' is perfect, and 'to hold the mirror up to nature' is neat. And the public condensed Carroll's *Through the Looking-Glass, and What Alice Found There*, again bringing Alice to the forefront.

There's no such thing as a synonym. Which is why compilations of them are so splendidly serviceable: not merely helping you to find the right word but leading you towards the exact thought. As for 'wrong' words, a foolish but instructive parlour game is to rewrite Shakespeare with recourse to a thesaurus: 'Be extinguished, be extinguished, short-term source of illumination!'

What is essential to children's books—as distinct from some others—is good sense. In *Alice Through the Looking-Glass*, for instance, the explanation given by the Tiger-lily of why the flowers thereabouts can talk while others can't: because the ground is hard, whereas in most gardens they make the beds too soft and the flowers are always asleep. Also in Carroll, the punning version of the old saw is as valid as the original, or more so: 'Take care of the sense, and the sounds will take care of themselves.' A rose by *some* other name could smell as sweet.

Without a basis of logic, or at least a strong presence, fantasy is mere whimsy.

'The reader looks in vain for any immediate reason why Alice should have dreamt such a dream or for any very edifying result deriving from it': *Illustrated Times*, 16 December 1865, reviewing *Alice in Wonderland*. But easy to see why the author chatted fluently to children and started to stammer as soon as grown-ups came on the scene.

May 1994: an American correspondent, Harry Frissell, sends a cutting from the *New York Times* book review section featuring imaginary letters of rejection. An editor writes 'with great regret' to Mr Dodgson/Carroll listing a variety of objections to his novels. Given the dangers of smoking and the impressionable nature of children, the caterpillar should not be smoking a hookah; nor should a child be represented as eating a portion of mushroom, since some young reader might be led to eat a toadstool, and this could result in death and catastrophic litigation against the publisher. The Red Queen is found sexist and in other ways offensive: 'Think again—must she be fat? need she be female?' Finally the titles are lacking in warmth, and could profitably be changed to something like 'Jennifer Goes on a Magical Adventure'.

Early on, Brecht had in hand a private publication, by a press in Augsburg, his home town, of some erotic or (as a friend said) 'priapic' poems under the title *Meine Achillesverse*: 'My Achilles Verses', or punningly, 'My Achilles' Heel' (*Ferse*). He, or someone else, had second thoughts, and the plates were destroyed. When the poems eventually appeared, it was under the less witty, more dignified title, *Augsburger Sonette*.

'I hate quotation. Tell me what you know.' Thus Emerson in 1849. (The saying is daringly highlighted on the front of *The International Thesaurus of Quotations*, with 'quotation' changed to 'quotations'.) But Emerson was thinking about immortality, and wishing that people would express their own views on the subject. Some twenty years later he observed that there were a few points to be made distinctly in 'this old matter of Originality & Quotation'; among them, 'the apparently immense amount of debt to the old. By necessity & by proclivity, & by delight, we all quote.' There is 'wise quotation': some people quote so well that the quoter 'honours & celebrates the author', in some cases giving more fame than he receives aid. By implication there must be unwise quoting, though Emerson adduces only the variety in which the quoter draws a conclusion or suggestion of which the author was quite innocent. As for originality, what is it? It is being somebody, being yourself, and reporting accurately what you are and what you see. 'If another's words describe your fact, use them as freely as you use the language & the alphabet, whose use does not impair your originality.'

This runs counter to the modern style of DIY as a matter of proper pride. An ill-favoured thing, it may be, but almost a virgin, and one's own.

'There are, indeed, things that cannot be put into words. They *make themselves manifest*. They are what is mystical.'—Wittgenstein, *Tractatus Logico-Philosophicus*, 1921.

'The handiest of the marks by which I classify a state of mind as mystical is negative. The subject of it immediately says that it defies expression, that no adequate report of its contents can be given in words. It follows from this that its quality must be directly experienced; it cannot be imparted or transferred to others.'—William James, *The Varieties of Religious Experience*, 1902.

Wittgenstein's statement is shorthand for James's. It throws light (some would say darkness) on his celebrated dictum, in the same work: 'Whereof one cannot speak, thereon one must remain silent', making it less 'refreshing', sturdy, no-nonsense, positivist than is often supposed.

So there are things that can't be expressed in words? A useful secondary definition of 'mystical', no doubt, but . . . Perhaps it's just that one resents people telling one to remain silent.

'The injunction to practise intellectual honesty usually amounts to sabotage of thought,' Theodor Adorno declares in *Minima Moralia*. Indeed, the injunction is itself dishonest. The writer cannot show every step he has taken towards his conclusion without misrepresenting, devaluing, vitiating the whole thing.

'Knowledge comes to us through a network of prejudices, opinions, innervations, self-corrections, presuppositions and exaggerations, in short through the dense, firmly-founded but by no means uniformly transparent medium of experience.' Experience has this in common with that particular experience, 'what is mystical': it cannot

46

be imparted, it cannot be written down. And much the same, it would seem, is true of knowledge. And it would seem wondrous that we manage to communicate as scrappily as we do.

What we do write down, however 'false' or fictive or foul, becomes our experience. Which means we should be careful what we write down. And also that we should be careful what we read— unless we can rely for safety when necessary on our ordinary carelessness. Not a wholly safe assumption.

The height of the Tower of Babel has been reported as 81,000 Jewish feet. In his *Dictionnaire philosophique* Voltaire cites a scholar who claimed to prove the truth of the Babel story thus: before the Tower was built, the Chinese language was the same as High German, but afterwards it wasn't. No one has yet refuted this argument.

Aristeas (3rd century BC) says that 72 scholars working separately translated the Old Testament from Hebrew into Greek and all the versions proved to be identical. Of the sizeable number of translations of *Ulysses* produced in Japanese, it is said that the only thing they have in common is the title of the work.

Foreign languages, foreign devils. Stendhal noted in the *London Magazine* (May 1825) that the English customarily made extraordinary blunders when they ventured into French. The *Memoirs* of Harriet Smith, otherwise admired in France for their wit, became ridiculous as soon as the author made pretensions to understanding that tongue, and for example put down *à la distance* instead of *à distance*. (The lady in question also wrote novels best described as *romans-* —let's get it right—*à-clef.*)

Conversely, in *À la recherche du temps perdu* Proust observed that in France 'we give to everything that is more or less British the one name that it happens not to bear in England', instancing *smoking* for dinner-jacket and, 'by an ill-judged piece of Anglomania', the term *water-closet* for what he claimed was called a lavatory in England.

More entertaining is the common expression, *les waters*, Gallicized by Raymond Queneau as *ouatères*.

Not that Proust was in a position to wax satirical. He was led to believe that Scott Moncrieff's title for the first part of his novel, *Swann's Way*, wouldn't do because 'way' meant 'manner', as in 'winning ways'; his own preference was for 'To Swann's Way'. 'I cherish my work, and I won't have it ruined by Englishmen.' Yet some early opinions of the translation rated it superior to the original.

A friend of mine, a diplomat serving in the East, took lessons in Thai from a distinguished elderly princess. In Thai the form of words can depend on the status relative to yourself of the person you are addressing. Whenever my friend went astray on the point, the princess would reprimand him thus: 'That, Mr——, is the word you would use in speaking to a pedicab driver, not when speaking to *me*.' Once, when a dog came up in conversation, she corrected him: 'You would not use *that* word when addressing me.' He apologized. 'Of course not, Your Highness, I would use it when speaking to a pedicab driver.' 'No, Mr——,' she replied, 'that word you would use when addressing a dog.'

For a comparably devastating rejoinder, albeit in a morally lower setting, we have to go to Voltaire. He was giving a lesson in tragic diction to a young actress, who recited a powerful passage of verse with extreme coldness of expression. 'My dear young lady,' he remonstrated, 'Act as though the devil were in you! What would you do if a cruel tyrant had just separated you from your lover?' She answered: 'I should take another.'

The new Rupert Murdoch Professor of Language and Communication at Oxford appears to follow the demagogic principle, Whatever is, is right. In an interview printed in one of Rupert Murdoch's papers, she condones the use of 'may' in the sentence 'The Queen may have married several suitors before she met Prince Philip' (a libellous insinuation, one would have thought), on the grounds that the distinction between 'may' and 'might' has grown irretrievably blurred. 'I'd like to stop people worrying about linguistic trivia like whether it should be graffito not graffiti.' And in a similar spirit she approves of the double negative: 'the more negatives you have the more negated it is.' People who fuss about words, she concludes, usually make fools of themselves. There are worse things to make of ourselves.

Double negatives have become *de rigueur* in *EastEnders*; you never hear a single one around Albert Square nowadays. Concurrently I note a hectic degeneration in manners and morals, the women turning into slags, the men into louts and not-so-petty criminals, all of them given to virtually continuous lying.

Their attachment to the demotic does not inhibit such pompous pronouncements as 'I don't think I'm ready for a commitment.'

Punctuation is pointless   Commas trip us up   Colons are intestines leading from little to less   Semicolons neither one thing nor the other   Quotation marks to be purged of irony and ostentation   Dashes fall over their own feet   The long dash is afraid to speak its mind   Inverted commas are plainly bent   Question marks are commonly rude and exclamations loud   Accents remain in use until defunct by natural wastage   Hyphens serve only to prevent mis-conception   Italics are foreign and to be treated as such   Brackets encourage second thoughts and secret sneerers   The full stop is a last resort.

ELIAS CANETTI's jottings, in *The Human Province*, don't always make striking sense. To stay with one theme: 'The word "civilization" seems nowhere so apt as in everything connected to China. Breeding and counter-breeding in their interplay can be most accurately studied here.' 'Of all thinkers, only the ancient Chinese have an endurable dignity.' 'The silkworm is a deeper expression of what is

Chinese than even the script.' 'Chinese names have something of the ultimate language, in which all human language will end.' 'A real Chinese revolution would be the abolition of the cardinal points': that, in some sense, one can believe.

Racial stereotypes, the politer side of them, have it that the Chinese are wise, the Japanese inscrutable, the Indians spiritual. Tell a Chinese he is wise, and his mouth will fall open foolishly. Tell a Japanese that he is inscrutable, and he will turn pale and stammer while seeking desperately for a suitable response. Tell an Indian he is spiritual, and he will suppose you are insulting him. What you have said conflicts with their myth of the Englishman, reticent, averse to flattery, down to earth, and hence they will all imagine you are engaged in a subtle plan (*perfide Albion*) to cheat them.

Another of Canetti's reflections reads thus: 'An Aztec as a cook in Hampstead. "Quetzalcoatl," I say to him; he doesn't understand me. "Steak au poivre," I say, and his face is wreathed in a grin.' But how boring is the thought that we are all brothers under the skin. There *is* something in these myths, even if they are best kept for one's private speculation. Perhaps they are needful, as long as their application is abstract and general, not concrete and individual. They help us to define ourselves—not invariably as *better than*, quite often as *not so good as*. Who would describe the English as wise, inscrutable, spiritual? Racist attacks have little to do with the victims (not that this will console them), and a lot to do with the attackers, who have had a hard time trying to define themselves, and don't much like the conclusions they foggily arrive at.

But we don't want too much of this self-defining. I used to think the Japanese the most self-conscious of all races, sedulously determining themselves according to their differences from other nations, and by stoutly denying their ordinary humanity, a commonplace commodity to be found more or less anywhere on the planet. (I employ the past tense in that things may have changed radically after forty years, even though I can't altogether believe it.) Ethical teaching typically ordained that whatever one liked should be avoided and one's attention devoted to unpleasant duties. The samurai virtue of self-control was summed up thus: 'He shows no sign of joy or anger.' The Japanese were forever informing the benighted though well-disposed foreigner that something or other was a 'tradition'; or a 'Japanese tradition', in the way the uniquely indigenous rice wine, *sake*, was pleonastically referred to as 'Japanese *sake*'. The occupying Americans were quietly blamed for introducing disinfectants into the water supplies of the bombed cities (a patently advisable measure) because this interfered with the traditional tea ceremony, an exercise in ritual etiquette and self-composure.

In general, however, the occupation was an unexpected success, being interpreted as another system of prescribed relationship and mutual obligation; people continued to be model citizens, albeit the model had changed somewhat. 'The occupiers,' wrote Frank Gibney, one of them, 'had a weird sense of being adopted.' The Garrison Army was also the Emperor's Army; and a doubtfully authentic but apposite story tells of the US colonel who asked an old farmer what he thought of General MacArthur, and was answered, 'The Emperor couldn't have picked a better man.'

To the eyes of foreigners the Japanese were a fascinating but disquieting people, both a stern reproach and a dreadful warning. Cribbed and confined in their behaviour, a prey to perpetual nervy formality, burdened by the demands of 'the expected' (in some ways convenient), and—for who could steadfastly meet such exalted standards?—enormously sad. Unless, which was rare during the spartan years I spent in the country, strong drink swept away their inhibitions; whereupon sober citizens averted their eyes from the unexpected behaviour that followed, but which could by these means be tacitly held not to have happened.

The unsolicited advice I boldly offered was: 'The Japanese have had Shintō, the Way of the Gods; and Bushidō, the Way of the Warrior; and Kōdō, the Way of the Emperor. What they might try now is the Way of the Human.' No wonder a British reviewer (1955) deplored the governessy tone of the book! The local verdict was 'very interesting, Enraito-san'. The Japanese were always and amiably interested in the views of outsiders, however banal or uninformed, for such views inevitably stressed their cherished differences.

What we didn't notice in those hard times was that, underneath the tragedies and the comedies, the ruined Japanese, embracing the Way of the Bootstrap, were being inscrutably successful—that is, *different*.

A peculiar characterization came from Lady Diana Manners (Diana Cooper), in a letter to Raymond Asquith, son of the Prime Minister, in December 1915, describing how she and Raymond's wife, Katharine, had lain 'in ecstatic stillness through too short a night, drugged in very deed by my hand with morphia . . . It was a grand night, and strange to feel so utterly self-sufficient—more like a Chinaman, or God before he made the world or his son and was content with, or callous to, the chaos.'

Quoting this account, Marek Kohn (*Dope Girls*, 1992) comments that it points to 'an ingenious resolution of an apparent paradox in British views of China'. The word 'Chinaman' evokes the conventional connection with opium, whereas the association here with God suggests something distinctly grander. The Chinese people, in the figure of this representative, are credited with 'an elevated level of spiritual consciousness' and, Kohn says, with a civilization of considerable antiquity, God being fairly remote in time; but simultaneously they are pictured as impassive to the point of callousness, devoid of humanity, since, unlike God, the said Chinaman never provided a son, a redeemer.

In his biography of the lady, Philip Ziegler gives a cooler appraisal of her attitudes, along class lines: 'To reduce oneself to a stupor with morphia was risky, perhaps immoral, but to drink a whisky and soda would have been common—a far worse offence.' At least there's no visible snobbery in the current drug scene.

Michel Foucault has averred that the *ars erotica* (in which 'truth is drawn from pleasure itself'), as developed in India, Japan and elsewhere, is one of the two great procedures for eliciting the truth about sex, the other being the Western world's *scientia sexualis*, the procedure of the 'confession' adapted to scientific discourse: 'Western man has become a confessional animal' (*The History of Sexuality*).

To master the analyses set out in Indian erotology you will need first of all to renounce sexual activity—if only in the interests of that famous spirituality. Rather as most commentators on Shakespeare are themselves neither poets nor dramatists. Only the spectator can hope to see that much of the game.

The most entertaining passage in the medieval *Koka Shastra*, a text which mixes extreme explicitness with extreme poeticality, is this: 'Women are most inclined to love, and most easily conquered, at night and in pitch darkness—approached under these conditions there is hardly a man to whom they can say No. Lastly, for seduction avoid any place inhabited by an old lady who has enjoyed carnal copulation in her time, for where one person has been successfully wooed, it is unlucky to woo a second' (Alex Comfort's rendering). So remember to ask: Are there any old ladies living around here? Do you happen to know whether in their earlier years they . . .?

Among complicated and minute exhortations and admonitions, more *scientia sexualis* than *ars erotica*, one might think, some manifest good sense is found in the ancient *Kama Sutra*. A list of twelve classes of women 'not to be enjoyed' includes a leper, a lunatic, and the wife of the king.

Light in the night

In an alley just around the corner
From the Singapore Methodist Book Shop
Lighted by coconut candles
Stands a hawker's glittering barrow.
The wares laid out so lovingly
When at last you recognize them
Are not for humdrum or unseemly uses
As foiling conception or fending off diseases
But designed to ENHANSE THE MARRITAL PLESSURES.
Some akin to vacuum-cleaner fittings

Sprouting circlets of frisky goat's hair
Or the painted feathers of little birds
While others are stoutly buttressed
Or bulge with beads in garish colours—
Knick-knacks and gewgaws set out neatly.
A Sikh presides, ancient and sleepy
With sacred appurtenances and saintly smile.
If you were a woman, you reflect
You'd gather up your skirts and run a mile.
The guru flicks a pack of faded papers
Affirming the contentment of MARRITAL CUPPELS
Whose names are past deciphering.
Many are the matrimonies he has saved
Just around the corner from the Methodists
But peoples of now, he warbles sadly
Are too much working to joy their blessings.
Only bats play curiously about the barrow.

Universal history. The ancients held that God was a sphere, this being the perfect shape in that all points on the circumference are equidistant from the centre. As it was written: 'His body is perfectly spherical, He has many friends, laymen and clerical.' Other spheres, commonly named after false gods, were fashioned unequal; bodies much less celestial: barren, cursed with awful weather, temperatures intolerably hot or cold, with insufferable atmospheres, or disfigured by the saturation bombing of meteorites. In one case the spoiling tactic took the form of inhabitants set down there, male and female, who created quasi-heaven on earth and also quasi-hell, the latter more successfully. Spheres all of them, but all of them far from perfection.

Through the centuries God was defined as the sphere whose

centre was everywhere and whose circumference was nowhere. As an adjunct of God, Nature came in for a similar description. Pascal, however, had reservations. According to the printed text, he declared that Nature (the universe, space) was an infinite sphere of which the centre was everywhere and the circumference nowhere at all—but a study of the manuscript reveals that his first impulse was 'fearful sphere', and then for *effroyable* he tactfully substituted *infinie*. Subsequent and more jaded centuries preferred the expression 'frightful sphere' or 'fright' *tout court*. Later even fear waned, following sphere (in the first elevated sense) into desuetude.

Yet something remained intransigent and unappeased. Spherical phenomena were observed in the sky, whose centres were enigmatic and whose circumferences undetermined, and which came to be known therefore as unidentified flying objects. Could God be about to show his face again? Hungry sheep looked up to be fed.

'Perhaps universal history is the history of the diverse intonation of a few metaphors' (Borges). Yes, but what we want is less reverence and more referents, less of what the savants call 'vehicle' and more of 'tenor'. Or, to put it plainly, wonders rather than signs.

God as referent? Highly problematic. But as metaphor, symbol, point of reference, he remains prime and eternal. (Which explains 'If God did not exist, we would need to invent him', for otherwise our phrase-making would be sadly impoverished.) He even makes an appearance in secular squibs like Karl Kraus's 'God made man out of dust; the analyst reduces him to it', and Chief Inspector Morse's answer when asked if he believed there was a God: 'There are times when I wish to God there were!'

For example, 'Those who are quick to take offence are quick to give it', or 'People who keep on about their roots must be dreadfully insecure.' The point about aphorisms is that you don't have to elaborate, debate and refine, and end up boring everybody. 'A man who can write aphorisms should not fritter away his time writing essays': thus Kraus, the Viennese satirist who died in 1936. He also said, 'An aphorism never coincides with the truth: it is either a half-truth or one-and-a-half truths.' Aphorisms embody a majority view; that is, they are true 85 per cent of the time, or 70, or 51. Or even true of 0.02 per cent of the population who haven't been noticed before.

But aphorisms are not invulnerable to aphorisms. Anton Kuh, a reluctant aphorist who died in 1941 (no admirer of Kraus, whom he labelled 'Zarathustra's ape'), had this warning: 'The aphorism is the biggest swindler. Through economy it simulates backgrounds which it doesn't possess.' Like people who mug up dictionaries of quotations. Whether in 'He lays sentences like eggs, but he forgets to hatch them' Canetti was thinking of aphorists isn't clear, but he may have been; the entry comes just before the even briefer 'His well-papered mind'. La Rochefoucauld, himself notoriously *enrhumé*, was of the opinion that one catches the desire to make maxims as one catches a cold. And in introducing *The Oxford Book of Aphorisms*, John Gross writes: 'Wagner said that collections of aphorisms always reminded him of performing fleas—an unfair reaction, needless to say, prompted by hostility to Nietzsche, but one knows what he meant.' Wagner's view might seem to accord with the third part of Dr Johnson's definition: 'an unconnected position'. While a jump-start is characteristic of both fleas and aphorisms, it is debatable whether the latter consist in making a lot go a little way or a little go quite a long way.

I am indebted to Harry Zohn, translator of Kraus, for Kuh's variation on a well-known Latin aphorism: 'Ante coitum omne animal est Tristan.'

Food for thought

The aphorist wrests himself from his desk
To attend a dinner
A rare event, but it might prove fruitful
Mustn't forget, literature feeds on life.

There's just room for a sentence
Between mouthfuls of pâté, you'd think
But the guests speak in paragraphs

Or even at chapter length
He utters an epigram, which
Falls flatly into his napkin
A bon mot sticks in his throat
During the fish course
His tongue is tied in moussaka
Stories see-saw over the cheeses
Long and circumstantial, irreducible
He doubts he has wind enough
Or else wind is what he has
Then coffee comes in tiny delicate cups
The night's nearest to an apophthegm
He starts on a Japanese joke
An amusing confusion between *kohi*
Meaning coffee, and *koi*, carnal love
It's not only quite unsuitable
He forgets the punch-line.

It is late when they turn homeward
The food was rather good, says his wife
Who has eaten virtually nothing
So was the wine, he mutters
Of which he drank virtually all
He worries about the morning after
About aphorist's block
Caused by a surfeit of table talk
Babel talk, he groans
While swilling a handful of aspirins
With milk of magnesia—
Life doesn't do so much for literature
It can be quite indigestible.

Aphoristic, anecdotal—the short wind of age, the long (selective)
memory.

Anecdotiana; or, A Library of Anecdote is a work in two hefty volumes published in 1841, collected and recorded, the title-page says, by an Eminent Literary Character. Either he—internal evidence points to a man—wasn't notably eminent or he was uncommonly modest. For as he notes, authors have 'a more than parental attachment to the productions of their pens': a fourth-century bishop, Heliodorus, forfeited ecclesiastical preferment rather than burn or even disclaim a novel he had written in his youth. This novel, called *Aethiopica*, 'appears to have been composed of material far less inflammatory than the modern furniture of a circulating library': when it comes to tell of the loves of Theagenes and Charicles 'the heroine is warmly rebuked by her lover for bestowing on him, in a frolicsome moment, an innocent kiss'.

The entry on *Booksellers* deals with a class of men who in some eyes are best qualified to introduce the productions of genius and taste to literary circles; indeed, 'such is the supposed dexterity of *the trade*, as they are emphatically called, in deciding on the probable success of any publication' that it has been considered rash and presumptuous to undertake any book without consulting them first. However, the Literary Character continues, this submissiveness can be carried too far, for 'booksellers, like other men, are subject to mental as well as corporal debility'. Many books which the trade have exercised themselves to promote are now forgotten, while many others, which they condemned vigorously, have since passed through many editions.

Concerning the purchase of copyrights, a publisher is quoted as claiming that the considerable sums paid to authors in modern times had once and for all rescued him and his like from 'the censure of thriftiness and illiberality so often pronounced against them by wits and wags'. There is some truth in this, the Literary Character admits, yet we should note that profits have often been proportionately high. 'If six hundred guineas have been paid for a single volume of sermons (Blair's) or seven thousand for an historical production (Gibbon's), let it be recollected that the profits, in both instances, have been after the rate of two thousand per cent.'

Under *Literary Men* we are reminded that such persons have frequently been blamed for 'their irritability, seclusion, and inaptness for performing the common duties of life'. Yet we should consider the other side of the coin: pitied by the merchant, the sportsman, and the man of pleasure, the author, buried in retirement, 'derives from past evil, or present folly, instruction, amusement, and employment'. His consolation is to imagine fondly that 'at some distant period tardy posterity may render the unavailing tribute of praise to that merit which has been unnoticed by his contemporaries'. Having made allowance for 'the keen sensibility of genius, and the pangs of real misery', the Literary Character turns indignantly—discount his flowery diction and what he says applies today—against those individuals, 'degraded by vice and folly' or 'debilitated by profusion and luxury', 'wild theorists, mad politicians, and affected enthusiasts', who 'overwhelm the town with volumes of self-bigoted mischance and reams of fictitious woe', crying on heaven and earth 'to heal wounds which, with a little common sense, would never have been inflicted, and to soothe sorrows which a minute portion of prudent activity might effectually prevent and speedily remedy'. There was less self-congratulation in those days, it would seem—were it not that self-lamentation can amount to the same thing.

There is something here to add to our Chinese stereotyping. Having such brilliant minds—inventing printing, gunpowder, and the compass, and said to have acquainted themselves with the circulation of the blood over 4,000 years before William Harvey—why was it that at some stage they came to a sudden intellectual stop, as if something had told them, 'Thus far shalt thou go and no further'? One theory cited by the Literary Character (who grows more eminent by the hour) puts it down to their strange and arduous language, 'which requires half a man's life to speak easily, and indeed is not generally understood by the natives below a certain rank; one word often bearing twenty meanings by the addition of a slight tone, an inflection of the voice, or some trifling variation'. Such a medium of communication, sadly unsuited to the diffusion of knowledge or the promotion of general improvement, is likely to create 'national paralysis' and a proliferation of semi-literate warlords. (True, I have observed Chinese gentlemen from different linguistic groups inserting bits of English into their earnest discussions or tracing ideograms in the spilt beer on the table.)

Elsewhere we read of a French bishop unctuously promising to give a boy an orange if he tells him where God is. To which the pert nine-year-old replies, 'I will give you two, my lord, if you tell me where he is not.' Bishops appear to be universal figures of fun.

Under *Mad Dog, bite of*, the Literary Character apologizes for departing from his usual urbane and scholarly manner. For the truth cannot be too forcibly impressed, that THE BITE OF A MAD DOG IS INCURABLE, and furious madness and violent death are sure to follow. If bitten, the most you can do is cut out a large and deep chunk of flesh round the bite with one of those keen-edged clasp-knives 'which most men carry with them for convenience': never mind if you sever an artery or lose a limb in the process. If this is to work, it must be done in the first half hour. After that recourse may be had, 'I think justifiably', to large and frequent doses of opium—though few men, I imagine, carried it with them—for the humane purpose of ending the unfortunate's life. (Not very much has improved since then. A friend in a hospital in Bangkok found the screams of a rabies sufferer in a nearby room so dreadful—not human, indescribable—that, ill as he was, he had himself transferred elsewhere.)

Joe Miller's Jests, or The Wit's Vade-mecum (1739) was among George Eliot's favourite reading in her early years. She would amaze her family by telling stories out of the book. Naturally I hunted for a copy. Alas, the book has only two good jokes. One is this: A moving ('melting') sermon preached in a country church had reduced the whole congregation to tears. All but one man, who, being asked why his eyes alone remained dry, replied: 'Oh, I belong to another parish.'

The other joke is that Joseph Miller, though a competent comic actor, was in person taciturn and utterly unhumorous. The compilation of jests then going the rounds, notably in taverns where Miller might be seen sunk in gloom, was made by a playwright of the time, John Mottley, and part of the proceeds went to the family of the late improvident comedian.

In one of her 'character' essays George Eliot has a servant worrying over the surprise Adam must have felt when faced with the assembled animals, for he hadn't been used as a boy to the sight of travelling menageries. It would have been better for us all had Adam and his mate felt surprise at times, surprise as distinguished from pious appreciation. Milton relates that Eve 'marvelled' at the serpent's articulateness, his tongue 'organic, or impulse of vocal air', though only because she took it complacently for granted that language had been withheld from the beasts. Milton was a poet, however, and this fit of marvelling, on a minor point, served as an unhappy distraction from what was being said. True, if a tree spoke, or an anaconda, we wouldn't start to debate the rightness or wrongness of what it uttered: but we expect better judgement in our prime mother. Surprise as a first step towards suspicion and circumspection was naturally absent before the Fall. The pair were *grateful* for the produce of the garden, Milton's 'vegetable gold'; had it given them bellyache they would have been *surprised*. Surprise might have been held legitimate as a step towards thoughtfulness, were it not that there was, or should have been, nothing to think about. Merely one simple little thing to remember.

There's much to surprise us now. *The Oxford Book of Friendship* features a story—quite fetching, I would have thought—concerning St Francis and St Clare. As they journeyed together through a countryside blanketed with snow, the two saints gathered that people were whispering about their relationship. Francis told Clare that they would have to separate. 'Father, when shall we meet again?' she asked sadly. 'When summer returns and the roses bloom again,' he replied. Then, miraculously, all the juniper bushes and the frosty hedges were covered in roses. And so, the legend says, the saints were never parted.

The reviewer in the Jesuit periodical, *The Month*, himself a member of the Order, dismissed the piece as 'romantically idealized' and regretted that some 'more earthly relationship' hadn't replaced it— 'like that between Shaw and Dame Laurentia of Stanbrook'. One is reminded of the distrust of miracles common to most of the clergy (including, I understand, the Islamic): miracles win adherents of an inferior grade (there's snobbery in heaven?), are unsuitably sensational (it's sober faith that counts), and can spread disaffection through their arbitrariness (if so-and-so enjoys a miracle, why can't I?).

All the same, the reviewer's comments are of a kind one would rather expect to meet in the pages of the *New Statesman* or the Rationalist Press. Are we to believe that with its present, up-to-date standards, *The Month* would have accepted Hopkins's *Wreck of the Deutschland*? I doubt it; the poem might still be found distinctly odd. More welcome would be an account of a boating mishap on the Cam or the Isis involving a controversial playwright and a prioress.

Coleridge imagined that a man passed through Paradise in a dream and was given a flower as a pledge that his soul had truly been there. 'If he found that flower in his hand when he awoke—Ay! and what then?' (*Anima Poetae*). Flaubert told a story, recorded in the Goncourt *Journal*, of an atheist who went fishing with a friend. They fished up a stone on which was carved the words 'I do not exist. *Signed*: God'. And what then? The atheist crowed, 'What did I tell you?'

The men appear to have devoted their lives to court ceremonies, elaborate robes, building snow-mountains, competing in games of riddles, playing on the lute, flute or zither, and politely seducing readily seduced ladies—this latter activity followed the next morning by the composition and dispatch of bread- (or bed-) and-butter letters and poems. An artificial, self-absorbed little world—yet somehow it produced Sei Shōnagon of *The Pillow Book* as well as Lady

Murasaki, author of *The Tale of Genji*, both of them ladies-in-waiting at the imperial court. The great age of women writers came early in Japan, around the year 1000, and went early.

From *The Pillow Book*, in Ivan Morris's exemplary version:

'A lover who is leaving at dawn announces that he has to find his fan and his paper. "I know I put them somewhere last night," he says. Since it is pitch dark, he gropes about the room, bumping into the furniture and muttering, "Strange! Where on earth can they be?" Finally he discovers the objects. He thrusts the paper into the breast of his robe with a great rustling sound; then he snaps open his fan and busily fans away with it. Only now is he ready to take his leave. What charmless behaviour! "Hateful" is an understatement.'

'A man with whom one is having an affair keeps singing the praises of some woman he used to know. Even if it is a thing of the past, this can be very annoying. How much more so' if he is still seeing the woman! (Yet sometimes I find that it is not as unpleasant as all that.)'

Among embarrassing things: 'Lying awake at night, one says something to one's companion, who simply goes on sleeping.'

Among hateful things: 'One has been foolish enough to invite a man to spend the night in an unsuitable place—and then he starts snoring.'

Among pleasing things: 'Finding a large number of tales that one has not read before. Or acquiring the second volume of a tale whose first volume one has enjoyed. But often it is a disappointment.'

'One is telling a story about old times when someone breaks in with a little detail that he happens to know, implying that one's own version is inaccurate—disgusting behaviour!'

'One has written a poem for someone, and then one hears people praise it as though it were that person's own work. It makes one sorry; yet at the same time it is rather gratifying.'

'When I met Yukinari a little later, he laughed and said, "I am sorry that my poem was too much for you and that in the end you never answered. By the way, all the senior courtiers have seen your letters." "Well then," I replied, "you must have a very high opinion of me. If one has been impressed by a letter one finds it a shame not to let other people see it. Since *your* letters, on the other hand, were rather poor, I hid them carefully and didn't let anyone get a glimpse. So our intentions were equally good."'

We must conclude from *The Pillow Book* that however effete the men around Sei Shōnagon appear, at least they had enough character to put up with her, her fearlessness, her sharp tongue, and her alarming cleverness, and even, it seems, to admire her uneasily. In the West she would have been consigned to a distant nunnery.

Get thee to a girls' school. Organizing extramural classes in the Black Country in the early 1950s could be a grim undertaking, and recourse was had to any means, however desperate, of insinuating oneself and whipping up interest. I tried to recruit the mayor of Dudley; catching the word 'extramural', he told me they already had one, a huge one on the wall of the council chamber, I should take a look at it.

On this particular occasion insinuation meant visiting a girls' school to talk to the sixth form about Modern Verse Drama.

A bus dropped one in the middle of nowhere. (I say 'one' because these experiences were common to all of us operating out of Birmingham.) The local people hadn't heard of the well-known local school in question. Eventually, by chance, one came to what looked much like a school. In the foreground was what looked like a playground, surrounded by railings, through which one peered in the hope of attracting attention. A girl was glimpsed in the distance. One waved and called, fruitlessly.

A hand fell on one's shoulder. A voice said, 'And what might you be wanting, sir?'

One explained to the policeman that one was wanting a school.

The officer confirmed that this was indeed a school, but *why* was one wanting a school, a girls' school at that? To give a talk. Oh, a *talk* is it? Yes, a talk on Modern Verse Drama. A smart guy, this, the officer must have been thinking. 'Then we'd better go and have a word with the headmistress, hadn't we?'

The headmistress was busy. She couldn't be expected to know about all the talks going on in the school, people were always talking. She sent for the senior English mistress, who at once vouched for one. The headmistress dismissed the policeman with what seemed excessive commendation. One was led away by the English mistress, who disclosed that for some time past the girls had complained of a strange man hanging around the playground.

The afternoon continued as badly as it began. It was plain from the giggling and smirking of the girls that one's views on the respective merits of Modern Verse Dramatists differed radically from those of the English mistress. One saw from her expression that she wished she had left one to the mercies of the police.

As I say, a common experience, of a kind all missionaries are familiar with.

Shōnagon relates a legend of 'long ago' which is—especially in the somewhat chilly context of *The Pillow Book*—quite heart-warming.

At that time the Emperor of China was thinking of annexing Japan, and therefore set puzzles to test the Japanese Emperor's abilities. Among these was a small jewel with seven curves and a passage that ran through all the curves and was open at both ends. 'Please pass a thread through the jewel,' he wrote: 'This is something that everyone in our country knows how to do.' All the craftsmen of Japan were summoned, but all failed. Then a Captain of the Guards consulted his father in secret, and the old man advised him to capture two ants and tie narrow threads round their middles. Honey should be smeared outside one of the openings and the ants placed at the other. This was done. The ants smelt the honey and crawled through the passage, emerging at the other end. The threaded jewel was returned to China, where it was decided that the Japanese were clever people after all and it was pointless to send them any further puzzles.

The real point lies here: the Japanese Emperor liked only young people and (in defiance of stereotypes) had decreed that everybody over forty should be put to death. ('Why should His Majesty have decided on this policy?' Shōnagon interposes mildly, finding it difficult to criticize even a legendary emperor: 'After all, he had no need to concern himself with people who lived quietly at home and minded their own business.') Thereupon the older people ran away and hid themselves in remote provinces. The Captain of the Guards was a devoted son and couldn't live without seeing his parents at least once a day, so he had dug a hole under his house and installed them there.

After the great success in threading the jewel, the Japanese Emperor offered the Captain promotion to whatever rank he desired, but the Captain's only wish was that the old people who had hidden themselves should be sought out and returned in safety to the capital. This was agreed. The Captain was appointed Great Minister and, Shōnagon says, 'evidently the Captain's father became a God'. Quite right too.

The RSPCA has brought a prosecution against the owner of a pet rat, abandoned for six days. Ziggy, aged 2, was said to have become 'extremely depressed', and died of pneumonia and starvation despite a course of steroids and antibiotics. The owner—'I loved Ziggy to death,' she declared—was fined £80.

Though scorn has been poured on the RSPCA, I find the affair oddly cheering. *The Times* complained that 'it trivializes the serious philosophical debate on animal rights'—ah, philosophy! ah, debate!—and detected misanthropy in it. As if the implication were, Why should a human being have life and thou—a dog, a horse, a rat—no breath at all? Or as if the case threatened to egg the world's warring tribes on to further atrocities.

Our mistake was to take too literally God's prelapsarian remark, that men and women should have dominion over every living thing that moved on the earth. The point, hardly to be termed philosophical, is simple: once we take in an animal, we make ourselves responsible for its welfare. I would even extend the principle to include children.

Arthur Schopenhauer and Samuel Johnson, though they couldn't be much further apart in their philosophical views, were at one on the subject of vivisection.

'. . . by knives, fire and poison, knowledge is not always sought, and is very seldom attained. The experiments that have been tried, are tried again; he that burned an animal with irons yesterday, will be willing to amuse himself with burning another tomorrow. I know not, that by living dissections any discovery has been made by which a single malady is more easily cured. And if the knowledge of physiology has been somewhat increased, he surely buys knowledge dear, who learns the use of the lacteals at the expense of his humanity. It is time that universal resentment should arise against these horrid operations, which tend to harden the heart, extinguish those sensations which give man confidence in man, and make the physician more dreadful than the gout or the stone.' (Johnson, 1758)

'Another fundamental error of Christianity is that it has in an unnatural fashion sundered mankind from the *animal world* to which it essentially belongs and now considers mankind alone as of any account, regarding the animals as no more than *things* . . . When I was studying at Göttingen, Blumenbach spoke to us very seriously about the horrors of vivisection and told us what a cruel and terrible thing it was; wherefore it should be resorted to only very seldom and for very important experiments which would bring immediate benefit, and even then it must be carried out as publicly as possible so that the cruel sacrifice on the altar of science should be of the maximum possible usefulness. Nowadays, on the contrary, every little medicine-man thinks he has the right to torment animals in the cruellest fashion so as to decide problems whose answers have for long stood written in books into which he is too lazy and ignorant to stick his nose . . . Have these gentlemen of the scalpel and crucible no notion at all then that they are first and foremost men, and chemists only secondly?' (Schopenhauer, 1851)

Which can also be read as covert misanthropy, no doubt. As if in other respects philanthropy were in full bloom, uninterrupted and universal.

We like to give animals a run for their money before eating them. (The freakish exception to the rule is the fox.) Hence the popularity of free-range eggs and chickens. But a recent purchase from the supermarket carried a chilling story: 'Chicken reared with freedom to roam outdoors WITHOUT GIBLETS'. Surely not much of a run?

PROFESSORS of literature: assassins hired to put an end to literature (but not quite in their time).

Or, it may be, literature is killing literature; or one, once minor, branch of it is killing the rest of the tree. Biography, I mean, the great growth industry, the stealer of review space, greeted by a thousand pens, the crowder-out of bookshops, 'What are you reading?' 'Oh, it's only a novel,' says the other, laying the book down with affected indifference or momentary shame. 'Of course I'm waiting for my copy of X's marvellous biography of Y.'

We learn (say) that Philip Larkin was most unadmirable in person, mean, sour, woman-despising, racist etc. And—since we unthinkingly embrace what C. S. Lewis called 'the Personal Heresy', whereby the 'Life' and the 'Works' are 'simply two diverse expressions of this single quiddity'—we can no longer admire and enjoy his poems (but for which no one would have written a biography of him or edited his letters) because, despite what we may say to the contrary, we don't really believe that a bastard like that could write perfectly shaped, plangent lyrics. We should ask ourselves whether someone who wrote such poems could ever be such a bastard. Why don't we? Because we trust the biography or the letters more than the work, although the work comes from deep down in the man while the best biography in the world only scratches the surface. (I'm not saying that to know all would be to forgive all, but simply that a little knowledge is a deceptive thing. By the way, does *tout comprendre c'est tout pardonner* imply that since we can't understand all, we forgive nothing?) Can you, dear reader, envisage with equanimity a biography of yourself? Aren't you pretty sure it would be a travesty of the self which—though you cannot be a fair judge of it either—is more complex, more mixed, than anyone else could know?

In Lewis's words, 'Very few care for beauty, but any one can be interested in gossip.' Biography is easier to digest than a writer's work is to judge; it rarely declines into profundity; it does the judging for you.

In my day, biography hardly existed in literary studies, aside from Johnson's *Lives of the Poets* (which we read for the criticism). Of course there had to be a revulsion from this rigid dogmatism, which we didn't then see as such. Now serious people tell you, 'We read about the life in order to understand the work better.' Why not read the work in order to understand the life better, if the latter does interest you? The moving accident is not their trade: unlike that of explorers, soldiers, politicians, and brothel-keepers, the life of writers is usually humdrum. The work is the best side of a writer's life, most likely the biggest. Who needs the rest of it? Our own lives will give us that.

'Poets present themselves to the world in the radiance of their works; and, especially if you look at them from a distance, you will be dazzled by their glory,' said Heine. 'Oh, let us never observe their lives at close quarters!' One great step towards removing literature from the syllabus and diverting youth into more profitable channels would be making students read only literary biographies in their first year. On second thoughts, it might attract them in huge numbers.

An advertisement: 'WASH & GET OFF: Dual action that first cleans areas soiled by poets and then helps deter them from further unwanted fouling and territorial marking both indoors and out. *375ml £3.75.*'

Advice to writers. Burn everything you wouldn't care to publish, and write nothing you wouldn't care to see published: you can't be sure of retrieving it and burning it in time. Do not temporize. Do not rely on the discretion of others. Do not kid yourself that anyway you'll be dead then so what does it matter? Have more respect, not for the way you lived, not for yourself, but for what you have written.

Kipling's verse, 'Seek not to question other than/The books I leave behind', is well known, much quoted, and disregarded. Less well known are the words of William Faulkner, in a letter to Malcolm Cowley (11 February 1949): 'It is my ambition to be, as a private individual, abolished and voided from history, leaving it markless, no refuse save the printed books . . . It is my aim, and every effort bent, that the sum and history of my life, which in the same sentence is my obit and epitaph too, shall be them both: He made the books and he died.' Of course there are anecdotes that are well worth preserving, not because they 'help to understand' the work, but because they reflect it, and—for entertainment is of the essence—are entertaining. To stick to Faulkner: for instance, the story of him on a visit to Japan, perpetually surrounded by sundry intellectuals and State Department officials—the former hoping for *obiter dicta*, the latter fearful of drunken outbursts—and breaking away from them, hoicking up his trouser-legs, and wading eagerly into a paddy-field to join peasants at work.

An epitaph once to be seen in Guildford Churchyard:

> 'Reader, pass on, ne'er waste your time
> On bad biography and bitter rhyme;
> For what *I am*, this cumbrous clay ensures,
> And what *I was*, is no affair of yours.'

Once, in the course of a (well-disposed) review of a new life of Heine, I passed some remarks about the dubious enterprise called biography. Thus, 'It was perhaps the suspicion that God alone knew the whole truth and he was too busy to write it down which provoked the theory that biography should and would aspire to the condition of fiction or poetry.' And, 'One extreme to which the ostensibly liberalizing theory of biography has led is "psychobiography", a practice which bears much the same relation to truthtelling as necrophilia does to love.'

This incidental skirmishing drew a sarcastic letter from a reader of the *Times Literary Supplement*: so I believed—he was forced to conclude—that a future biographer should be born along with his or her future subject and live in continuous, intimate association with him or her? Momentarily I was tempted to reply that alas even that wouldn't suffice. But I should have settled for the temperate words of the biographer Samuel Johnson: 'Nobody can write the life of a man, but those who have ate and drunk and lived in social intercourse with him.'

Reality is so complex and history so fragmentary and so simplified, Borges writes, 'that an omniscient observer could write an indefinite, and almost infinite, number of biographies of a man, each of which would emphasize different facts; we would have to read many of them before we realized that the protagonist was the same man.'

And the repugnance that biography can generate . . . For the continuance of the race, as something worth continuing, it might appear we have to rely on such worthies as the two maids in Proust, Céleste and Marie. 'They will never read any books, but neither will they ever write any.'

Rather comical to come across this in a book published in 1989: 'At this point in the twentieth century, we look for different priorities in a biography. We find little inspiration in somebody who is perfect. We want the truth, the living, breathing sinful character who does make mistakes, does have foibles, does find life difficult, but is able ultimately to triumph. Only that sort of person is believable or identifiable in our world.'

Some of us might find considerable inspiration in somebody who was perfect; but very well, nobody is. The announcement soars from 'perfect' (here conceivable, but lowering) to 'truth' (always a good thing), by a natural transition to 'sinful', and then, lest it should seem to grow extravagant, drops back to homely 'mistakes' and 'foibles'.

Yet it is far from ingenuous, for it advertises on two notable fronts: sin and ultimate triumph, and its closing sentence hints discreetly at a further attraction: 'Why, this might be *your* life.'

Incidentally, the passage comes from the preamble to a biography of George Eliot.

Ian Hamilton offers an admonitory instance. Among his papers he came on a perfumed postcard from a Priscilla, thanking him for a 'wonderful, enriching encounter' and hoping that they might 'do it again very soon'. Who was Priscilla? Eventually he remembered: she was a student researching on literary magazines and he had spent half an hour discussing the subject with her in a noisy London pub. That was all. What would his biographer make of her, he wondered. Would Priscilla figure as a mysterious woman 'who clearly meant so much to the ageing Hamilton as he approached the end'?

One thing his biographer will now have to agonize over is whether Hamilton was telling the truth about the postcard, or not, or making up a telling story.

Such is the power of the printed word that one inclines to believe what it says. One is often impressed with the value, with the truthfulness, of what one reads. Not always, however, when the subject is one that one happens to know something about. For instance, this passage from a new autobiography:

'X had already left Japan when I arrived there; but a number of people, English and Japanese, were only too eager to tell me of the latest disaster which had precipitated yet another move for him. At a club for the foreign community in Kobe, some drunken American had suggested, totally erroneously, that X—whose manner might indeed be thought slightly camp—was a "faggot". There had followed an altercation, after which X, who had been asked to leave the club, returned to smash the glass panel of its front door. Although, because of this incident, X spent only a year in Japan, he wrote one of the best books about the country that I have ever read (*The Year of the Monkey*).'

I never entered any club for foreigners in Kobe. No American, drunken or sober, ever suggested I was a 'faggot'. I was never asked to leave a club, and certainly didn't smash any part of its front door. I spent three years in Japan, and left after the completion of my contract with the university, in reasonably good order as it happened. As for the book about that country—thank you all the same for the compliment—it was called *The World of Dew*.

Perhaps it's as well that we forget much of what we read.

GOOD and evil in this world grow up together almost inseparably; we know little of good if we have no knowledge of evil. Therefore, Milton wrote in championing the freedom of printing, 'I cannot praise a fugitive and cloistered virtue, unexercised and unbreathed, that never sallies out and sees her adversary.' Further, he declared grandly, 'Let truth and falsehood grapple. Who ever knew truth put to the worse, in a free and open encounter?'

Nevertheless Milton was prepared to extirpate the productions of popery and what he considered manifest superstition, in that they were extirpators of true religion. 'I deny not but that it is of greatest concernment in the church and commonwealth to have a vigilant eye how books demean themselves [here, how they behave], as well as men, and thereafter to confine, imprison, and do sharpest justice on them as malefactors. For books are not absolutely dead things, but do contain a potency of life in them to be as active as that soul was whose progeny they are.' As a good book can do good, so a bad book can do bad. No free and open encounter there.

Censorship has always existed, often in minor and defensible forms. When my wife was a schoolgirl in France, her textbook had it that in Villon's 'Ballade des dames du temps jadis' Abelard was vaguely *punished* for his offence: the word being *châtié*, chastised. Later she discovered that Villon had really said *châtré*, castrated: only one letter had been changed in the school version. Britain of course prides itself on its freedom of speech. (And of art, as indignant makers of videos cry out when one of their products raises disquiet.) After the Falklands war, Argentine widows and bereaved mothers were shown grieving on BBC television, as well as their British counterparts. An MP complained in the Commons that these Argentines had no right to feature on British television—because they hadn't paid the British television fee. This struck me as so sick a joke that I wrote a temperately worded verse praising the BBC for its even-handedness and observing that what apparently didn't need a licence was wit, however disgusting. The poem was accepted by the literary editor of a leading weekly, and I passed the proof. The poem failed to appear, though, and eventually the embarrassed literary editor confessed that his editor had vetoed publication on the grounds that it might ruffle feelings or reopen wounds, the time wasn't ripe. The time was soon overripe. Here censorship came in the shape of good taste. It has to be said—'C'est avec les beaux sentiments qu'on fait de la mauvaise littérature'—that the poem was a poor one.

Most of us draw the line somewhere, even if we don't notice ourselves doing it. And where I draw the line—well under my pamphlet on divorce, as it were, and well above yours on the late, saintly king—probably isn't where you do. Which is the trouble with that necessary thing, censorship. (Though some stuff, you might think, is too plainly, irredeemably awful for any general principle to save it.) Milton also noted that those who are appointed to be judges 'to sit upon the birth or death of books' will have to be people of outstanding qualities, 'studious, learned, and judicious', and such people are unlikely to accept the fearful loss of time involved in poring over heaps of volumes which they would never have chosen to read. Talking of the licensing of plays, Conrad opined however that the censor would need to be an utterly unconscious being, one who has done nothing, expressed nothing, imagined nothing, who knows nothing of art, or of life—or of himself, 'for if he did he would not dare to be what he is'. An equally unlikely person, if not to locate, then to sign up.

My favourite player on this stage is the eponymous hero of Heinrich Böll's novel of 1963, *The Clown*, a gifted mime whose dearest satirical turns are called 'Meeting of the Board of Directors' and 'The Party Conference elects its Presidium'. If he were content to do the first of these in Leipzig and the second in Bonn, he would make a handsome living. Unfortunately he insists on offering the first in Bonn and the second in Leipzig, arguing that making fun of Boards of Directors where they don't exist or of Electing Presidiums where there are no presidiums to be elected seems pretty low. This troublemaker is soon reduced to beggary.

In January 1993, apropos of the Calcutt report on the conduct of the press, the editor of the *Sun* stated: 'We're not going to have some clapped-out judge deciding what goes into our paper.' *Areopagitica* raised that question, of who is to decide. But 'some clapped-out judge': is this the voice of Milton in our day? I remembered a remark in one of Tom Stoppard's plays: 'I'm with you on the free press. It's the newspapers I can't stand.'

A whole convoluted 'philosophy' has sprung up around horror films, 'the effect and affect' (to borrow a headline from the *Times Literary Supplement*); its lines of inquiry darting in every direction, feminist, political (as in the phrase 'the politics of pornography'), semiotic; its language the judicious quasi-scientific brand so dear to arts theorists; its manner that of the analyst of the likes of Shakespeare and Milton; its points of reference ranging widely, through Foucault, Lacan, Freud (that old devil of a myth-maker), clouds of witnesses summoned to cast darkness on a lurid subject.

What this has to do with teenagers, or—for we mustn't be emotive—grown-ups, seated in a cinema or living-room, remains obscure. Or, since this consideration is too near to the real heart of darkness, best left aside, or left to such figures of fun as Mary Whitehouse, policemen, judges, and the backward little boy who couldn't appreciate the Emperor's new clothes.

The true horror of this new school of films, remote from the old vampires and werewolves: that they are made, that they are watched, and—lagging well behind—that they are dignified with philosophy.

'Situations of torment, and images of naked horror, are easily conceived; and a writer in whose works they abound, deserves our gratitude almost equally with him who should drag us by way of sport through a military hospital, or force us to sit at the dissecting table of a natural philosopher.'—Coleridge, reviewing M. G. Lewis's *The Monk*, February 1797.

IN HIS affectionate exhortation to young people who feel disposed to take up writing, Coleridge offered sound practical advice: *never pursue literature as a trade*, but furnish yourself with 'some *regular* employment, which does not depend upon the will of the moment, and which can be carried on so far *mechanically* that an average *quantum* only of health, spirits, and intellectual exertion are requisite to its faithful discharge'. A few hours of leisure, eagerly looked forward to, will prove more productive than a whole week of full-time compulsion. An extra benefit—by no means minor, since we cannot all afford a cork-lined room—is that 'the habits of active life and daily intercourse with the stir of the world' will enable you to cope easily with the noise of a family. (Coleridge put this more poetically.)

Naturally, when you retire, or are made redundant, you can devote to writing as much time and exertion as your health and spirits allow. You are unlikely to think of pursuing literature as a *trade*. You will have no illusions about trade.

So much in Gissing's *New Grub Street* (1891) 'still rings horribly true,' says John Gross.

'I think it isn't at all unlikely that I might make a good thing of writing against writing. It should be my literary specialty to rail against literature. The reading public should pay me for telling them that they oughtn't to read.' Jasper Milvain is being slickly facetious. But a true reviewer would be doing something like that: telling the reading public what they oughtn't to read, or what they don't need to. He wouldn't find himself overemployed, I fear.

On that point rests the difference between the literary critic, who has cut his teeth on the established literature of the past (and goes on chewing it), and the reviewer, who risks his arm on new writing. Except that the literary critic, when turning to contemporary publications, becomes a reviewer. As for the reviewer, you won't find him declaring himself a literary critic; he simply assumes he is that— and, to his moral credit, without benefit of a university teacher's steady income.

'What an insane thing it is to make literature one's only means of support!' says the unfortunate Reardon, a man of principle. 'To make a trade of an art! I am rightly served for attempting such a brutal folly.' When his wife scolds him for destroying what he has written, enough to make a three-volume novel, and 'all good enough for the market', he cries out, 'Don't use that word, Amy. I hate it!'

Amy considers his attitude 'unmanly', for a man ought to be able to provide for his family. Before long she leaves him.

More news from Grub Street. 'Sometimes the three hours' labour of a morning resulted in half a dozen lines, corrected into illegibility. His brain would not work; he could not recall the simplest synonyms; intolerable faults of composition drove him mad. He would write a sentence beginning thus: "She took a book with a look of—"; or thus: "A revision of this decision would have made him an object of derision" . . .'

'To assail an author without increasing the number of his readers is the perfection of journalistic skill.'

'You have to become famous before you can secure the attention which would give fame . . . If a man can't hit upon any other way of attracting attention, let him dance on his head in the middle of the street; after that he may hope to get consideration for his volume of poems.'

'The growing flood of literature swamps everything but works of primary genius. If a clever and conscientious book does not spring to success at once, there's precious small chance that it will survive.'

'Oh, to go forth and labour with one's hands, to do any poorest, commonest work of which the world had truly need! It was ignoble to sit here and support the paltry pretence of intellectual dignity. A few days ago her startled eye had caught an advertisement in the newspaper, headed "Literary Machine"; had it then been invented at last, some automaton to supply the place of such poor creatures as herself, to turn out books and articles? Alas! the machine was only one for holding volumes conveniently, that the work of literary manufacture might be physically lightened.'

'Reardon can't do that sort of thing, he's behind his age; he sells a manuscript as if he lived in Sam Johnson's Grub Street. But our

Grub Street of today is quite a different place: it is supplied with telegraphic communication, it knows what literary fare is in demand in every part of the world, its inhabitants are men of business, however seedy.'

Human nature and hence human experience don't change in essentials. (Which suggests that we shouldn't place too much faith in 'the verdict of posterity', quite aside from the low consideration, voiced by Milvain, that by then, if you're alive at all, you will be hoary and sapless and nothing under the sun will delight you.) It's too late, it always was of course, to go forth and labour with your hands. Dancing on your head in the streets may earn a coin or two from home-going commuters, but you need to be a famous politician, actor, sportsperson, newscaster or gangster before you think of setting up as a famous writer. And the last item quoted above might be a proleptic glimpse of the modern Frankfurt Book Fair. (The great hit at the fair in 1587, destined for a longer life than most best sellers enjoy, was the eagerly awaited *Historia von D. Johann Fausten*, a mixture of black magic, devil worship, riotous comedy, exotic locations, elevated sentiments, freaky sex and gruesome violence.)

There are two truths in Baudelaire's remark: 'On the day a young writer corrects his first proofs he is as proud as a schoolboy who has just caught his first pox.' And a total truth in Gide's reply to young writers who asked him whether they should carry on: 'What? You can stop yourself writing and you hesitate?'

But poor Reardon! For the other side of the coin, or rather for the coin, see Arnold Bennett, *The Truth About an Author* (1898). 'Serial fiction is sold and bought just like any other fancy goods': as Bennett knew since at the time he was the editor of a weekly paper for ladies. He had sworn never to write down to the public, but this consideration went by the board 'the instant I saw a chance of earning the money of shame'. So he set to and in twenty-four half-days composed a story consisting of twelve instalments of 5,000 words each, and incorporating 'generous quantities of wealth, luxury, feminine beauty, surprise, catastrophe, and genial, incurable optimism'. His artistic conscience, or its 'lingering remains', urged him to sign the work with a pseudonym, 'Sampson Death', but oh no, his employers ruled, reading that name at the head of every instalment would depress their readers mightily. So he signed his own name: 'I, apprentice of Flaubert et Cie, stood forth to the universe as a sensation-monger.' The serial was well received and led to further and greater successes in the same line.

In a later edition of *The Truth About an Author*, Bennett commented on the reception the book had, the worst press of all his books, though why he could never understand since he had 'merely destroyed a few illusions and make-believes'. Some of his best friends were so shocked that they couldn't bring themselves to mention it in front of him. Ah well, 'many fine souls can only take the truth in very small doses'—especially when it concerns something they hold dear.

'Do not imagine that I should work for the future, if my services were accepted or acceptable in the present,' Emerson confided to his journal. 'Immortality, as you call it, is my *pis aller*.'

Curse the Present, by all means, but the appeal to Posterity is neither seemly nor effective. Far manlier is Lamb's remark to himself when a poem of his was rejected: 'Damn the age; I will write for Antiquity!'

Extracts from a genuine commonplace book

'Those who write clearly have readers; those who write obscurely have commentators' (Albert Camus). What a glow this brings to the pens of those of us who lack commentators! But remember, it is perfectly possible to have neither the one nor the other. Nietzsche has a similar thought: 'Good writers have two things in common: they prefer to be understood rather than admired; and they do not write for knowing and over-acute readers.'

'I have always honoured the defenders of grammar or logic. We realize fifty years later that they have averted serious dangers' (Proust). How true! You would expect it to be the last word on the subject. But . . . it was M. de Charlus who spoke these words, an ageing poseur and snob, with whom no schoolboy, however logical and grammatically impeccable, would be safe . . . You can't have last words on anything. It might appear that Christopher Hitchens pronounced the last word in saying that one has to side with Salman Rushdie 'because there is no other side to be on'. But no, you must always have new words, or else, it seems, the world would grind to a halt.

Defending Byron against the charge that pure culture gained nothing from him because of his questionable morality, Goethe asked whether Byron's dash and boldness counted for nothing. We should take care, he added, not always to look for the cultured in 'the explicitly pure and moral'. Thomas Mann adduces this as an instance of the great bourgeois's unbourgeois attitudes.

'That everyone is allowed to learn to read will in the long run ruin not only writing but thinking, too' (Nietzsche). One sees what he means. ' "I haven't read a book since I left school. Reading could destroy my instinct for what is popular," says the man who is Britain's most successful magazine publisher' (interview with Paul Raymond, *Independent on Sunday*). One sees what he means.

A love of literature, Virginia Woolf wrote, is often roused and initially nourished, not by good books but by bad ones. 'It will be an ill day when all the reading is done in libraries and none of it in tubes.' And vice versa, too.

'Literature has now become a game, in which the booksellers are the kings, the critics the knaves, the public the pack, and the poor author the mere table, or *thing played upon*.' When was that said? In 1820, by the Revd Charles Caleb Colton.

'"Sir," said the publisher, "Goethe is a drug; his *Sorrows* are a drug, so is his *Faust*, more especially the last, since that fool —— rendered him into English. No, sir, I do not want you to translate Goethe or anything from the German."' Reported a couple of months ago? No, in 1851, by George Borrow.

'How long most people would look at the best book before they would give the price of a large turbot for it!' Said last week? No, in 1865, by Ruskin.

And what about this? Spot on!: 'Let me mention a crafty and wicked trick, albeit a profitable and successful one, practised by littérateurs, hack writers and voluminous authors. In complete disregard of good taste and the true culture of the period, they have succeeded in getting the whole of the world of fashion into leading strings, so that they are all trained to read in time, and all the same things, viz. the newest books; and that for the purpose of getting food for conversation in the circles in which they move . . . Literary newspapers, too, are a singularly cunning device for robbing the reading public of the time which, if culture is to be attained, should be devoted to the genuine productions of literature, instead of being occupied by the daily bungling of commonplace persons.' Schopenhauer writing, in *Parerga and Paralipomena*, 1851 (translated by T. Bailey Saunders). Some things don't change; but they can always get worse.

And finally, to escape from literature (or to show that you can't), Goethe's remark that the burning down of a farmstead was a real catastrophe, whereas 'the decline of the Fatherland' was just a phrase. Adopted, this criterion would signify the death of the world's press, leaving only the strictly local newspapers. Goethe was talking like a poet: poems are local newspapers.

Trollope's saying that he had always thought of himself as a preacher of sermons has been the cause of much uninnocent mirth. 'I do believe that no girl has risen from the reading of my pages less modest than she was before, and that some may have learned from them that modesty is a charm well worth preserving.'

But let's hear him out. No one can work long at any trade, he contends, without being forced to consider the effect of what he is doing. Poetry is the highest form of literature, but people read more fiction because the reading is easier. Yet it is the case that by both the poet and the novelist 'false sentiments may be fostered; false notions of humanity may be engendered; false honour, false love, false worship may be created'. And equally, true honour, true love, true worship, and true humanity may be inculcated by both: 'and that will be the greatest teacher who will spread such truth the widest'. The greater honour goes to poetry, but, the suggestion is, to the novel goes the larger public, and the graver responsibility.

Trollope didn't always appear to the eyes of others as a preacher of sermons. In his autobiography he tells how a friend, a Presbyterian minister, asked him to write a novel for his magazine, *Good Words*; the material did not need to be religious, and he felt himself safe in Trollope's hands. The minister had made a wrong choice of contributor, Trollope told him: if he wrote for the magazine he would necessarily be 'as worldly and—if anyone thought me wicked—as wicked as I had heretofore been'. The minister persisted; terms were agreed; and with his usual expeditiousness Trollope sent him a novel called *Rachel Ray*. It was returned: alas, said the minister in a letter 'full of wailing and repentance', it wouldn't do for the readers of *Good Words*. It was all his own fault, he should have known better, he would willingly pay the fee— which, Trollope adds, 'I exacted, feeling that the fault had in truth been with the editor.'

Not a brilliant tale, this *Rachel Ray*, according to the author, but not very wicked either. What wouldn't do, he surmised, was the dancing that went on in one of the chapters, 'described, no doubt, with that approval of the amusement which I have always entertained'. Whatever the age, whatever the spirit of the age, there's bound to be something that won't do. Often something not very wicked.

While German radio emitted great waves of Wagner, the BBC sent out sugary ripples of Vera Lynn. The philistinism of the British people is closely related to their political continence. They may not read your books, but they don't throw you into gaol for writing them.

It might be good for literature if on occasion they did. The purveyor of porn would then need greater conviction or courage than he customarily possesses. More to the point: the writer works against resistance, he does a better job if the job is made hard for him. Up to a point.

In Singapore during the decade of the 1960s I gave perhaps three public poetry readings. These were 'exciting', they drew quite an audience, because it was surmised (perhaps wrongly, but you never know: these people need to justify their existence) that Special Branch officers would be present, and there was the chance of an 'event'. Returning to England, I found that poetry readings had become an institution, often a rather dull one; you could say anything, do anything, and no one twitched an eyebrow. The nearest to an event in my experience came when I read some poems involving Adam and Eve, and a scornful gentleman asked me if I believed in the existence of this couple and, if so, how I managed to reconcile them with Darwin. A second man intervened to the effect that he found it much easier to believe in Adam and Eve than in Darwin. The rest of us trooped out, leaving them to it, hammer and tongs. On another occasion a woman rose to deplore the holding of Eve responsible for the world's woes, while magnanimously allowing that it wasn't altogether my fault, she supposed, it was the way I'd been brought up.

Though the intrinsic difficulties of writing ought to be enough without such extraneous ones as penury, imprisonment, or death, there persists a faint suspicion that unless a writer is under threat from the authorities, then he isn't being taken seriously—or he isn't *being* serious. But it would be idiotic to hanker after a tyranny, let alone a world war, so that a few individuals could achieve their finest hour. The writer has to find his own suffering, his own 'edge', without implicating too many others. This shouldn't prove hard, given that we are all children of Eve—I mean, of Adam.

'What I did not pursue, except in the most offhand way, was the world of the poetry trade, now open to me as a "writer" and you might say "an established poet" instead of a mere civil servant. In what was almost my initiation, I arrived at Leicester with a group of well-briefed poets, myself not having given a thought to what I should read. Naturally it did not take me long to correct this slackness, and to manufacture the bits of nonchalant chat expected of a creative writer: no one wants to listen to poems all the time, and who can blame an audience for that? I quickly learned to distinguish between those audiences, largely middle-aged, or geriatric cases like myself, who stoically go to "poetry readings" whatever the fare, and those which contain a kernel of people who have read something of the author and, understandably, want to know what he sounds like. It must be said that the business of poetry readings is overdone.'— C. H. Sisson, 1989.

Going by reports, international poetry festivals, less nonchalant, can be rather more overdone: 'I think I can recognize the word *freedom*/In seventeen languages. It seems to be popular.'—Anthony Thwaite.

Sisson had his spot of trouble. '*An Asiatic Romance* . . . was of course to establish my place as a writer. In a mild way I was avenging myself on the office, which took all my time, by making my most villainous character an eminent civil servant. His original name, in my manuscript, was Sir Wisdom Tooth, but when at last the book came to be printed the printer objected to that, on the to me extraordinary grounds that it might be considered a libel on a politician whose rather dissimilar name had certainly never entered my head.'

The same author on another relevant issue. 'A septuagenarian may be allowed regrets, but they are no more to the point than the hopes of earlier years. One can hardly do better than to turn to the visible world, and there I am fortunate. Before my window the fields stretch away to the Dorset hills; the willows, no longer pollarded, have not all been removed. The river flows or overflows among them, according to the season. What it all means, God knows.'

'Never trust the artist. Trust the tale.' True, writers discussing their own writing often appear to be talking about something altogether different; they tend not to notice, or prefer not to admit, that the hand that held the pen didn't invariably wield the whip. And so, Lawrence said, the critic's proper function is to save the tale from the artist. Saving is an enterprise which doesn't always know when to stop; as for trusting, how far can one trust oneself? In these matters there is no overriding rule or safe assumption, no uniformly valid procedure. William Empson has cited the Wimsatt Law, 'which lays down that no reader can grasp the intention of any author'. He adds, 'As that is just what the reader ought to be trying to do, the Law is a powerful means of destroying all literary appreciation.' It has been noted in other connections that laws can betray a curious ignorance of human nature.

In *The Engineer of Human Souls* Josef Skvorecky quotes a line of Czech: 'The poet's fleeting heart beats strongest in small stories.' Like this small story from Christina Rossetti. A wagon has run over a frog; unaware, the wagoner goes on his way, whistling 'A froggy would a-wooing go':

'O rich and poor, O great and small,
Such oversights beset us all.
The mangled frog abides incog,
The uninteresting actual frog;
The hypothetic frog alone
Is the one frog we dwell upon.'

Come to that, without small stories the biggest novel has no heart.

Touching little stories. In 1904 Freud was consulted by a young poet and university student, Bruno Goetz, who suffered from persistent headaches. After an hour's discussion, in which it emerged that Goetz spent what little money he had on books, Freud gave him a sealed envelope, containing a prescription, and also warned him that psychoanalysis might not be good for poetry. When Goetz opened the envelope, he found both diagnosis and cure: the headaches were caused by hunger, and money was enclosed to spend on food.

In the late eighteenth century, Johann Paul Friedrich Richter was forced to abandon his university studies through lack of money. Later, under the pen-name Jean Paul, he wrote a story about a country schoolmaster, Maria Wuz, who loved books but couldn't afford to buy them. So Wuz appropriated the titles of new books announced in the Leipzig Book Fair catalogues and wrote his own versions to go with them, including a *Critique of Pure Reason*, a play called *The Robbers*, and *An Account of a Voyage Round the World*. He came to believe that his were the canonical texts and the printed books no more than plagiarisms.

Did Goetz buy food for himself? Did his headaches cease? How did his poetry fare? How good were Wuz's writings? Did anyone ever read them? What size did his self-created library grow to? If you relate such anecdotes orally, people will ask questions of this kind—and spoil the stories. If you are to be exemplary, the art is to stop short. The shyer class of symbols mustn't be interrogated.

'*Men as bad poets*.—Just as in the second half of a stanza bad poets seek the idea that will fit the rhyme, so men are in the second half of life accustomed to become more anxious to seek actions, positions, relationships, suited to those of their earlier life, so that externally it all sounds in harmony: but their life is no longer dominated and repeatedly directed by a powerful idea, in place of which there appears the objective of finding a rhyme.'

It's something if you can find a rhyme! Nietzsche died two months short of his 56th birthday, but for the last twelve years of his life he was insane and silent. Powerful ideas had destroyed him. Along perhaps with syphilis, once a common preservative against declining into the second half of life. At the age of 35 he observed that he had reached what was by ancient convention the middle of life.

It was after he had embraced a horse
In Italy, a broken-down old cart-horse,
That they knew there was something amiss—
This and curious remarks to his friends
On how he had had Caiaphas thrown into chains
And arranged for every anti-Semite to be shot.
All of which was distinctly alarming.

It wasn't because of curious or alarming remarks
To be found in his philosophical books.

He may have confused the horse with Incitatus
Fallen on hard times
And the brutal driver with Caligula
In hiding from assassins.
The sun does strange things to us northerners.

But to throw his arms round a horse in public—
A man who during his military service
Had tumbled from one of them, thereby incurring
Severe and permanent injuries to the chest!—
He had to be irredeemably mad.

> The remarks in the philosophical books prove nothing,
> Foibles are a feature of the profession.

Nietzsche as a television pundit? You can't imagine it! But perhaps you can. With the right coaching—could you be more obviously sincere, a little less peremptory, smile from time to time—it would have done him a power of good. Steadied his mind, tempered his extravagances, alerted him to the virtues of the man (and the woman) in the street, and bred a firmer sense of responsibility towards his (much enlarged) public. Before long he'd have been co-opted onto influential EC committees, drafting new legislation, helping to eradicate blond beasts and firebrands, invited to deliver the Reith lectures, given an honorary knighthood by Britain ('Sir Freddie'), appointed a Chevalier of the Légion d'Honneur, awarded the Order of the Chrysanthemum for Excellence in Prose Poems, and asked to open innumerable fêtes. In short, he would have spent an agreeable, useful, sane old age, in the bosom of an admiring world. *Sic non transit gloria*.

'As a man living alone one thinks not only of one's past but also beyond one's own being. In a word, I have a considerable fortune and I would like to name you as my heir in my testament. This is a great honor for me because in this way I want to express my appreciation of your work.'

Isn't that handsome? From a German gentleman, typed on a tasteful letterhead, and in perfect English, aside from one word: 'I hope that with this help you would be able to attend to your important literaric work more intensively.' (Oh, has one been slacking off?)

If I care to send him a little present, the writer suggests a few handwritten lines from *Academic Year* (an old novel), with dedication and signature.

Cheering, if not wholly credible. Won't hurt to send him a few lines, incorporating an apt quote from Rainer Maria Rilke ('O Lord, give everyone his own death') and wish him a long life. No need to point out that he'll have to be pretty ancient if he isn't to outlive me.

At any rate more compelling than the usual requests for autographs or signed photos, mentioning some long-forgotten poem ('I am a bit of a bookworm'), if not a work by somebody else. 'Dear Sir Tennyson, Please write out for me my favourite poem of yours and sign it. The poem is called "Where Claribel low-lieth" . . .' 'Dear Mr Robert Browning, I am an old admirer of your work and my most favourite is "In Memoriam" . . .' 'Dear Dr Louis Carol, At school I am very interested in mathematics . . .'

It soon appears from the grapevine and then the press that half the poetic population of the British Isles, and a number of novelists too, have received similar letters from Herr Rainer Böhlke of Neustadt, appointing them his sole heir. An unnecessarily elaborate mode of soliciting autographs, but not unendearing.

Long ago, a letter from a male person forwarded by *The Listener*, which went like this: 'Dear D. Enright, Can you be the vivacious Dorothy Enright I met on a cruise to South Africa five years ago? Do you remember those nights on deck, gazing at the moon? . . . You didn't tell me you wrote poems, but I should have guessed . . .', et—somewhat embarrassingly—cetera.

'DAMNOSA quid non imminuit dies?'; or, in James Michie's version of Horace's odes, 'Time corrupts all. What has it not made worse?' Don't be too quick to scoff. I can remember when academics were expected to speak scrupulously and forthrightly where others, such as journalists, might perforce trim their sails to the wind, when universities were supposed to be, in a certain sense, shaky but real, *au-dessus de la mêlée*. Now they are the *mêlée*. An acquaintance tells me he has been forced out of the university where he taught linguistics for over twenty years, in the wake of a lesbian feminist coup. (His words.) Others report that from being teachers they have become managers, fund-holding and fund-raising. But let us spare ourselves the horror stories.

Something similar has happened in publishing, if less alarming since it has always been a balancing act between art and trade. (In Brecht's neat oxymoron, the book is a 'sacred commodity'.) In tune with the prevailing ethos, the less glorious face now the more acceptable one, some publishers embraced the seemingly inevitable, kissing the rod, or connived at their own ruination. (Albeit they rarely emerged ruined in person.)

Are these developments a symptom of national bankruptcy, or are they the apotheosis of an elementary Thatcherism which Mrs Thatcher loved her country too much to dream of? (She ought to have dreamt of it, it should have given her nightmares.)

We must wait, if we have time, for the famous swing of the pendulum.

'Alas!', Thoreau lamented, 'paper is cheap and authors do not have to erase one book, before they write another.'

Thirty years ago it occurred to Michel Butor that he couldn't return to a chicken drumstick he had already eaten. Just think, if the same were true of books, and you couldn't reread them because the ink had faded from the page or the paper had disintegrated. This would encourage the purchase of another book.

Publishers had become aware of this, he continued, and not long before, a well-known house was terrorized by a new edict: any work not sold out in the course of twelve months was to be pulped. The 'brightest and bravest' of the editors—there were bright and brave editors then, there still are—strove to convince their boss that there was something foolish in applying this rule to books, to his own products. But the boss was unmoved: such were the laws of modern industry.

Butor sees hope here, thanks to another law: competition. Newspapers, radio, television, and films will take over the day-to-day trade, the ephemera, thus forcing books to become 'increasingly "fine", increasingly dense', and the book will cease to be an object of consumption and become one of study and contemplation. H'm.

It strikes me that of the ten years I spent in publishing around six went in puzzling over borderline offerings, striving vainly to push them over the borderline, many of them coming from 'friends of the firm', and in concocting nice, unhurtful, not too discouraging ways of saying No. But No is never very nice.

It is hard to be not too discouraging without seeming to encourage. It might be thought sufficient to point out that the story of a novel is minimal and its characters invisible. But after a few weeks the author turns up again: 'I have expanded the story and strengthened the characters, as you advised, and am sure you will now want to publish my book.' And then the sadnesses. There came a collection of poems written, the husband said in his letter, by his dying wife, whose last days would be brightened if . . . Hardly had the poems been ashamedly returned than they came back. She had died, and the husband longed to see them published as a memorial. The second No was just a little easier than the first.

Later on, a former colleague was kind enough to remark that I had saved the firm money by turning books down. No one could claim that I had made money for the firm. This is generally left to a different class of person, who knows what will sell, often without the time-consuming chore of examining it. Publishing can be a question of mind over matter, the publisher's mind over the author's matter—of prophecies that fulfil themselves through the passionate intensity with which they are promulgated. An enviable gift, passionate intensity.

Sorrows of a publisher

Proposing to rephrase a sentence of Leavis's, in the typescript of one of his last books, for the sake of readier comprehension, and he replies: 'Nobody would believe *I* had written that!'

Querying Empson, as a reprint of his *Collected Poems* goes to press: did he really intend 'Heaven me' (*sic*) as an expletive? 'Yes, my aunts always used it.'

Down in Reception a disappointed poet collapses in tears. A secretary takes him a cup of tea. You hide in the lavatory.

Suggesting to Iris Murdoch that a word doesn't exist in that form. 'It does now.'

Searching for an intruder, a black man who has scared a secretary on the stairs, and catching Nirad Chaudhuri, gentlest of gentlemen, who was looking for a glass of water.

Tactfully persuading a woman poet, over from America, that while she may be prepared to go to any lengths to get published, one isn't oneself.

'In a queer way Connolly did enjoy his schoolboys'—what? At the very last moment, phoning the printers: 'Make it schooldays.'

Struggling to persuade a shocked author that remaindering his last book will clear the way for his next.

Re Proust, convincing the typesetters that 'Soddom and Gomorrah' won't quite do as a running headline.

A picture on the jacket of the General's account of being stranded in Arnhem and how the local people pinned a badge on him, inscribed with the Dutch for 'Hard of Hearing', so the Germans wouldn't expect him to speak—and a Dutch reader writes in: what the picture of the badge actually says is 'Hard Whoring'.

Sorrows of an author

Hurrah, proofs have arrived. The title-page attributes the book to D. J. Wainwright. Not a cheerful beginning.

Hearing from your editor, the Poet Laureate of the time, that he has spent the whole weekend removing 250 sets of brackets from your novel.

Told your book will come out in midsummer—'when there are no big books about'.

A typesetter engaged on your large anthology of verse and prose has set prose as verse and verse as prose. His partner is his wife; their marriage is breaking up.

Lunching with your publisher at his club and handing over your new book. As you part fulsomely at the door you have to remind him that he has left the typescript under his chair.

A generous publisher has advanced considerably more than you have earned. You can't look him in the face.

The editor you deal with leaves under a cloud. The cloud descends on you.

Asked to reduce its size, you actually enjoy cutting the book—you've improved it! The publisher says: 'You've removed the bits I liked best.'

Being lectured on the ineluctable good sense of remaindering.

Being both a publisher and an author, and unable to tell whose side you are on.

A publisher asks you to comment on somebody's detailed proposal for an ambitious, wide-ranging reference book. You give a lot of time and thought to it. The publisher offers books from his list in lieu of monetary recompense. You have too many books already. Grinning inwardly, you suggest a book of stamps. Months pass, and then you receive a book of ten first class stamps. You have asked for it.

Conspirators in retirement, they met in a pub near the offices. As it were, a government in exile, chewing over the past, gasping at the present, foretelling the future. And sipping beer. Week by week, the years went past, the offices were moved again and again, the firm was merged, was taken over. The pub remained its suitably shabby self. The price of drinks went up and up. By now they could hardly tell which government they were in exile from, who the enemies, who the allies. Elsewhere no doubt were other generations of dissidents, from later discomfitures. But there was always something to marvel at and bemoan. From bygone scores to latter-day revolutions, from inflated advances to deflated pensions. Old publishers never die—as the ditty had it of old soldiers, the young ones wish they would—they sit in pubs and gossip.

There's an old story about a computer used in translation work which rendered 'out of sight, out of mind' into the Japanese equivalent of 'invisible, insane'. Recently Professor Tom Shippey mentioned a Japanese-built computer whose spelling-checker threw out 'Jesus' in favour of 'Jesse'—evidently being better up in outlawry than in theology. Just as a British spelling-checker might incline to replace 'Bashō' with 'Basher' or 'Bisto'. In an article on 'bitic literature' (works of non-human origin), Stanisław Lem speaks of the habit machines have of creating neologisms 'along so-called semantic axes'; thus one well-equipped computer came up with the following expressions as equivalents for 'little prostitute': tartlet, screwball, bedrabbled (i.e. bed-rabbled), layette, claptrap.

The day of Artificial Intelligence, the mighty mental machine, hasn't quite arrived yet. The golems of Jewish legend, we recall, were of considerable practical use until something went badly wrong. They had feet (and rather more) of clay. Perhaps by default —a pleasing paradox!—AI will eventually succeed in persuading us of the reality of the human soul.

The Princess Royal has said that the need to master the skills of reading and writing is all the more pressing now that there is 'practically no such thing as an unskilled job'. There *are* two left—reading and, more especially, writing.

There's another side to the story. A friend in his early forties, who has worked for years in various spheres of publishing, at responsible levels, is now told, when he puts in for jobs, that he's overqualified. And recently, when I remarked that I hadn't been getting much work from a leading literary periodical, someone on the staff explained that, confusingly, I seemed able to deal with quite a wide range of subjects, and consequently wasn't down on any of the specialist lists to which they resorted for the 'right reviewer'. Maybe I was overqualified.

In effect overqualified equals not merely underqualified, which can be remedied, but unqualified. (Mind you, 'He's going to be theatre critic on the *Sunday Times*, apparently they're impressed by his lack of qualifications': Simon Gray, *The Common Pursuit*.)

A strange world, in which talent has become superfluous. It can't be solely ascribed to computers.

Computers? Wouldn't have one in the house. A good servant, you say! There's a model that ticks you off for using 'gender-specific' words like 'policeman'. Somebody who typed in the word 'freeman' reports that it spat back 'citizen' at him. And you can imagine how taken aback was the director of the Institute for Jewish Learning in Toronto when his computer told him to avoid the word 'Jew' because it was an 'offensive term'. Why, not long ago I was borrowing a couple of books from the public library, and the computer trumpeted that I already had thirty out and flashed up a list of titles I'd never even heard of, fishing, midwifery, Rudolf Steiner, mountaineering, Jewish humour, the Third Reich, and so on. Later it accused me of having lost a book, which fortunately I was able to find on the shelves. And then it pretended I had incurred a fine earlier in the month and failed to pay it. This time the computer triumphed, the librarian sided with it, and after some undignified expostulation I coughed up. And that was only a library computer, a petty functionary!

You have a computer? You swear by it? I shall count the spoons after you've left.

Even so, there are probably some things these machines wouldn't stoop to. 'If a computer could write a Nicholson Baker novel, it might come up with *The Fermata*' (*Times Literary Supplement*). That's unfair.

REALISM and fantasy are reckoned uncomfortable bedfellows, and if a writer makes his bed that way he will have to lie on it as best he can. Surprisingly often we rest content with the outcome. No doubt it helps when the fantasy is black, as it generally is these days. So much that is literally true in Günter Grass's novel, *Dog Years*, reads like the wildest, most horrendous imaginings; hence we hardly raise our eyebrows when, at the end of the war and in the cause of denazification or purification, the character Walter Matern pays court to the wives and daughters of former party officials. 'Anyone who takes a look at the statistics on venereal disease in Germany during the first postwar years will be struck by a sudden increase [in gonorrhoea] beginning in May '47.' Undeniably, this is 'a highly original, if for him somewhat debilitating, revenge' (blurbs can be small works of art!). It must be realistic, for no one would romance about venereal disease, would they? And there aren't any salacious pleasures to be had; it's all strictly business.

Eventually, 'Physician, heal thyself': which Matern does with the aid of a wall-socket. Painful, but Matern needs to be punished too; a risky, unconventional method, but true, an unbroken stream of urine does conduct electricity; and in the interest of credibility the treatment has to be repeated five times. 'From this moment on, the clap is on the decline in Germany.'

The bed shared by fact and fantasy will need to be king-size, as it is here, with plenty of room to manoeuvre. Ordinary realism—

watery beer, black market, overcrowded trains—serves to domesticate, as do Grass's lashings of lowly colloquialisms, poles apart from the airy-fairy. The one jarring note occurs when circumstance rules out the chosen retribution—the man's wife is dead, his six-year-old daughter has gone away to her grandmother—and Matern kills the pet canary: only too naturalistic. Otherwise one bout of the unbelievable renders another more believable, one flight of fancy opens the way for the next. In short, an unexpectedly happy marriage between genres.

Not that the fantasy *has* to be black. Flann O'Brien once suggested in *The Irish Times* that well-to-do people who buy books to furnish their houses and impress friends but don't have time or inclination to read them might welcome a 'book-handling' service, a professional body who would give the library a good mauling for so much per shelf.

Two days later O'Brien outlined three classes of handling. The 'Popular' guarantees to dog-ear four leaves in each volume and insert a tram ticket or cloak-room tag as a forgotten bookmark (price: £1 7s. 6d. for a shelf of books four feet long); the 'Premier' provides as extras the underlining of suitable passages in not less than twenty-five volumes and the insertion as a bookmark of a leaflet in French on the works of Victor Hugo (£2 17s. 6d.); the 'De Luxe' throws in the damaging of selected spines to show that the books have been carried about in pockets, exclamation or question marks in the margin against underlinings, old Gate Theatre programmes as if accidentally left there, the enrichment of not fewer than thirty volumes with old coffee, tea or whiskey stains, and the inscription of at least five with forged signatures of the authors (£7 18s. 3d.).

Subsequently a fourth class was announced, the 'Handling Superb' or 'Traitement Superbe', in which fifty per cent of the books will have underlinings and such phrases inserted in the margin as 'Rubbish!', 'How true, how true!', 'Yes, but cf. Homer, Od., iii, 151', and 'I remember poor Joyce saying the very same thing to me'. Six volumes will carry forged messages from the author: e.g., 'From your devoted friend and follower, K. Marx', 'To my old friend and fellow-writer, in affectionate remembrance, from George Moore', 'Your invaluable suggestions and assistance in entirely rewriting chapter 3 entitles you, surely, to this first copy of "Tess". From your old friend T. Hardy'. The fee for this superlative service: £32 7s. 6d.

Here a simple-minded joke, a far-fetched fancy, gathers substance by accretion, and as it grows in elaboration, sustained by the reasoned gradations of provision and price (comparable to the impeccable logic with which patently lunatic propositions are commonly argued), it becomes increasingly likely, even acquires an air of everyday reality. A business venture you might consider investing your redundancy pay in.

For children only

The author is telling a story
About a band of animals in an unmanned ark
Who have many adventures
They try to imagine what People were like
They find a large book
Called the 'Shorter Oxford English Dictionary'
Which has no pictures in it
And in the vicinity of the National Gallery
A painting of two People looking tired
And labelled 'Venus and Mars' . . .

Sometimes it is art
Sometimes it is an ark
Sometimes an arkful of art
With optional archangels
And other cute angles—
Authors are artful
But not always thoughtful.

The publishers are not happy
They ask the author to furnish a preface
Explaining why there is so much water around
And where all the People have got to
(Migrated to Mars, evacuated to Venus?)
And why the animals talk just like People
(A slight equally on humanity
As on the dignity of animality)
In short to mitigate what might be considered
A harmful, hurtful, fateful fantasy . . .

Quite as ill-advised as 'Alice'
Where oysters come to sticky ends
And butterflies are made into pies
In the skies
And tyrants rant and rave
And babies and words are misused—
Which is never going to help People
To cope with the realities of reality
But only incite them to fall down holes
Embark on arks and childish larks
Or cower in ivory towers.

Such books should be kept away from adults.

(Apropos of which, see Penelope Lively's *The Voyage of QV 66*, 1978. 'She is now writing for adults as well,' said the jacket note in extenuation or relief.)

Money doesn't need to talk much. In 1976 I published a children's novel which featured Mr Spock, Inspector Barlow, and Herr Brush, popular television characters of the time, as a band of what in modern parlance would be termed ghost-busters. The book had also been accepted by a small American firm, whose lawyers subsequently took fright at the appearance of Mr Spock. They approached Paramount Pictures, who promptly threatened to sue them for unlawful use of their famous personage, first officer of the starship *Enterprise*.

This took me aback: a huge corporation bracing itself to annihilate a negligible little book for children! I was asked to furnish Paramount Pictures with an explanation of my behaviour, in which, unwisely, I suggested that the book might serve if not as a small ad for *Star Trek* then as a compliment to it. This failed to appease, and I was told to meet in person a senior Paramount executive who happened to be in London on business. Assuming an expression of mixed amazement, hurt, righteous anger and contriteness, I went along to his Park Lane hotel: he was polite, seemingly unaware of any crisis, but very busy and able to spare only a couple of minutes. I said my pathetic piece and forced on him a copy of the British edition to read on the plane.

I heard no more from Hollywood, but the threat still held, and the US publisher declined to go ahead unless I de-Spocked the story. I obliged, turning him into Mr Mock, deleting his pointed ears, changing his planetary origin, and cutting out a joke about his brother, a Doctor who knew all about children. Quite an engrossing little job, since the revisions had to occupy the same space as the offending passages. Publication went off without incident. And without reviews, as far as I know. In due course the American firm were offered a second novel, a sort of follow-up. Thanks, but no thanks.

Power: cracking little nuts with large sledgehammers, breaking butterflies on wheels; or merely being in a position to do so. Frail fantasy doesn't stand much chance against rude reality.

Practically every day we see them passing the house, a small boy and a small girl, six or seven years old, and a large long-haired collie, the children hand in hand perhaps, leaning one on the other, loitering to play or expostulate, the dog a few paces ahead, patient and dignified, never lifting a leg or sniffing at the undergrowth.

We have seen them passing slowly by for years, ten or twelve years now, this unchanging little group, the two children in cheerful dirndl or shirt or jersey, faintly old-fashioned clothes, and the dog, spruce, attentive, noble. A fairy tale, ageless; happier babes in the wood, skirting the field, with their guide and protector.

We never looked for rational explanations. Then one Sunday morning the whole family were out with the dog. Six children, all dressed much the same, ranging from four or five to sixteen or seventeen. That could account for their never growing up, as one took over from another down the years. Perhaps even the collie has been replaced.

Less of a fairy tale now? No, even more. More of it to come.

O NE bad thing about ageing is that death happens more and more. To others, that is. With the effect, not that there fewer people to think about, but more. The lady down below, whom we had lived above for twenty-two years, died recently, aged 91. She was a lively lass, even her fantasies—men under the bed or lurking outside the bedroom window—were life-enhancing. Not that she *believed* her stories; it was 'just the sort of thing' someone of her age, and clearly never a man-hater, would be expected to entertain. With advancing years one tends to live up to the expectations of others, to stereo-types, as a private joke, a self-recompensing irony—and why not a little recompense for growing old? Every age has its disadvantages, so every age should have its peculiar perks.

My mother, too, who died nine years ago, at 95, whom we, my sister and I, 'idly supposed' (which is different from 'believed', and stronger) was immortal; at least to the extent of seeing *us* out. (After that, it was up to her.) Her death was at the same time 'only to be expected' and a considerable shock.

An old friend this month, and another old friend a few months back. Old as friends, a little younger in years. A kind of resentment sets in: they are interlopers, jumping the queue, their time isn't yet, such incontinence leads to overpopulation of the memory, premises already decayed and tottery. What to do? Tipp-Ex them out of our tablets?—a trivial act, yet hard to do. Everybody's death diminishes somebody's address book.

Often the dead prove more alive than they were when living: as if one has inherited a concentrate of their past. More present in the spirit than they were in the flesh, popping up without prior notice, no telegrams over there. There is at least this on-off immortality, available to all who have at least one friend, or one enemy.

We told the old lady living below to thump on the ceiling with her stick if ever she needed anything. She never did, she was proud. Now that she's dead, we hear a thumping nearly every night.

Meeting a young Chinese poet, said to be a descendant of Confucius, and asking whether he had suffered from the relationship during the anti-Confucius campaign, in the last stages of the Cultural Revolution, when the sage was accused of having spoken for the slave-owning aristocracy. No, he smiled, he hadn't; he was only one among untold thousands of descendants. We didn't ask whether he had suffered because of his poetry.

Short thoughts for the day

'The ruling class thinks of punishment, the lower classes hope for benevolence.'

'Clever talk disrupts virtue; a little lack of forbearance disrupts great plans.'

'If you act on the basis of profit, you will be much resented.'

'If you make a mistake and do not correct it, this is called a mistake.'

'When everyone dislikes something, it should be examined. When everyone likes something, it should be examined.'

While he was visiting a national shrine, someone remarked of him, 'How can that old man be said to know the classical rites? He has to ask about everything!' Hearing this, he commented: 'Asking is part of the rites.'

Hearing that an elder statesman was reputed to act only after reflecting three times, he said: 'Reflecting twice will do.'

Of a student given to sleeping in the daytime, he said: 'A manure wall cannot be plastered.'

'It is hard to find anyone who has studied for a few years without seeking a grant.'

'Enliven the ancient and also know what is new; then you can be a teacher.'

—Confucius, 551–479 BC; mediated by Thomas Cleary.

Confucius: 'How I've deteriorated! It's been such a long time since I last saw the Duke of Chou in dreams.'

Last night I dreamt of my friend R. G., he whose Thai was polished by a princess, and who died in Bangkok nearly three months ago. 'But . . .' I stammered, as he approached, 'Why . . . ?' 'I am not at liberty to explain at the present time,' he replied, tapping his nose. Then it sank in. He wasn't dead after all, he was working undercover for MI6 . . .

How my bedtime reading has deteriorated!

Or, how desperately dreams strive to succour us, twisting and turning as they see one effort failing and grab at another scenario.

In 1969 the external examiner in English collapsed while out in Singapore, the day before his return and his 48th birthday. It was during a farewell dinner at a Chinese restaurant, the Celestial Room. I held his hand in the ambulance; he was dead when we reached the hospital, of a heart attack. I talked to the police, went home and rang a mutual friend at Leeds University. He told the unbelieving wife, widow, and rang back to say I must speak to her myself. Which I did, hardly able to believe what I told her. It was three in the morning by then, around seven in the evening in England.

There was nothing more to be done till later that day. Eventually I fell asleep. I dreamt that the dead man's wife was present in the restaurant, and a doctor too, and he was treated in time, and saved. So we hadn't done enough for him? I slept again, and the dream resumed. He had indeed recovered, for a moment, but then he became enveloped in flames, no one could help him, he died slowly and in agony. I awoke, appalled, and then faintly comforted. In reality, at least he had died peacefully.

As De Quincey said, 'The machinery for dreaming planted in the human brain was not planted for nothing.'

But how cruel dreams can be too. By inspiring in us a sheer, absolute emotion, overriding in its intensity, uninhibited by shame or pride, unrelieved by everyday dilutions and adulterations, the compensatory 'nevertheless' or 'on the other hand' or 'at least'. Here nothing is weighed judiciously in the balance, you are yourself the scales, borne down by an unrelenting pressure of pure feeling. And of thought, too, since in dreams of this sort feeling and thought are indissolubly at one; there's no reasoning your way out of it. Here Hazlitt was right in saying that we are not hypocrites in our sleep.

The emotion may be one of terror: whereas in waking life we would think of something to do, however vain, here there is nothing to do except suffer. Or one of loss and desolation: whereas in waking life we should try our best to shrug it off, to find mitigations (sometimes the best gain is to lose; when one door shuts . . .), here there is no fudging. This dream is akin to the simplest idea of hell: you have lost God, your deprivation is eternal, and you know it.

No matter how desolating the dream, the next day perhaps you feel cleansed, paradoxically at peace. Possibly a little proud, for you have undergone an experience which waking you could never endure, and which, through delusion, distraction, or drugs, you would have made sure that you didn't have to. Asleep though you were at the time, you have risen above yourself for an indeterminate, brief, immense-seeming span of time.

A meticulous demonstration of dream-configuration occurs in *Sodom and Gomorrah*, where the narrator and his grandmother seemingly stand in for the author and his mother, and fiction follows fact. Proust's narrator has been thinking of his dead grandmother, the grief he caused her, and the ease with which he has forgotten her living reality. The 'ingenuity of the mind in safeguarding us from pain' prompts him to a happy recall of the opinions she held, as if she could hold them still. Then he falls asleep and in 'that more truthful hour', in the dream that follows, he remembers that he hasn't written to his grandmother for weeks. 'Oh God, how wretched she must be in that little room which they have taken for her . . . where she's all alone with the nurse they have put there to look after her . . . She must think that I've forgotten her now that she's dead; how lonely she must be feeling, how deserted!' (She is both alive and dead; the dream gives with one hand and takes away with the other, unsparingly in both respects.) He must hurry to see her, but has forgotten the address. He calls to his father: 'Where is grandmother? Tell me her address. Is she all right? Are you quite sure she has everything she needs?' His father tells him not to worry: 'Her nurse is well trained. We send a very small sum from time to time, so she can get your grandmother the little she needs.' His grandmother had been told he is going to write a book, and this seemed to please her. (Such intimations ought to console the dreamer, but 'safeguards' don't always work; the intimations only remind him of his remissness.) 'Quick, quick, her address, take me to her' (the dreamer fights the dream), but his father says she is very frail, and he would find it rather painful. Also he cannot remember the exact address. (A temporary resolution of conflicting emotions, desire and fear.) 'But tell me,' the dreamer persists, 'it's not true that the dead have ceased to exist. It can't possibly be true, in spite of what they say, because grandmother still exists.' (A clever twist, conceding much but retaining something.) The father smiles sadly: 'Oh, hardly at all, you know, hardly at all . . .'; and it's better for her to be alone, better for her not to think: 'Thinking often makes people unhappy.' (Dreams don't object to commonplaces, they refresh them.) 'Besides, you know, she's quite faded now.' (That she has faded from his memory is the cause of his guilt; but because she is faded he shouldn't feel too guilty about not seeing her.) 'But you know quite well,' the dreamer is just declaring, 'I shall always live close to her . . .', when he tails off into the utter nonsense which at the time seems limpidly logical and apropos—on the threshold of waking as on that of sleeping—since for one reason or another the dream is letting the dreamer go: 'stags, stags, Francis Jammes, fork.'

Freud insists that every dream is a wish-fulfilment. Then this Proustian dream, we must suppose, fulfilled two contrary wishes.

Of dreams in which the dead person is confusingly treated as alive and dead by turns, Freud writes: 'I at last divined that this alternation of death and life is intended to represent the *indifference* of the dreamer ("It is all one to me whether he is alive or dead"). This indifference, of course, is not real, but wished; its purpose is to help the dreamer to deny his very intense and often contradictory emotional attitudes, and so it becomes the dream-representation of his *ambivalence*.' As so often, Freud is semi-persuasive; there must, you reckon, be more to it than that, or less. In fact he admits to a feeling that interpretation is far from having brought to light all the secrets of dreams of this kind.

Incidentally, in introducing *The Interpretation of Dreams* Freud states that he could choose only his own dreams or those of the patients he was treating, and the latter were inadmissible because of 'the intervention of neurotic characters'. He was forced, therefore, to reveal to strangers 'more of the intimacies of my psychic life than is agreeable to me, and more than seems fitting in a writer who is not a poet but a scientific investigator'. Sir Thomas Browne held that since there are undoubtedly demoniacal dreams, there must be angelic ones too. But there are no innocent dreams, Freud maintains: 'they all show "the mark of the beast"'. Innocence is unrevealing . . .

Although at one point he must refrain from elucidating part of a particular dream 'because the personal sacrifice which this would involve is too great', and of another he says he cannot give a detailed interpretation of one of its scenes 'out of sheer regard for the censorship', Freud's own dreams are respectable enough, not remotely beastly. Things are different when none the less he comes to the dreams of his patients—or to his interpretations of them. (Primo Levi has remarked on how suggestive such dreams are, and how stupid and flat *our* dreams are.) But after all he is the author, he calls the tune. As a 'creative writer' (cf. Nietzsche and Schopenhauer) Freud is more a novelist than an autobiographer.

Shirley Jackson (1958) takes a sturdier view: 'Let me just point out right here and now that my unconscious mind has *been* unconscious for a number of years now and it is my firm intention to keep it that way. When I have nightmares about a horrid building it is the horrid building I am having nightmares about, and no one is going to talk me out of it.' This seems to check with Jung's opinion, that the dream is a natural occurrence and 'there is no earthly reason why we should assume that it is a crafty device to lead us astray'. Or to the truth.

But 'an uninterpreted dream is like an unread letter', it says in the Talmud, where a neat theory is put forward: the good man has bad dreams, because bad dreams are more conducive to heart-searching; the bad man has good dreams, to compensate for the joys he will be denied in the next world. This may comfort those of us who suffer from nightmares.

A story here illustrates both the vagaries of interpretation and the waywardness of man. Abbai and Raba dreamt the same dream, in which the words from Deuteronomy appeared to them: 'Thine ox shall be slain before thine eyes, and thou shalt not eat thereof.' Bar Hedja, an interpreter of dreams, told Abbai: 'Thy business will prosper, and thou wilt have no desire to eat because of the joy of thy heart.' To Raba he said: 'Thy business will fail, and thou wilt have no desire to eat because of the grief of thy heart.' As it happened, Abbai had paid him a fee in advance, while Raba gave nothing. After many ramifications, the story ends with Raba picking up a book on dreams which Bar Hedja had accidentally dropped and spotting the words, 'All dreams follow the mouth of the interpreter.'

Dr Umar Azam's book, *Dreams in Islam* (1992), bears this dedication: 'To Allah Almighty, of whose mercy dreams are an example'. Divine mercy can sometimes pass our understanding. But Dr Azam confines himself to 'good' dreams', granted to good men, 'happy dreams, which relate to the righteousness stipulated in Islam'. These are messages from God, not warnings from the unconscious mind.

The commonest features in the dreams recorded are weddings, children (the more the better, they being gifts from Allah), fine apparel, schools and universities, golden castles, trees, and—interestingly—religious books, often written by the dreamer. One dream goes thus: 'Mr R got a message in his dream that he had been given 10,000,156 trees, and that Mr X had been given 10,000,056 trees in Paradise. These trees were packed with absolutely everything—food, clothing and so on. When one required an item, the trees read one's mind, and the correct type of branch would lean down.' During the day, the items that had been picked would grow again.

The dream tallies with John Selden's comment of long ago, that while the Christians speak of a heaven 'where we shall enjoy we can't tell what', the Muslims tell of a heaven 'where there is sensible pleasure'. Here the sensible pleasure of a truly super market. And reminiscent of the tree in 'The Cherry-tree Carol', which Jesus, speaking from the womb, commands to bow down its fruit 'for my Mother to have some'.

No dreams for weeks, or none of any interest remembered. A consequent feeling of flatness, of mild unease—as if it portends the big dreamless sleep. This dearth coincided with a lengthy stretch of enervating flu, but has continued since. Perhaps to dream at all vigorously one has to be in good health, physically at any rate: prepared (or able) to take risks, romp or crawl through the lower or higher levels of, er, of the spirit, engaging in foolhardy or ridiculous acts, submitting oneself to unsuspected discoveries and unrecognized ironies, wish-fulfilments and wish-denials, experiencing sensations either depraved or elevated, putting together by sheer force garish or crepuscular pieces that come from disparate and never to be completed jigsaws . . . Pretty demanding! No wonder one needs lots of sleep.

A dream at last, but no great shakes. A reprise of a recurrent dream of childhood. I would find myself walking along the suspension bridge over the river Leam, a route often taken to get to our Aunt Nellie's; halfway across I shrank to paper thinness and slipped haplessly between the railings, waking up with a shudder just as I was about to hit the water. So frequent was the dream that eventually I would tell myself as I began the crossing: 'This is only a dream, it will soon be over.' Which made not the slightest difference.

On this fresh and belated occasion I had forgotten it was only a dream. Before I was halfway across, the dream veered off in another direction. I was closeted first with a surgeon, then with a woman doctor, both of them real persons I know in real life. The surgeon was brisk, as he is in reality, but uncommunicative, and soon stalked off to some more pressing engagement. The doctor, in life now retired, was sympathetic, almost tender, at least solicitous, without saying anything to the point. Rather worrying, I felt.

No great shakes . . . See what complaining gets you: an appalling nightmare that you'll never tell anyone, and certainly not write down; which left you shaking and gasping, afraid to fall back into sleep and perhaps—not a sequel, there couldn't be one—into reiteration. You can only pray that the soul-doctors are right and the dream comes from some sickness or vice, no matter how revolting, inside you, and that, for all its devilish touches of actuality, it has absolutely nothing to do with—with the world outside.

A TELEVISION show called *J'accuse*: here are two men, keepers of the nation's liberal intellectual conscience, but looking like one's idea of KGB bosses, trying to hide their glee under a façade of grave regretfulness, more in sorrow than in anger, and just failing. The prisoner in the dock, whose life and work are at stake, one Philip Larkin, is absent because dead, and this is a posthumous dishabilitation. Several witnesses appear, who one assumed were well disposed, including a close friend of the accused. Could they possibly have thought they had been called by the defence, itself nonexistent? The two accusers, one standing in what seems to be a hospital ward, the other seated on what seems to be a chair, are actually Professors of English Literature at English universities. Substitute pages setting the record straight will be sent out for insertion in encyclopedias, literary histories, and companions to literature. This will ensure that whatever survives of the man certainly won't be love.

In *The Varieties of Religious Experience* William James quotes Cesare Lombroso: 'Genius is a symptom of hereditary degeneration of the epileptoid variety, and is allied to moral insanity', and J. F. Nisbet: 'Whenever a man's life is at once sufficiently illustrious and recorded with sufficient fullness to be a subject of profitable study, he inevitably falls into the morbid category . . . And it is worthy of remark that, as a rule, the greater the genius, the greater the unsoundness.' James asks whether these experts, having established to their own satisfaction that works of genius are fruits of disease, go on to impugn the value of the fruits, and whether they forbid us to admire the productions of genius from now onwards. But no, they are not literary critics. 'Their immediate spiritual instincts are too strong for them here, and hold their own against inferences which, in mere love of logical consistency, medical materialism ought to be only too glad to draw . . . for the most part the masterpieces are left unchallenged.'

George Eliot, in an essay, 'Moral Swindlers': 'Doubtless there are many sorts of transfiguration, and a man who has come to be worthy of all gratitude and reverence may have had his swinish period, wallowing in ugly places; but suppose it had been handed down to us that Sophocles or Virgil had at one time made himself scandalous in this way: the works which have consecrated their memory for our admiration and gratitude are not a glorifying of swinishness, but an artistic incorporation of the highest sentiment known to their age.' Elizabeth Barrett Browning: 'Books are men of higher stature.' More recently, Stephen Spender, in an interview: 'Biography can become a form of pornography in fact.'

Talking of companions to literature: when reviewing one long ago, a German one, I failed to resist the obvious witticism, 'With companions like this, literature doesn't need enemies.' Though in fact the book wasn't at all bad, and I have often had occasion to consult it since. See George Herbert on wit, that 'unruly engine': 'Hast thou the knack? pamper it not with liking: /But if thou want it, buy it not too dear', and, ah me, 'Make not thy sport, abuses; for the fly/That feeds on dung, is colourèd thereby.' It *was* a shitty thing to say.

Having just used the word 'unsentimental' in reviewing a book—if a trifle ironically as it happened—I stop to ask why unsentimental is reckoned such a good thing to be. 'A short story about a four-course meal from the point of view of a fork will never be sentimental,' wrote John Irving in an essay on Dickens; 'it may never matter very much to us, either.'

Ah, irony . . . A confusing mode, certainly unsentimental in being the converse of 'Say what you mean'. Efficacious perhaps in the right place at the right time, but, like wit, an 'unruly engine', changing gear without warning, dodging up a side-street instead of keeping to the main road. ('The irony was an obvious part of the meaning,' Ernest Gellner protests *re* a hostile review of one of his books. But never obvious enough, my dear social anthropologist.)

Once you have been detected in committing an irony everything you say, no matter how frank or amiable the intention, will be interpreted ironically. Think of the person watching a satirical programme on television and later discovering that what he took for a mordant send-up was an earnest commercial screened during the break. You can make enemies that way. But enough on this subject; talking sincerely about it is almost as sticky as anatomizing humour.

To return to 'unsentimental'. There is so little chance these days of sentimentality arising in the *Concise Oxford Dictionary*'s eighth sense: 'a mawkish tenderness; the display of this', that we could surely and safely allow sentiment (from the Latin: 'to feel') back into literary discourse. How nice to have a modern novel called (and in no spirit of coarse irony) *The Man*—or *The Woman*—*of Feeling*!

I'd have thought there was, or could be, a good deal of feeling in irony; but never mind.

On sentimentality. Note in his poem, 'Tursac', Douglas Dunn recalling the counsel given by his dead wife 'in her best sardonic style': 'Write out of me, not out of what you read.'

On irony. Observe how this entry in Camus's notebooks, 'The whole of my work is ironic', is followed by this one, 'My constant temptation, the one against which I have never ceased to wage an exhausting struggle: cynicism.'

The scribbling cat, Kater Murr, solemnly clever and a shade conceited, is a stranger to irony. Not so his creator, E. T. A. Hoffmann. Murr reflects that the divinity of poetry can be seen in the fact that, although the search for rhymes makes one sweat at times, the writing of verse produces a feeling of ease and vanquishes all earthly sorrows, even (some say) overcoming hunger and toothache. A certain man, for example, was thought to be quite rightly beside himself with grief when his wife died, but found consolation in the splendid elegy he was composing, which filled his mind. Indeed, he married again solely to preserve 'the hope of having another tragic inspiration of the same kind'. (See *The Life and Opinions of Kater Murr*, 1820–21; translated by Leonard J. Kent and Elizabeth C. Knight.)

There's a true writer for you. Thoroughly unsentimental. Not an ice-cube in the heart, but a whole fridge. Poets behave towards their experiences with impudence, Nietzsche observed: 'They exploit them.' The most notorious offenders in this respect, they are deficient in the softer feelings, wrote James Clarence Mangan, simply because they have already 'vented them in verse': 'Pour the wine out of a flask and you leave the flask void.'

Kater Murr again (a fluent writer and a good trencherman): 'Youthful cats, be modest as I am and not always ready with a poem when simple honest prose will do to spin out your thoughts. Poems should do for prose what lard does for sausage: namely, they should be sprinkled through to give the whole mishmash more glistening fat, more sweetness of taste.' He speaks 'as a cat of aesthetic education and experience'. And he is confident that his colleagues in the art won't consider the metaphor vulgar or ignoble, since it is drawn from their favourite food. I was less fortunate, when at a reading someone asked why people wrote poetry; at a loss, and reluctant to cite Keats on leaves coming naturally to a tree (too self-congratulatory a metaphor, or too noble), I suggested it was as natural, and for some as necessary, as emptying the bowels. 'That one's a troublemaker,' I heard a lady in the front row say grimly to her neighbour.

How embarrassing it is, to speak about such matters, like discoursing on Death or Love. No wonder that when writers get together they talk exclusively of publishers, editors, and fees. Compare Kater Murr with Cyril Connolly's Sir Mortimer Gussage (*Shade Those Laurels*): 'After all, what's literature? An arrangement of vowels and consonants—that's poetry. And prose then?—an arrangement of consonants and vowels.' And, alas, that persistent, graceless, ungrateful thought, that *you* wouldn't go to a poetry reading given by the likes of you. Or if you did, you certainly wouldn't ask the fellow why he writes poetry.

Cats might be said to be wise in that they decline to do what humans suggest, at any rate until three or four minutes have elapsed, during which, it appears, they weigh up the matter, examining it from all angles. Their demeanour betokens judiciousness, with a strong hint of distrust, even censoriousness, which is never the case with dogs, hence considered man's nicest friends. It is not surprising that human scribblers have chosen cats as the mediators of wisdom, although the wisdom in question, such as it is, commonly derives from the scribblers. Any foolishness inadvertently incurred can be tacitly ascribed to the feline mouthpiece.

The hero of Natsume Sōseki's *I am a Cat* (1905)—or rather, since cats, unlike dogs, don't care to make a spectacle of themselves, the narrator—is a case in point. While he considers it a reasonable proposition, in view of their habit of drowning kittens, that cats should wage all-out war against the human race, he thinks it still more reasonable to wait in patience for the Day of the Cat and scrape along as best he can in the meantime.

Cats are logical and direct, whereas the mental and emotional processes of humans are always jumbled and obscure. Cats eat when they want to, they sleep if they desire to, when they are angry they are wholeheartedly so, and when they cry, the narrator says, they cry 'with all the desperation of extreme commitment to our grief'. Therefore they feel no obligation to keep diaries. (Never mind that in the interests of art and knowledge this is what Sōseki's cat is doing.) No doubt humans find diaries necessary 'in order to display in a darkened room that true character assiduously hidden from the world'. Cats, on the contrary, pursue their occupations quite openly. 'We live our diaries, and consequently have no need to keep a daily record as a means of maintaining our real characters.'

The four main occupations listed are walking, standing, sitting, and lying down. It might be noted that Hoffmann's Kater Murr has no luck with the ladies, and Sōseki's nameless cat has never contrived to catch a rat, though he claims that he has contrived never to catch one. These two cats are not like other cats. This is the well-known—once well-known—price they pay for belonging to the 'sickly aristocracy of literature', as Mann put it, rather than the healthy bourgeoisie.

Wisdom and foolishness are sometimes hard to tell apart. An instance arises when Sōseki's cat muses briefly, and with a precision unknown to Hamlet, on a subject apt to exercise humans albeit not among his own main preoccupations: 'Since I have not yet had the experience of being dead, I cannot say whether or not I would like it.' (Translation by Aiko Itō and Graeme Wilson.)

In Christa Wolf's 'The New Life and Opinions of a Tomcat' (1974), her footnote to *Kater Murr*, the speaker, like all good felines, manages to have it both ways. Max is subjected to a hunger test conducted by the professor, his landlord—the pets' committee has decided to drop the old-fashioned expression 'master' in favour of 'landlord'—but without any damage to his health, since the daughter of the house feeds him in secret. 'I ate whatever she offered me although, in view of my scientific objectivity, I naturally couldn't share her anger over her father's experiments.'

The only other thing of consequence this cat has to say is: 'What is it that urges the true author to speak of the most dangerous things again and again?'

Am engaged in an amicable argument with Luke Di Matteo of Ventura, California, who contends that irony is a purely verbal phenomenon, and that 'situational irony', as espoused by me (e.g.

Lolita found alongside *Alice in Wonderland* on a bookshelf), is merely coincidence arising from thoughtlessness or plain error. He adduces the juxtaposition of the Tailhook Association's convention with a Mrs America pageant. The former, an 'infamous' naval get-together, features strippers, blue movies, waitresses dressed as Play-boy bunnies and, on a recent occasion, the sexual harassment and assault of dozens of women. While this event, typifying male ex-ploitation and abuse of females, is happening on one floor of a San Diego hotel, the Mrs America pageant, purporting to celebrate womanly beauty, dignity and charm, takes place on another. 'Ironically', according to the journalists, but, says Mr Di Matteo, no more than the result of carelessness on the part of the hotel management—or, I'd think, their simple desire to rent out as many floors as possible, and to hell with irony hunters.

But do we want to diminish the gaiety of nations by banishing the irony of situation? There is a nice, innocuous instance of it in *The Times* of 7 December 1993, involving books, not women: in a letter from a reader who couldn't find any religious books in his local bookshop and asked an assistant for help. Showing him 'an inconspicuous handful of bibles and prayer books', she explained: 'We have had to move them down to the bottom shelf because of Christmas.'

SURELY we have never before had such a mixed bunch of simple-minded, shifty, on occasion downright fraudulent bosses! They must have been childishly overjoyed to hear (from some tattered old ghost come from the grave?) that Market Forces Rule, that making money—for themselves, for the country, and thus creating jobs (which jobs were those?)—was the supreme moral aim. This being the case, it didn't really matter *how* they made their money—by insider dealing, by bribery, in the shape of golden handshakes for having caused leaden flops, or through some other form of urbane peculation. The higher morality ousts the lower ones. At worst they would be punished by being sent to an open prison or a hospital; cf. the penalties for stealing from a supermarket, a *real* crime, jeopardizing market forces and commonly committed by the sort of person who is 'not one of us', the sort who wouldn't rate the character reference invoked for a bank manager who absconded with £100,000: 'a very pleasant and affable man much respected for his patience when playing with golfers of a lesser standard' (press report, 17 May 1994).

Who was responsible for this enthusiastic, tumultuous, ingenuous transformation of values? Surely not Mrs Thatcher, with her pep-talk about pulling up one's socks and paying one's way, and her homely patriotism? It's as if greed were something shiningly new, a condition never before properly appreciated; as if it were the triumphal Arthurian knight who knows exactly where the Holy Grail is located. These people weren't born yesterday. They were born today.

The fact is, Mammon has always been an easy god to worship, and his votaries are generally admired. Even Johnson allowed that there are few ways in which a person can be more innocently employed than in making money. And Lichtenberg observed that 'Once he has stolen his 100,000 talers a rogue can walk through the world an honest man.'

Government, too: not an exact science, but the art of the possible. So why go and make it virtually impossible? Surely our masters could contrive to be a little cleverer in their (no doubt inescapable) deviousness, and avoid insulting our intelligence quite so blatantly? They hire PR men to improve their images; they talk of morality; they write pretty dreadful novels, e.g. about hanky-panky at Westminster, and publish tell-all diaries ('I know the truth, they know the truth, God knows the truth,' says Alan Clark). It's not that we expect very much; we know democracy has its unspoken limits. But in this unending hubbub of open debate and closed doors how can we tell what is fact, what is fiction? A distinction of some moment, one would think.

Cash flows out as well as in, so people needed to borrow money. Christians were forbidden to engage in money-lending, seen as a form of sexual misbehaviour ('the usurer lives by the lechery of money, and is bawd to his own bags, taking a fee, that they may engender': Dekker, 1606; in this rather muddled allegory the borrower derived no satisfaction from the deal), and so it was left to Jews to oblige. (They had plenty of time, there being few other occupations they could take up.) People needed to have Jesus killed, that Jewish son—*O felix culpa*, absolutely essential to our future well-being—so the Jews obliged. We hate those who do our dirty work for us, or simply those who have done us happy favours. Makes no difference if it was ages ago, and for long since we have carried out our own money-lending, or our own killing, lawfully, unworriedly, even enthusiastically. Ingratitude? As Johnson observed, obligation can be quite a pain.

'This always happens when social progress proceeds at too fast a pace and when society, in its impatience, passes from penny bribes to bribes amounting to thousands of pounds. The philologists, unable to follow so quickly the changes which life introduces into the meanings of certain expressions, fall into error and continue to call a "bribe" something which in justice should have been given the name of a "bonus". Hence a confusion in terms arises . . . Luckily, life gives the lie to such explanations and affirms stolidly that the "bribe" is definitely dead and that its place has been taken by the "bonus". But it is plain that a "bonus" is quite a different thing and that for the elucidation of the question as to what extent this new economic force promotes or hinders the welfare of the people one would require a great deal of time.' (M. E. Saltykov-Shchedrin, *The Pompadours*, 1863–74; translated by David Magarshack.)

Strange, while there has been ample reporting of bonuses given and received, there has been little questioning as to how they affect the welfare of (to use an old-fashioned term) the people.

Why then, given its obvious qualifications, is the cat not among the twelve animals of the Chinese zodiac (*zōion*: animal)? Explanations vary. For instance, that when the Buddha summoned the chosen animals, the Rat, charged to inform the Cat, decided it would present itself instead. That the Rat found the Cat asleep, and the Cat preferred to go on sleeping. That the Cat was dropped from the list because of savaging a pet mouse of the Buddha's mother.

The story that the Cat subsequently tried to usurp the fourth sign by ousting the Rabbit—believed by some to be a poor relation: the Malay name is *kuching bĕlanda*, Dutch cat—is surely apocryphal. Give a cat a bad name . . .

It is just as well that the Rat did make the final list, by whatever means, for otherwise (Rat: scratch, scratch, amasses money) the world would lack its fair share of tycoons (Japanese: great lord, from Chinese: great ruler; English: businessman).

Canetti at his best: 'The name "moralist" sounds like a perversion, one wouldn't be surprised at finding it suddenly in Krafft-Ebing.' No more surprised than one would be to find scopophilia, undinism, and paedophilia in a book on family life; uranism and necrophilia in a biography; algolagnia and zoophilia in a library novel.

That Western countries supplied Iran and Iraq with armaments and helped Libya build a chemical weapons plant—this has been described not as morally wrong but as injudicious and unfortunate. Good business which innocently turned out to be a bad business, so to speak. Should somebody decide to wage biological war on us— Russia is said to have developed a 'superplague' with a 'production capacity' of 500,000 deaths a week—we wouldn't be in a position to protest that this was immoral, even wrong. It would be undoubtedly unfortunate.

The most exciting part of today's *Times* is the appointments section. 'Want to Play in a Band of Winners? . . . We are looking for very special people who can truly make things happen . . . You will be joining a creative, visionary, hard working, fun loving team that is set to achieve great things . . . a 1990s' company, horizontally structured with hands on management . . .' Not a dodgy dating agency, as you might think, but to do with European telecommunications.

'[blacked out] is a future global leader. (And that's the only lead we can give you.) Why is such a successful organization unable to reveal its name? We can't tell you that either. All we can say is that you won't be disappointed . . . It's a highly performance-driven environment where successes are recognized and rewarded—and where you'll be expected to make an immediate impact.' Sounds much like one of the secret services, or a terrorist group. For further details contact an outfit called 'Response and Assessment'.

A third item, concerning employment in Arabia, offers a princely salary plus incentive bonus and a range of 'attractive benefits'. The intention is to 'exploit the enormous potential market within the Kingdom'. The white slave trade? Please write in confidence to 'Search and Selection'.

It must be the same class of trained communicators—'business writers' they term themselves, serving inarticulate (or perhaps merely bashful) tycoons—who are responsible for the junk mail which has just arrived. 'Companions Introductions Ltd' is offering to interview me and ask 'lots of questions' about my hobbies, likes and dislikes, my income, do I smoke, do I have O levels or even a Ph. D., what nationalities I would like to meet (ranging from British to Oriental and Doesn't Matter), and do I want (a) companionship, (b) marriage, or (c) serious relationship (presumably more serious than marriage) . . . 'Companions' use 'sophisticated methods' to 'open new doors' for me, 'doors you would probably not open yourself', and they do not take on their books anyone 'of doubtful character or motive'.

Lest I should feel that making use of their facilities is a trifle lowering, an admission of defeat, they insist that they have 'the upmost [*sic*] respect' for me. I am not one of the losers, 'people who don't take action' and 'end up accepting second best'. Members of 'Companions', on the other hand, are 'sincere', 'they're fun', 'they're interesting', and 'very serious' about filling that 'empty space in their lives'.

But why have 'Companions' contacted *me*? They have the answer: personal situations change daily, and it is 'almost impossible' for them to keep up with events and know who is single, divorced, widowed, or in a relationship, at any given moment. (Thank heavens for that.) A polite little tightening of the screw there?

It is all extremely dignified, combining gentility, tact, allure, and firmness. No mention at this stage of money changing hands, only a promise that 'when we are sure that we can be of assistance, we will discretely [*sic*] contact you'. Prepaid envelope enclosed.

A friend in the States has sent me a photocopy of a letter to Salman Rushdie which, against all rational inclination, I have to assume is authentic. In it the representative of a New York talent consultancy engaged in 'matching up companies with spokespersons for their products' makes Mr Rushdie 'an exciting proposition'. After extensive consultations with the 'image coordinators' of a highly reputable company planning to promote a new cholesterol-free turkey meat in 1994, it has been decided that, in view of his 'ongoing confrontation with the threat of death', comparable to the dangers associated with excess cholesterol, Mr Rushdie is the ideal person to endorse the product on television.

Other such offers, the precise nature of which it would be tasteless to dwell on, are bound to follow. Mr Rushdie has a great future in front of him. Truth is far more inventive than fiction.

Religion still carries some clout. I have a nagging impression that somewhere I came across a catering firm ready to serve up a full Last Supper with appropriate menu, but this may be the sick fancy of a damaged imagination. The following at all events is true: a classified ad in a California newspaper, which reads, 'JESUS BREAD. Authentic last supper recipe. Delicious, easy! $2.00.'

An opportunity there for a talent consultant. 'Dear Mr Jesus, I am acting on behalf of a highly reputable timber merchant . . .'

There is something untapped, unsuspected, lying idle in all of us. It should be brought out, to the last ounce, and put to practical uses. In the past they resorted to whips, threats, banishment, starvation. Not in our gentler day. Now they have psychological weekends in country hotels with every modern convenience, where something untapped, maybe unsuspected, will be drawn out by a variety of amusing techniques, including charades, twenty questions, Rorschach blots, spelling-bees, table manners, and writing poems or playlets on heroic figures of your choice. All paid for by the benign employer.

Injudicious saying of old Mencius (4th century BC): 'Only when a man will not do some things is he capable of doing great things.' But great things often are those some things, aren't they?

If only people would admit that they do it for money. Which is recognized as a perfectly creditable motive. Or for kudos, fame, notoriety, all identical and equally acceptable. But no, tribute has to be paid to insignificant virtue. As in November 1993 by the editor of the *Sunday Mirror*, who defended the publishing of surreptitious photographs of the Princess of Wales exercising in a private gym—on the grounds that this action served to expose deficiencies in the lady's security arrangements. He only wanted to keep her safe and sound.

The arguments in favour of the monarchy are less than potent. The best: that instead we might get some superannuated statesman to shake hands; that we had better hang on to something 'traditional', if only to remind ourselves that we have a past. The arguments against have a touch of churlishness about them, and are either meaningless (everything is changing therefore everything should change), mistaken (that the Royal Family is responsible for the poverty of other families: would it were that simple), or modish, offering to make the 'issue' look a *real* one (that the hereditary principle is racist; that the monarchy encourages snobbishness: take but degree away and social concord will prevail).

A more respectable argument against the Royal Family is that, simply by existing, it attracts the grubby attention of the media, and the media's subsequent behaviour infects us all; envy, resentment, voyeurism, prurience, and *schadenfreude* (the laughter of hell, Schopenhauer said) permeate the nation. No doubt, if the Royal Family didn't bear the brunt, other celebrities would, transiently, less colourfully, more trivially.

Much of the charm of latter-day monarchs has been that they symbolize authority and—through a mixture of pomp and circumstance and homeliness—make it seem almost natural, without wielding power and therefore running the risk of unpopularity. Symbols may be *de trop* in literature, but they still carry some weight in the shared life of a country. And we don't have all that much holding us together. In seeking to make himself *useful* rather than symbolic, Prince Charles is bound to incur the sneers of superior persons, who know about architecture etc. and prefer that royalty should remain in the state of happy ignorance into which they were born. Good luck to him.

In other connections—if only the Royal Family could behave a little better, or not so foolishly (beating breasts, baring breasts), and the newspapers much less badly.

May 1994: 'Prince enrages the Left with attack on "trendy dogma".' That is, he has put in a good word for grammar, suggested it might be sensible to smack your child once in a while, and criticized 'fashionable theorists' in university English departments who are trying to 'tear apart' many of our writers 'because they do not fit the abstruse theories of the day' (cor!). Perhaps his worst offence was to quote the closing sentence of *Middlemarch*, about our debt to those who have lived quiet unremarked lives and were never seen on television. But why are these views thought to be Tory? Why should the Conservative party be credited with them? One Labour MP says the Prince is talking rubbish, another, a woman, that he has 'lost his marbles': yob-speech which helps to explain why, no matter how abject they prove, the Tory party has remained in government for fifteen years.

A tip for parents, royal nannies, child-minders, and constables on the beat: 'If anyone is going to spank him, it will have to be done this summer; by next summer he will be doing the spanking' (Kafka's diaries, 1914).

The EC. Might as well put one's pennyworth in, or ecuworth... 'Europe' might seem a more attractive proposition if the businessmen, whom we have no reason to trust unhesitatingly, weren't so mad keen on it. In theory they stand to gain a large market, and hence the country a lot of jobs. But the market, the number of people with money to spend, remains the same, and presumably the number of businessmen operating in it. (Unless—I don't trust myself unhesitatingly—I am naïvely mistaken.) In which case the toughest of them, not necessarily 'ours', will prevail. As for jobs, one can be out of work in Europe just as easily as unemployed in Britain. Competitiveness is something we don't seem to be very good at, but maybe the idea, the 'philosophy', is: better to be uncompetitive inside than out of the competition altogether.

By now we must have irritated the rest of 'Europe' past forgetting, perhaps past forgiving. Some of us may feel, despite intermittent evidence to the contrary, that kinship of language is a stronger bond. But then, writers would, wouldn't they?

A columnist in the *Times Literary Supplement* relates that when Peter Quennell received the CBE, Her Majesty enquired, 'Still writing, Mr Quennell?' Similarly, when Philip Larkin went to receive his, she asked if he was 'still writing'. (He replied that he was still trying.) The columnist suggests that the next writer to receive an honour from Her Majesty might like to investigate the point and report back.

The question 'Are you still writing?' is a customary courtesy, and shouldn't tax our wits. It shows that the Queen knows you are a writer and not a hero of the Gulf War, a captain of industry, or a long-serving borough councillor. (One wonders, does she ask 'Are you still a hero?' or 'How's business?') Moreover it insinuates that she is acquainted with earlier work of yours, perhaps current at a time when she had more leisure for ordinary reading. Writers ought to be appreciative of such rare solicitousness; maybe they are, deep down.

On a like if lowlier occasion Her Majesty asked me the question in a voice so tentative as to suggest that she feared I was past it. I thought to remind her of an earlier meeting at the Palace, a pleasant quarter of an hour you might say, in the company of Sir John Betjeman, when the conversation touched on books as disposables, the difficulty of recycling glass, and the relative intellectual merits of the then Prime Minister of Singapore and his wife. But my seven seconds were up and the chamberlain was urging forward the next recipient. The Queen had a lot on her plate.

Honours. As the years mount up, the odd one flutters down. But ah, the one that got away, that's the one you covet.

Long ago, in Thailand, a voluntary job for the Ministry of Education, supervising the making of English manuals, simplified tales like Of Two Cities abridged to One. And the official i/c Textbooks promised an honour in lieu. Fine, the Order of the White Elephant, one suggested, and it must be Third Class or nothing. Perfectly possible, he said, you may rest assured, Third Class it will be.

Something went wrong. Surely not that night one mistakenly spent in the lock-up. A mere trifle, said the Thais, it happens to the best people. No, it was the man from the Min. of Ed., who announced that he had finally achieved perfect enlightenment and turned into a Buddha. What were textbooks, or civil servants, or worldly honours, let alone a night in the cells? Mere illusion. This proved too much for the Min. of Ed. He was quietly put away. As was the White Elephant, Third Class. Such is the price one pays for the holiness of others.

The disarming joke has it that the best thing about a knighthood is that it gets you a table at the restaurant. The Goncourts report an earnest discussion between two high government officials in Paris, 1852, as to whether one should wear one's decorations when visiting a brothel. One of them says one certainly should not. The other says one certainly should, for then 'they give you women who haven't got the pox'.

Need for sex education. The Australian poet, Gwen Harwood, of two small girls overhearing their fathers talking about the Great War:

> '(We thought a brothel was a French
> hotel that served hot broth to diggers.)'

How charming is divine philosophy! 'Some critic called me the Nothingness Himself and that didn't help my sense of existence any. Then I realized that existence itself is nothing and I felt better' (*The Philosophy of Andy Warhol*). Sweet are the uses of 'philosophy'!

A Nissan promotional video. 'Who wouldn't want a hunk like this?' gasps a pretty girl. 'Not just a new car,' comes in sterner tones, 'a new lifestyle.' Then talk of the philosophy of the automobile. (Sexy word, 'philosophy'.) Followed by routine stuff, a scurry of clever senseless graphics, clips of brain-addling computerized virtual reality or total unreality, with voices-over prophesying that a car shall become man, a man become car . . .

So we have truly corrupted the East! All this to sell cars. A far cry from the old amalgam of Buddhism, the sadness of things, spartan constraints, ritual observances. But then, remember Johnson on making money as a relatively innocent way of employing oneself. The less innocent ways can be left for writers, Eastern or Western, to entertain us with.

In the *Times Literary Supplement* Roger Kimball speaks of the 'kind of inverted Romanticism' that set in at the end of the last century and has remained with us. He cites Allan Bloom (*Love and Friendship*): 'He who has the most terrible message possesses the most truth', adding in his own words, 'We live at a moment when it seems best to think the worst of ourselves': a proposition which Bloom is asking us to reconsider.

There is little chance of any return to a comfortable 'romanticism', a confidence in our essential goodness. Memories of the Holocaust, if they are not undying, are revived by current events—these days thoroughly publicized; Brecht's man who laughed because he hadn't yet heard the news doesn't exist any more. Yet this anti-romanticism has become a cluster of easily exploited stock responses, has hardened into a set of literary conventions no different in kind, though at the opposite pole, from the sentimental old ones. This does us no chastening good. Believing we are rotten makes us, not humble, but complacently rotten. The increasingly 'terrible messages' are self-fulfilling, they are what we live down to, what legitimizes our debasement. Perhaps it is time we gave ourselves, however cautiously, however—from the artistic point of view—boringly, the benefit of the doubt.

The ending of *Middlemarch*: '. . . the growing good of the world is partly dependent on unhistoric acts; and that things are not so ill with you and me as they might have been, is half owing to the number who lived faithfully a hidden life, and rest in unvisited tombs.' While the growing good may be an overstatement, the half owing is surely an understatement. The words are still to the point, despite the communications explosion.

It's not so much that one is out of sympathy with the age, it's the only age one has, as that the age is out of sympathy with one.

But then, the age is out of sympathy with itself.

Still, once everybody is alienated, nobody will be alienated.

'Unsettling': another favourite fiction-reviewing epithet. As if we were nicely settled before we opened the book.

'The principal aim of some writers seems to be to *put us down*. Are we so up, then, still, after all these years?': Michael Frayn, in *Constructions*, 1974. He continues: 'Of course, in unsophisticated literature things often turn out to be better than they look. Dark clouds have silver linings, cowards summon up their courage, bounders turn up trumps, cads are redeemed by love. Perhaps literature of this sort is intended primarily for people whose lives are hard. The sort of literature where the good is bad underneath is intended for consumption by the privileged classes.'

But how did this come about?

'Let us make man in our image,' God announced, 'after our likeness.' With God all other things are possible; this was too much even for him. 'Hear, O Israel: the Lord our God is one Lord', one only. He had to lower his sights.

So God made men and women after other likenesses, other likings. He made those who naturally preferred to hear about good things, like dark clouds that had silver linings, bounders who turned up trumps, cads who were redeemed by love, and so forth. This class of humans, he reflected, would get by, with an effort, no need for special concessions. Of course, good things require the co-existence of bad things since otherwise they wouldn't be perceived. So God then made men and women who were more interested in hearing about silver linings that had dark clouds, courageous men who were cowards underneath, nice people who were destroyed by love, and so on. Poor wretches, he mused, we must give this lot special privileges to make up for it.

Later, Thomas à Kempis came along and threw cold water: 'At the Day of Judgement, we shall not be asked what we have read, but what we have done.'

Remember the scorn with which the intelligentsia greeted Martyn Lewis's suggestion that items of *good* news should be reported as well? As a newscaster he had to utter the bad news day after day; they only had to listen to it, if they so chose.

Aspiring to the Best no doubt exacts a full look at the Worst. But may we not suggest that contemplation of the worst should accommodate a brief glance at the better?

'The news is always blood and dead,' observes our small grandson during lunch, waving his fork at the television. 'I don't like it.' Repeating this opinion rather loudly in the underground, he draws grave, approving nods from fellow passengers.

He knows something about the killing of James Bulger. 'Bullies,' he mumbles sorrowfully, perhaps with the school playground in mind. He doesn't yet read the newspaper, that daily emetic.

'The London Library does not accept responsibility for injuries incurred by members in handling volumes of newspapers' (notice board).

'There is nothing either good or bad, but thinking makes it so.' That was Hamlet, exchanging cynical quips with his smart varsity chums.

But an impeccably serious psychologist, brought in to deal with the eccentric Martyn Lewis, says this: 'It is not news itself which determines how we think, feel and act but our interpretations of it . . . "The news" is a figment of our imagination. It does not exist.' So if we turn the television off, or turn our imagination down, these terrible things—a dead mother, a starving child, a civil war—will cease to exist, like the tree in the quad when there's no one about to look at it?

Then there is the 'feel-good factor'. Bad news 'affirms' our belief in a 'just world', and watching stories of tragedies far away enables us to create in ourselves feelings of compassion and pity which assure us that we are 'kind, generous, caring'. Who on earth are these 'we' who procure such satisfying feelings from the sight of others' sufferings? This—possibly an echo of the old idea that heavenly bliss consists largely in witnessing the pains of the damned—is theory run mad. In the 'just world', the psychologist proceeds, the wicked are punished, so when you see people suffering, you know they are wicked. No child would make that assumption; no one bright or imaginative enough to conceive of a just world would suppose for a second that in the real world those who suffer must be wicked.

After these simple-minded, perverse, and profoundly callous pronouncements, the secular guru advises us to strive, through critical thought and careful examination, to dissociate our interpretations from figments and bring them as close to reality as we possibly can. For 'what we need from the media is not good news or bad news but the truth'. We need the truth—that's true. But does she mean that the reports of massacre, famine, torture, murder and rape, far away or close at hand, are *false*? That the 'just world' *is* the real world?

The television listing says of a documentary: '. . . offers that awful cliché, a message of hope'. Most of the rest of the evening's viewing has to do with murder, sexual problems, sick comedy. No mention of awful clichés there.

It's Wednesday, and time for *Star Trek*, our weekly fifty minutes of morality as it functions still in outer space. Low-quality acting, high-quality pondering—the opposite of everything else in the world of entertainment.

❧

SCENES from a documentary about the new divided countries. (1) A blunt old shepherd says, 'Who do these hills belong to, except my sheep?' Heart-warming. (2) An old shepherd cuts a sheep's throat with a blunt knife. Can't be avoided, and it's his sheep. (3) Old shepherds of different ethnic groups beat one another up with blunt instruments. Might have known.

As was said by Vasko Popa, Serbian poet who died in 1991:

'Some bite off the others'
Arm or leg or whatever

Take it between their teeth
Run off as quick as they can
Bury it in the earth

The others run in all directions
Sniff search sniff search
Turn up all the earth

If any are lucky enough to find their arm
Or leg or whatever
It's their turn to bite

The game goes on briskly

As long as there are arms
As long as there are legs
As long as there is anything whatever'
      —'He', translated by Anne Pennington

Mencius asks whether the maker of arrows is really more unfeeling than the maker of armour. The former is afraid lest he should fail to harm people, the latter is afraid lest he should fail to protect them.

Mencius doesn't exactly answer the question. He merely compares the case with that of the doctor and the coffin-maker, presumably in that the doctor makes a living by trying to save people from death and the coffin-maker by accommodating those who die. The emergent moral, faintly disappointing, is: 'One cannot be too careful in the choice of one's calling.'

Less cryptic is the story of the king who notices an ox being led through the hall. When he asks where it is going, he is told that its blood is to be used in the consecration of a new bell. 'Spare it,' he says, 'I cannot bear to see it shrinking with fear, like an innocent man going to the place of execution.' In that case, the ceremony will have to be abandoned. But that, says the king, is out of the question: 'Use a lamb instead.'

The common people believe that the king was being miserly, replacing an expensive large animal with a cheap small one. And if he were truly distressed by an animal going innocently to its death, what was there to choose between an ox and a lamb?

But Mencius approves of the king's behaviour as the way of a benevolent man. Once having seen an animal alive, he cannot endure to see it die; once having heard an animal cry, he cannot endure to eat its flesh. What next, we wonder, a puff for vegetarianism?

The king is pleased. He had failed to understand his own heart, but Mencius saw into it and described it for him.

The moral is eminently practical: 'That is why the gentleman keeps his distance from the kitchen.'

Probably not for quite a time yet, but the day will come when we reflect with disgust and incredulity on how humans used to eat the flesh of animals, much as we now look back to the witch hunts and inquisitions of bygone centuries. No doubt we shall continue to steal, destroy, rape, and murder. The body's regime is more readily transformed than the soul's.

In Gwyneth Jones's science-fiction novel, *White Queen*, aliens have arrived on earth. Great excitement. And how appealing they are, the way they thank a waste-disposal unit, 'Good machine, eat up', and in their habit of getting our idioms slightly wrong: 'like as two peas in a pot'. Unfortunately they kill a thirteen-year-old girl who is surreptitiously taking a blood sample from one of them in the advancement of science. In their eyes this constitutes an act of war. Ah, those customs, nice or nasty, whether of races other than ours, 'cultures' is the word, or come to that of individuals within the race . . . The novel has a twist in the tail: the aliens are immortal, and cannot conceive of death. Oh dear, what have we done, we didn't know. This lets them off the hook, but doesn't bring the girl back.

Pictures of a child suffering evoke so much pity that we are even prepared to succour grown-ups at a pinch.

Coleridge on Ireland: 'I am quite sure that no dangers are to be feared by England from the disannexing and independence of Ireland at all comparable with the evils which have been, and will yet be, caused to England by the Union. We have never received one particle of advantage from our association with Ireland, whilst we have in many most vital particulars violated the principles of the British constitution solely for the purpose of conciliating the Irish agitators, and of endeavouring—a vain endeavour—to find room for them under the same government' (*Table Talk*, 17 December 1831). And 'I am deliberately of opinion, that England, in all its institutions, has received injury from its union with Ireland. My only difficulty is as to the Protestants, to whom we owe protection. But I cannot forget that the Protestants themselves have greatly aided in accelerating the present horrible state of things, by using that as a remedy and a reward which should have been to them an opportunity' (5 February 1833).

Wise words. But not one particle of advantage? My old dad was advantageous in his way.

I came on a group of people squatting on the grass who announced themselves as members of the IRA. In a mollifying way—I had no wish to be beaten up—I informed them that my father's parents had both been killed by the Black and Tans (a downright fib, as I was fully aware), but the IRA were no better, I insisted, indeed they were worse. The word 'Warrington' arose in my mind, with that peculiar clarity or resonance that attends the occasional irruption of specific reality into a dream. This didn't perturb them noticeably. I caught the eye of a beautiful young girl, whose confiding eye was willing to be caught. Finding myself alone with her, the others having left on some mission or other, I said, 'You must be the common-war life of the leader.' I realized that something was amiss in this utterance and briefly thought of rectifying it, but she seemed agreeable, even grateful. She grew more captivating by the second. Clearly I would have to rescue her from the gang. I had barely embarked on her salvation when, between the close-set trees, I glimpsed the shapes of the IRA stealing back. It was time to wake up and save myself.

The humanity Arabs show towards the mad . . . afflicted by Allah, or touched, which is tantamount to a blessing; and therefore not to be hindered or harmed. John Buchan wrote of an Englishman riding alone through Yemen that the Arabs let him go on his way, reasoning that 'the hand of Allah was heavy enough on him without their efforts'.

Once in Alexandria, during rioting, the university was closed, I was bored, and took it into my head to call on a Jewish friend, and bring her a little cheer. It was a curious sort of riot, even for those days; it had nothing to do with politics. The police had gone on strike, looters were busy, the army had been brought in to deal with both the police and the looters, several of whom (or perhaps innocent passers-by) lay dead in the streets. Shops were ablaze, a cinema was burning. I had miscalculated. But returning would be as tedious (to say the least) as going on. A group of soldiers stopped me. Didn't I know there was a curfew? Where was I going? It wouldn't do to give the address. 'Thalassa! Thalassa!' I thought of crying, since the apartment house where she lived was near the Corniche. But Greeks were even less popular than the British. Then a good word came into my head, meaning 'sick': it might lead them to think I was a doctor on an errand of mercy. 'Ayyan, ayyan!' They must have supposed I was the sick one, sick in the head, touched, and after some uncertainty they waved me on, abstractedly, turning away from me. 'Make hurry, effendi!' one of them hissed. They didn't want an officer to witness what might be deemed slackness rather than humanity.

Now I remember having told the story before—in a novel, published forty years ago, so much of which was mere reality as to be shameful in a work of fiction.

The drunkenness of things being similar

What Tel Aviv brought to mind was Alexandria
The same air, the same light, the same water.
Alexandria once waited to be bombed by Tel Aviv
Once Tel Aviv expected to be bombed by Alexandria.
So much in common in so many places you perceive.

Warsaw, September 1981. At a writers' club, everyone darting about with pens peering out of their pockets, papers tucked under their arms (samizdats in the making? Who makes anything else?), talking urgently or uneasily, smoking furiously (cigarettes kill you? What doesn't?), knocking back vodka or beer (it makes you drunk? So where's the difference?), all of them great writers it may be, writings tucked under their arms, heading for the ancient gestetner (it still works? They all still work).

'What shall we do with all our untranslated diacritical marks?' (Piotr Sommer, 'A song'). The cry of a writer proud of his native language, perhaps one of those languages which command a relatively small public—or someone whose writings for some reason can only be issued abroad, in foreign garb. Also the writerly thought, mischievous, pleasurable, that some things *are* untranslatable.

Goethe observed that it was precisely the untranslatable that gave a language its value and character.

> 'We know all about oppression
> and that we are very much against it
> and that cigarettes have gone up again
> oh we know . . .'
>
> —Hans Magnus Enzensberger,
> 'Song for Those Who Know'

It can't be denied, there are different sorts of knowing, and so many things to be against.

The end of the world as observed by the landlady of the Rovers Return in that epic, *Coronation Street* (13 October 1993): 'Communism doesn't work. Capitalism doesn't work. Marriage doesn't work. Work doesn't work.' And the price of beer keeps going up.

Another semiprecious stone from *Coronation Street* (20 May 1994): 'You can't live in the past.' 'You can when you have no future.' Note that the second speaker isn't a crumblie or even a wrinklie: he just can't find work.

Japanese soldiers straggling out of the jungle years afterwards, rusty guns at the ready: no one had told them the war was over. They discovered they had lost it. Later still, Japanese soldiers stumbling out of another jungle, bodies emaciated, uniforms in tatters. And it

looked as if they had won the war. There's a parable here, about
going on fighting, with nobody telling you it's all over. But let's
leave it for someone else to explicate. Some things are best not
looked into.

Package tour

The main thing is, not the famous yellow cotton
The main thing is, that many people
A great many people were killed here once
(So much is beyond dispute)
They were good people
Consisting of men, women, and children
100,000 of them (a conservative estimate is 60,000)
While 40,000 women were raped (alternatively 20,000)
Though this is not why they call it the Rape of Nanjing
All of which was the work of Japanese soldiers
(Reportedly they were bored and tired, but not
      sufficiently)
In those days the Japanese were not good people
Of course it was a long time ago
(Though some do not reckon 50 years is all that long)
But it is the main thing
One's attention is drawn to it repeatedly
Right up to the next scheduled meal
In a famous Buddhist restaurant as it happens
Where smiling monks serve elegant dishes
Totally vegetarian, which does not preclude beer
Yet it would not do to enjoy oneself too much
Despite the manifest attractions of this beautiful city
Which it is only right to admire openly
On the banks of the Yangtze River
With its abundant greenery and temperate climate
And (the guidebook hints) its 'unharried pace'
Which brings us back to the main thing . . .

'And Babylon, the glory of kingdoms, shall be as when God overthrew Sodom and Gomorrah. It shall never be inhabited, neither shall it be dwelt in from generation to generation: neither shall the Arabian pitch tent there; neither shall the shepherds make their fold there. But wild beasts of the desert shall lie there; and their houses shall be full of doleful creatures; and owls shall dwell there, and satyrs shall dance there. And the wild beasts of the islands shall cry in their desolate houses, and dragons in their pleasant palaces.'

Prodigious words! No wonder that some British West Indians use the name 'Babylon' of Britain, white Britain. ('I will punish the world for their evil, and the wicked for their iniquity; and I will cause the arrogancy of the proud to cease.') They feel themselves victimized, they live in exile. Exiled from where? What is the promised land? (Free airline tickets to Africa don't find many takers.) Surely the compromised land of us all: Eden, a place not on any modern map, where, in Isaiah's later words, 'the whole earth is at rest, and is quiet: they break forth into singing'.

How many miles to Babylon? Some of us feel we live in a land of captivity, a Sodom, a Gomorrah, where worse crimes are committed than any traditionally associated with the cities of the plain, even crediting Grimmelshausen's tall story, that in addition to their other vices the Sodomites were so averse to hospitality that strangers were consigned to beds of various sizes and, in Procrustean fashion, stretched or trimmed to fit them—a land where the keepers of the law, so we gather from the reference books specializing in common colloquialisms we hadn't met before, are known in some quarters as 'the Babylon'.

St John took up the theme in the 'great whore with whom the kings of the earth have committed fornication', the Scarlet Woman upon whose forehead was written 'Babylon the Great, the Mother of Harlots and Abominations of the Earth'. At this stage she was probably ancient Rome, drunk with the blood of the Christian martyrs. Subsequently Protestant divines transferred her name and features to the Roman Catholic Church, while their Catholic counterparts located them in the Protestant Churches. A whore for all seasons, a woman for all reasons.

Holidays fall in a class of their own. People like to refresh them-
selves in the more touted sinks of iniquity, to visit famous Babylon,
strictly as tourists. Such alluring brochures they put out! Wild beasts!
Dragons! Bird-watching! Palaces of pleasure! A chance to dance with
satyrs! As for the local women, doleful creatures they may be, but
the sight of hard currency soon gets them cracking.

A thank-you letter from abroad

It was gracious to have you with us, our jokes
have grown stale, but you made merry at them.
A freshened breath of air, as the chairman said
concluding your last appearance in our city
(one of our old heroes, by the way, very soft
of speech, perhaps you didn't hear him well)—
As he told, we must make your appearance last.
All enjoyed your poetry readings though not
appreciating all. If I say they came for coffee
and faded pastries, it is only our worn-out joke!
The one who asked the questions was a secret police,
he is 'given the boot' but cannot stop it.
It was not your failing you consumed the final
of the lady's cheese. And our currency is funny
so you never learned the payment of a drink.
Then I am shamed your wallet with small bills was
        robbed,
these bad persons are confused concerning property.
I think perhaps the liquor made you carefree!
The top hotel you stayed I fear was not quite up to it,
the widespread menu is before the war, with gravy stains,
one day a bacon, one day an egg, 'never the two together'.
And why we did not like to go inside, you know,
it was the favoured 'stamping ground' of upper echelons.
We are told of a new poetry magazine, uncensored,
but barely there is paper to print it on,

the unimpeded publishers use all for sex and crimes.
You see, my friend, we have still some reason of being!
Taboo or not taboo? We are a little lost without it.
There is much movement these days, upwards,
        downwards,
sidewards, but still we have our pride somewhere.
I promise my poor effort to turn your choicest poems
into our hard language, I think they are acceptable.
When we receive our imminent liberties
we shall come in your own country, which I do not call
Great because you do not like it. (Such modesty! I think
my country would be Great except for history's bad
        turns.)
There'll be lots to talk about, of little things,
And we shall visit far-famed pubs, where the 'booze'
flows freely and the Scottish eggs are ample,
and everybody speaks his mind unfearfully
(as we can now, if we only know our minds).
Also the Café Royal, to rub our elbows with the spirits
of Oscar O'Flahertie Wilde and Ernest Christopher
        Dowson
(see, I study the Oxford Friend to English Literature
you kindly presented me!) We shall call on Oxford too,
and—I think your nursing mother?—Cambridge is
        obliged.
I hope the British Council will agree my wishes,
so I bring my wife you took such pleasure in, and kiddies
        too,
in case. But too much of your costly time I am spending,
with love and memories . . .

NIETZSCHE is the one modern philosopher whom the layman has a fair chance of understanding. Perhaps this makes him *not* a philosopher. Perhaps it makes him a poet. (A *non sequitur*.) Or is there a connection in this sphere between being understandable and being insane?

Commenting on the unresolved contradictions in Nietzsche's writings, H. G. Schenk describes what he has left us as 'the intellectual echo of the recurrent oscillations of his soul, observed with the utmost sensitivity'. In introducing *Human, All Too Human* in R. J. Hollingdale's translation, Erich Heller remarks that even the most impressive of philosophical systems is perched uncomfortably on a throne of rock-bottom stupidity, the self-induced narrow-mindedness which leads a man to believe that he, a small part of an immense world, is capable of making absolutely coherent sense of it all. Heller is championing aphorisms, which, through their brevity, achieve 'a kind' of finality, one which we know, the world being so immense, isn't more than a kind of. One effect of eluding narrow-mindedness and resisting schematization, something more commonly observed in poets, is that over the years Nietzsche has proved to be a number of serviceable things to a number of men (and even a few women); and less obviously, for thinkers incline to welcome what looks like support and ignore what sounds like dissent, an occasional stumbling-block to an occasional creed.

To quote a few—or, come to that, many—of Nietzsche's aphorisms is to misrepresent, to do him less than justice (or to do him more). To quote all of them wouldn't be much better, since if he had lived longer he would have uttered more. In fact, denied immortality, he never completed his task. His writings are partial, in two senses of the word. Philosophical systems are equally disreputable; more so, rather, for the reason Heller gives: they think they are reputable. Nietzsche himself observed that when you have finished building your house, you realize that in the process you have learnt things you ought to have known before you started.

Partial, then . . .

'It is good to repeat oneself and thus bestow on a thing a right and a left foot. Truth may be able to stand on one leg; but with two it can walk and get around.' That will hearten some of us!

'Metre lays a veil over reality: it effectuates a certain artificiality of speech and unclarity of thinking; by means of the shadows it throws over thoughts it now conceals, now brings into prominence . . . Art makes the sight of life bearable by laying over it the veil of unclear language.' Sad; but then, there's always an element of sadness attending the experience of great art. Life tries to live up to it, but rarely can, no matter how much extra unclearness of thought we bring to it. As for that veil, it was Nietzsche's Zarathustra who said that the poets lie too much. A rider has it, 'But Zarathustra too is a poet.'

'It is neither the best nor the worst in a book that is untranslatable.' It's those little idiomatic touches, the unimportant bits where *tone* is important—and the workaday passages which induce apathy in the translator.

'We belong to an age whose culture is in danger of perishing through the means to culture.' Timely, all too timely. No need to mention names.

'He who lives for the sake of combating an enemy has an interest in seeing that his enemy stays alive.' What would the terrorist organizations do if their enemies suddenly vanished? Start a football team?

'Convictions are more dangerous enemies of truth than lies.' It all depends—on who's lying and how, on whose convictions and what they are. (But see Thoreau on Yankees, below.) And 'Linguistic danger to spiritual freedom: Every word is a prejudice.' A truth, but not a very helpful one; there's little we can do about it, aside from using as few words as possible.

'Not when it is dangerous to tell the truth does truth lack advocates, but when it is boring to do so.' Which accounts for a lot, including the silences of politicians—and our horror of commonplaces.

'. . . A god who begets children on a mortal woman; a sage who calls upon us no longer to work, no longer to sit in judgement, but to heed the signs of the imminent end of the world; a justice which accepts an innocent man as a substitute sacrifice; someone who bids his disciples drink his blood; prayers for miraculous interventions; sin perpetrated against a god atoned for by a god; fear of a Beyond to which death is the gateway . . . —how gruesomely all this is wafted to us, as if out of the grave of a primeval past! Can one believe that things of this sort are still believed in?' Indeed one can. (Worse things have been believed in.) Belief is another of our deepest hungers. The alternative to the kind of elaborate and comprehensive belief Nietzsche sniffily adumbrates is a succession of little beliefs, in this or in that ('I believe in exercise', 'I believe in the government', 'I believe in doing my own thing'), which are continually collapsing and being replaced by others of the same ilk. Personally I believe in believing—in what, and how unreservedly, I'm not sure. Incidentally, isn't there 'poetic justice' in a god atoning for sin perpetrated against a god, with that god's connivance? Moreover, the perpetrators (including some who have perpetrated nothing at all) are made to feel all the more guilty. Apropos of the 'pale, bloodstained Jew', Heine takes another view: 'Anyone who sees his god suffering finds it easier to endure his own pain.' He also mentions a legend current among stones that one day God himself would become stone, in order to redeem them from their fixity.

'A little seamstress is seduced and dishonoured; a great scholar of all the four faculties is the miscreant. But that surely cannot happen in the right nature of things? No, by no means! Without the assistance of the Devil in person the great scholar could not have brought it about.—Is this really supposed to be the greatest German "tragic idea", as Germans say it is?—But even this idea was still too dreadful for Goethe . . .' So dreadful that the little seamstress was received into heaven, and even the great scholar escaped hell through a legalistic quibble. But a great scholar ('Habe nun, ach, Philosophie, Juristerei und Medicin, und leider auch Theologie durchaus studirt': what an exhausting syllabus!) might well need the counsel and encouragement of some young devil when it came to having his way with an innocent, pious maiden of the lower middle class. Gretchen wasn't a seamstress—which we suppose implies an easy lay—but a respectable girl who, since there was no maid, had to keep her penny-pinching mother's house, cooking, cleaning, knitting and sewing, on her feet all day long. As for being saved—since Nietzsche didn't believe in heaven, the question doesn't arise. Nor did Goethe, but he raised the question. It would have been simple enough to make Faust a modern-style academic, say in the mould of Malcolm Bradbury's fictions, who has a brief affair with a sweet girl-undergraduate, independent of any supernatural soliciting, and then more or less politely drops her. Whereupon she changes to another faculty—there being more than four faculties by now—takes a degree in sociology, and is eventually enrolled among the saints of feminism. The Professor takes early retirement and writes a best-selling novel.

Aporia: more or less honest doubt—another ailment of old age. And with reason.

D'Alembert says that in the morning he sees probability on his right, and by afternoon it's on his left. When the evening comes he doesn't believe either the morning's opinion or the afternoon's. Diderot is impatient with this vacillating: if D'Alembert thinks it through, he will perceive that our real opinion is not the one we have never wavered from, but the one to which we most regularly return. D'Alembert agrees with him. It's getting late and D'Alembert wants to go to sleep. (Diderot: *D'Alembert's Dream*.)

Thoreau is less enervated. 'We Yankees are not so far from right, who answer one question by asking another. Yes and No are lies— a true answer will not aim to establish anything, but rather to set all well afloat.'

❧

IN INTRODUCING *Essays and Aphorisms*, a selection from Schopenhauer's *Parerga and Paralipomena*, R. J. Hollingdale notes that in literature Goethe reaped the whole harvest, with the result that original minds who followed him, if they weren't content with gleaning, had to turn to new fields. Schopenhauer, who might otherwise have expressed himself in fiction, poetry, or autobiography, was diverted to metaphysics, and became 'the first German philosopher to be read as "literature" by a public not primarily interested in philosophy'. Presumably there were predecessors in other languages, notably the authors of the Bible.

Always shrewd on literary matters, Schopenhauer says that the poet presents images from life and leaves it to readers to absorb his thoughts as best their mental abilities allow, thus engaging all sorts of men, fools and sages. The philosopher on the other hand presents not life itself but the finished thoughts he has abstracted from it, demanding that readers should think exactly as he himself does; which is why his public is so small. 'The poet can thus be compared with one who presents flowers, the philosopher with one who presents their essence.'

He is (to put it mildly) a gloomy soul—'The world is Hell, and men are on the one hand the tormented souls and on the other the devils in it'—where Nietzsche whips himself into a frenzy of enthusiasm or rage. The word 'whip' reminds us that neither of them will be found acceptable on the subject of women. Schopenhauer must be the more offensive of the two in that he takes them more seriously, 'big children' though he terms them. In fact it is in comparison with women that he says his nicest things about men. A visitor observed of the philosopher's conversation that it affected him 'as though I had felt an icy draught blowing in on me through the half-open door of nothingness'.

'The Creator created not only the world, he also created possibility itself: therefore he should have created the possibility of a better world than this one.'

'Evil is precisely that which is positive, that which makes itself palpable; and good, on the other hand, i.e. all happiness and all gratification, is that which is negative, the mere abolition of a desire and extinction of a pain. This is also consistent with the fact that as a rule we find pleasure much less pleasurable, pain much more painful, than we expected.'

'If you are asked about continued existence after death by one of those people who would like to know everything but refuse to learn anything, the most appropriate and approximately correct reply is: "After your death you will be what you were before your birth."'

On this theme there follows an amusing dialogue between Philalethes and Thrasymachus. Your immortality, Philalethes tells Thrasymachus, might be described as an indestructibility without continued existence. Thrasymachus won't give tuppence for immortality if it doesn't include the ongoingness of his individuality. Philalethes proposes a bargain: suppose he guarantees the other's immortality on condition that it is preceded by a completely unconscious death-sleep of three months. That's fine by Thrasymachus ('forceful fighter'?). But, says Philalethes, since we have no notion of time while we are unconscious, it makes no difference whether the death-sleep lasts three months or ten thousand years. Thrasymachus has to admit to the logic of this. Philalethes ('lover of oblivion'?) continues: Then, if after the ten thousand years it was forgotten to wake Thrasymachus up, it would be no great misfortune, since his period of non-being would have exceeded by far his brief period of being himself, and he would have grown used to it. Certainly he would have no idea that he had failed to be woken up.

Some very clever reasoning by Philalethes ensues—nothing so crude as an earlier pronouncement of Schopenhauer's, that mature consideration persuades us that total non-being would be preferable to the kind of existence we lead—but Thrasymachus departs in high dudgeon. He has more important things to do.

'More than nine-tenths of all literate men and women read nothing but newspapers, and consequently model their orthography, grammar and style almost exclusively on them . . . A censor should be instituted who, instead of receiving a salary, should receive one louis d'or for every mangled or stylistically objectionable word, error of grammar or syntax, or misemployed preposition he discovers in them, and three louis d'or for every instance of sheer impudent mockery of all style and grammar, with double the sum for any repetition, the amounts to be defrayed by the perpetrators.'

'According to Herodotus, Xerxes wept at the sight of his enormous army to think that, of all these men, not one would be alive in a hundred years' time; so who cannot weep at the sight of the thick fair catalogue to think that, of all these books, not one will be alive in ten years' time.'

On Christianity: 'It is best to communicate this [i.e. dogma] to the great masses, who are incapable of grasping truth directly, in the form of a beautiful allegory . . . But a small addition of absurdity is a necessary ingredient in such an allegory: it serves to indicate its allegorical nature. If you take Christian dogma *sensu proprio* [literally], then Voltaire is right. Taken allegorically, on the other hand, it is a sacred myth . . . Yet the weak point of all religions remains that they can never dare to confess to being allegorical, so that they have to present their doctrines in all seriousness as true *sensu proprio*; which, because of the absurdities essential to allegory, leads to perpetual deception and a great disadvantage for religion. What is even worse, indeed, is that in time it comes to light that they are *not* true *sensu proprio*, and then they perish. To this extent it would be better to admit their allegorical nature straightaway: only the difficulty here is to make the people understand that a thing can be true and not true at the same time.'

Difficult indeed! And alas nothing is as headstrong as an allegory; once you confess to one, once you let one in, it chomps away at everything.

'What a bad conscience religion must have is to be judged by the fact that it is forbidden under pain of such severe punishment to *mock* it.'

As witness Salman Rushdie, who may have thought (I certainly did) that he had written a religious book.

'If, having taken stock of human *wickedness*, you feel a sense of horror at it, you should straightaway turn your eyes to the *misery* of human existence. (And if you are shocked at its misery you should turn your eyes to its wickedness.) Then you will see that they balance one another; you will become aware of the existence of an eternal justice, that the world itself is its own universal Last Judgement, and you will begin to understand why everything that lives must atone for its existence, first by living and then by dying.'

Pessimistic? The wickedness and the misery balance out in the end, the above passage claims, but they aren't always equitably apportioned. Yes, but endearingly, almost enliveningly. (Though it still goes against the grain to concede that *how* you say may count for more than *what* you say.) Schopenhauer's passion for literature, in diverse languages, shines out in his writing, and in the most direct form: quotation. And literature is a product of the world he condemns: it wouldn't exist without it. And Schopenhauer is a part of literature. His style is fluent, lucid, forceful; the darkest thoughts unfold in light; a grim invigorating humour is never far away. The thoughts that a man is capable of, he said, always express themselves in clear, comprehensible and unambiguous language (cf. Wittgenstein: 'What can be said at all can be said clearly'). 'Those who put together difficult, obscure, involved, ambiguous discourses do not really know what they want to say: they have no more than a vague consciousness of it which is only struggling towards a thought: often, however, they also want to conceal from themselves and others that they actually have nothing to say.'

So Goethe didn't reap quite the whole harvest.

'A man's life of any worth is a continual allegory,' said Keats, whose life was a short-lived one. In 1930 Kurt Tucholsky, German satirist, cited a man who was religious, a lover of all living creatures, but also keen on fishing. Having cast his line, he would gaze into the water and pray to the Good Lord (Fish Division) that no fish should take the bait. There was a man who had learned how to reconcile heavenly ideals with sinful passions: 'a typical allegory, a symbol even'!

You move the dozing cat into the sun, which seemingly he hasn't noticed. This is a liberty he resents. Settling down, however, for a moment he is gratified. Then the sun goes in. He shoots a reproachful look—you have turned it off! This little drama gives you to pause. Here, you wouldn't wonder, is—what Borges perceives as a frivolous and intolerable aesthetic error—an allegory. Composing himself artistically, the cat agrees with Borges.

In addition to the great themes involved—eternal life, lifeblood, love or lust, power over others—one reason for the survival, the immortality you might say, of the vampire legend is that we have all met vampires: those who batten on others, who suck up their energies—perhaps in the most courteous of ways, but unrelentingly. Possibly even having pallid cheeks and red lips, never quite healthy yet tireless, in whose vicinity the hale and hearty droop and fade. Montaigne tells of a rich old man, very sick, whom he once visited in Toulouse. Having recovered, the old man informed his physician that he owed this transformation to 'fixing his eyes upon the liveliness and freshness' of his young visitor's face, 'setting his thoughts upon the jollity and vigour' of youth, and 'filling all his senses with my flourishing estate'. By these means his health was restored. Montaigne adds: 'But he forgot to say that mine might also be impaired and infected.'

In his fascinating and alarming *Concise Oxford Dictionary of Literary Terms* Chris Baldick says, 'An allegory may be conceived as a metaphor that is extended into a structured system.' To the two great evergreen or ever-black legends, vampire and Faust, we must add the story of Eden and the Fall, lagging behind these days owing to its lack of sensation-value (?) and its moralistic bias (!), yet the true basis, accounting for sins of diverse kinds, for death and, if pro tem, the loss of immortality, and prefiguring the activities of

Faust-figures, whether Promethean or diabolic in inspiration and effect, through the centuries. 'Structured systems', all three, which lend themselves generously to continual restructuring, even of a frivolous appearance. Allegories which it would be staggeringly absurd to spurn as 'aesthetic errors'.

GEORG Christoph Lichtenberg is held to have introduced the aphorism into German literature, although, as Mr Hollingdale remarks in his generous selection from notebooks dated between 1765 and 1799, this appears to have happened without intent on his part in that the aphorisms remained unpublished at his death.

Lichtenberg can be obvious: 'He ate so well that a hundred people could have had their *Give us this day our daily bread* answered with what he ate'; or pointless: 'In England a man was charged with bigamy and his lawyer got him off by proving that his client had three wives' (we have seen too much of the law's aberrations); at times obscure: 'Whenever he spoke every mousetrap in the neighbourhood snapped shut' (but be on your guard: 'To find something obscure poses no difficulty: elephants and poodles find many things obscure'). On rare occasions he is quaintly naughty: 'He travelled through Northeim to Einbeck and from there through Mlle P. to Hanover'; 'Her petticoat had stripes of broad red and blue and looked as though it had been made out of a stage-curtain. I would have paid a lot for a front seat, but there was no performance.' And the following suggests that he was loitering with intent after all: 'If I had not written this book then a thousand years hence between six and seven in the evening people would in many a town in Germany be talking about quite different things from what they will in fact be talking about.'

When he is good he is extremely good, as was perceived by Goethe, who considered him an amazing divining-rod since behind each of his jests there lurked a problem, and by Nietzsche, who included the aphorisms in a very short list of German books which merited repeated reading.

'No work, and especially no work of literature, should display the effort it has cost. A writer who wants to be read by posterity must not neglect to drop into odd corners of his chapters such hints at whole books, ideas for disputations, that his readers will believe he has thousands of them to throw away.'

'Nature has joined men at the heart, and the professors would like them to be joined at the head.'

'We say that someone occupies an official position, whereas it is the official position that occupies him.'

'We do not think good metaphors are anything very important, but I think a good metaphor is something even the police should keep an eye on . . .'

'It would have to be a quite fearfully dreadful translation that could spoil a good book for a man of intelligence who reads it as a whole without lingering over individual expressions or sentences.'

'There can hardly be stranger wares in the world than *books*: printed by people who do not understand them; sold by people who do not understand them; bound, reviewed, and read by people who do not understand them; and now even written by people who do not understand them.'

'Although I know, of course, that very many reviewers do not read the books they review in so exemplary a way, I none the less cannot see what harm it could do if one were to read a book one is intending to review.'

'Nowadays we everywhere seek to propagate wisdom: who knows whether in a couple of centuries there may not exist universities for restoring the old ignorance?'

'As soon as he receives a little applause many a writer believes the world is interested in everything about him. The play-scribbler

Kotzebue even thinks himself justified in telling the public that he administered an enema to his dying wife.'

'The forests are getting smaller and smaller, the amount of wood is decreasing, what shall we do? Oh, when the time comes that the forests cease to exist we shall certainly be able to burn books until new ones have grown.'

Is it because they have no time to bring in the specifically topical that good aphorisms strike us as so remarkably topical? Under certain regimes poets have got away with quite a lot simply because the police didn't scrutinize their metaphors. Dwindling forests . . . writers telling all . . . universities reinstating ignorance: Lichtenberg's couple of centuries brings us to around 1995.

On the subject of translation. You can see what Lichtenberg means, but ideally—and these days the standard is pretty high—the translator has to be himself a writer. He may not write outside translation, he may not write his 'own stuff', but he still needs to be a true writer.

'I myself have seen a horse who preferred Horace to Pope' (Lichtenberg).   •

Caligula on the subject of names

Though he had little Latin
He seemed to like his title
I named him Incitatus
Meaning to run swiftly
But also to excite, to incite
Or so to speak spur on
Me they dubbed Baby-Boots
I gave him iron ones

He was born in a tailored toga
I hoped he would spur on the others
So I made him a consul
There's a Pole called 'I think' who thought
He performed his duties perfectly
'That is, he didn't perform them at all'
Which is not entirely accurate
At times he intervened in the proceedings
He would hear-hear with his hooves
His neigh was his nay
And invariably well timed
His droppings were neat and odourless
Unlike most of the magistrates
And indispensable to market gardeners
As I pointed out when taking their money
He rode roughshod
He spurred on the others
Many of whom left the Senate hurriedly
Small committees I always argue
Are preferable to large ones
I found it quite stimulating
'My kingdom for a horse' I would say
Visiting his stable afterwards
(Yes, it was made of the finest marble)
His hay was his yea
What happened later I was not around to tell
And the pertinent books of Tacitus
(Not too ill named) are lost
I like to think he trotted off to Thessaly
And joined the centaurs
(No, not the same as senators)
He was partial to the wine-trough.

THE FIRST great riddle. On the arrival of a new baby, 'the child asks himself the question: *Where do babies come from?*—a question which, there can be no doubt, first ran: *Where did this particular, intruding baby come from?*' (Freud).

As when one asks: *Where do human beings come from?*, which really means, 'Where did this particular and altogether remarkable being, myself, come from?' Following up with the question, 'Who was my enormously perspicacious and potent creator, and what does he expect in return?'

This gratifying but also slightly alarming thought is subverted, to one's dismay mixed with relief, by the next question: 'But what misguided creator is responsible for bringing all these foolish, un-attractive, wicked persons into the world?' At least one doesn't owe *him* anything.

But proceed with caution. On the theme of immortality, William James plays with the prospect of an 'eternal perpetuation unreduced in numbers' of (as it happens) the Chinese. We might like to keep a few chosen specimens alive to represent 'an interesting and pecu-liar variety of humanity', but God himself could have no use for the whole pullulating lot of them! Be that as it may, when you go on reasoning in this fashion, asking at which precise number disquali-fication sets in, sheer giddiness can lead you to lose all assurance 'in the immortality of your own particular person', precious though you feel the latter to be. Safer to tell yourself, displeasing as it may be, that 'each of these grotesque or even repulsive aliens is animated by an inner joy of living as hot or hotter than that which you feel beating in your private breast'.

If your Father has anything approaching a house, it will need a multitude of mansions.

Plainly the body is a most unsuitable vehicle, let alone companion, for the soul. Consider its vulgar inconveniences, its shameful habits, its evil communications; always causing mischief. And the soul is an utterly inappropriate companion, or mentor, for the body; always whining, spoiling things, causing mischief. A couple of hangers-on with nothing better to hang on to.

But just try to imagine either without the other.

A scholar complains that the English translation of Proust's novel is too English, and that what is required is something more ecumenical. What—assuming that the word as used here isn't simply a pompous euphemism for 'politically correct'—is an ecumenical translation? A sort of Esperanto of the word and the spirit? (George Eliot defined Esperanto in one of her essays as 'a patent deodorized and non-resonant language'.) A mishmash of dialects suited to our not-quite global village? A protracted obeisance to all possible creeds, cultures, and ethnicities? Compromise rather than conviction, mending fences and sitting on them, keen to satisfy everybody and pleasing nobody. Also, if it matters, unProustian.

I was reminded of this when reading Stanislaw Lem's *The Futurological Congress*, about a time when non-biological intelligence is common and computers suffer existential dilemmas. A certain Father Chassis of the Nonbiologican Friars, a translation model, sets about revising the Holy Scriptures to make them relevant. 'Shepherd, flock, lambs—these are meaningless entries in the modern lexicon. While divine spark plug, ministering matrices, transmission everlasting and original sync speak powerfully to the imagination.'

Ecumenicalism aspires to the condition of believing in nothing— something many people arrived at long ago.

On the other hand, in 1846 Thoreau recommended a collective or selective printing of the sacred writings of the Chinese, the Hindus, the Persians, and the Hebrews, which together with the New Testament would make a super-Bible, the book of books. If we neglect the opportunity, 'will not at length the printing press itself by miracle address itself to so sacred & choice a labor?' Boiled down, this might go some way to answering the demand for multi-religious instruction in our schools. (Plus an ecumenical miracle.)

An intriguing story recounted by Kafka in his diaries. The Baal Shem, eighteenth-century founder of Hasidism, ordered his favourite disciple to get himself baptized. Whatever the distress he felt, the disciple obeyed. Winning the esteem of his new associates, he rose to become a bishop. One day the Baal Shem called the man to him and gave permission for him to return to Judaism. Again the man obeyed, presumably with relief, and did heavy penance for his initial apostasy. The Baal Shem then explained. Because of his outstanding qualities, the disciple had been in mortal danger from the Evil One, and by commanding him to convert to Christianity, the Baal Shem stole the devil's thunder. Since the disciple had no choice but to submit to his master, he was not at fault. Yet so grievous was the sin that Satan could not improve upon it. Satan: in Hebrew, 'the plotter'; but the Baal Shem proved the more adroit.

The story demonstrates the advantage of having a variety of religions in the world; one can be played off against another. God, you might think, would admire such creativity on our part, and his opposite number such double-dealing. Whether this is the case must depend on the particular circumstances.

Dean Swift on Christianity and Christians

'We have just religion enough to make us *hate*, but not enough to make us *love* one another.'

'Violent zeal for truth hath an hundred to one odds to be either petulancy, ambition, or pride.'

'What they *do* in heaven we are ignorant of; what they do *not* we are told expressly, that they neither marry, nor are given in marriage.'

'I never saw, heard, nor read that the clergy were beloved in any nation where Christianity was the religion of the country. Nothing can render them popular but some degree of persecution.'

In favour of preserving the Lord's Day: 'There hath been an old custom time out of mind for people to assemble in the churches every Sunday, and shops are still frequently shut in order as it is conceived to preserve the memory of that ancient practice; but how this can prove a hindrance to business or pleasure is hard to imagine. What if the men of pleasure are forced one day in the week to game at home instead of the chocolate-house? Are not the taverns and coffee-houses open? Can there be a more convenient season for taking a dose of physic? Are fewer claps got upon Sundays than other days?... I would fain know how it can be pretended that the churches are misapplied. Where are more appointments and rendezvous of gallantry? Where more care to appear in the foremost box with greater advantage of dress? Where more meetings for business? Where more bargains driven of all sorts? And where so many conveniences or incitements to sleep?'

Also: 'If Christianity were once abolished how would the free-thinkers, the strong reasoners, and the men of profound learning, be able to find another subject so calculated in all points whereon to display their abilities? What wonderful productions of wit should we be deprived of, from those whose genius by continual practice hath been wholly turned upon raillery and invectives against religion, and would therefore never be able to shine or distinguish them-selves upon any other subject? We are daily complaining of the great decline of wit among us, and would we take away the great-est, perhaps the only topic we have left?'

But what's this?: 'In a few weeks, there starts up many a writer capable of managing the profoundest, and most universal subjects. For, what though his *head* be empty, provided his *commonplace book* be full.'

After Cavafy

The people had grown neglectful
Concerning the day set apart as holy,
For theirs, as the priests conceded,
Was a highly mobile and leisure-oriented
Existence, and not always were they free
To worship at the time prescribed—
So in future, the priests proclaimed,
The entire week would be held sacred
And the temples permanently open.
The people knew what these words were worth.
They could cease to feel faintly guilty
In the matter of holy days.

We didn't really need the preachers. The ordinary lurking notion
of natural law was enough. (Natural, even if one didn't know the
expression.) When you think of the good things you did, or the
fairly good, then it looks as if it might possibly be heaven. When
you think of the other things, seemingly more memorable, when
for some reason you start thinking and can't distract yourself, it
must certainly be hell. Perhaps it was ever thus. Belief doesn't
seem to come into it—could it possibly come out of it?—nor any-
thing supernatural. Just that obstinate, innate, unwritten, natural
law.

And when natural law is at odds with itself? Some small adjustment
will have to be made.

Not long ago I ventured mildly that there was something sad
about abortion, however desirable, however necessary, and was
sharply reprimanded by a young woman. I backed off; I was in a
false position; it was easy for me to talk, or mumble, given my sex,
age, 'privileged' condition.

Hitherto abortion has largely been a case of 'this hurts me more than it hurts you'. Now scientists have advanced a grim possibility that foetuses may feel pain during terminations—and it would be prudent to administer painkillers.

Abortions won't be given up any sooner than cars, sex, and falling out of love. God bless anaesthetics is all one, this one, dare say. Useful for those of us at the other end of the course, too.

Octavio Paz: 'Nietzsche would say that Stavrogin was an "incomplete nihilist": he lacks knowledge of the Eternal Return. But perhaps it would be more precise to say that Dostoevsky's character, like so many of our contemporaries, is an incomplete Christian. He has ceased believing but he has been unable to substitute others for the ancient certitudes or to live in the open, without ideas to justify or give meaning to his existence. God has disappeared, but evil has not. The loss of metaphysical referents does not extinguish sin: on the contrary, it gives it a kind of immortality. The nihilist is nearer to Gnostic pessimism than to Christian optimism and the hope of salvation. If there is no God there is no remission of sins, but evil is not abolished either: sin ceases to be an accident, a state, and becomes a permanent condition of men.' ('Dostoevsky: The Devil and the Ideologue', in *On Poets and Others*, translated by Michael Schmidt.)

'Like so many of our contemporaries . . .' No one entirely sure of himself, no one who disbelieved confidently in *evil*, who believed whole-heartedly in psychological or social explanations, would show quite such livid fury at the mere mention of the word as so many of us do. While we shouldn't exactly congratulate ourselves on it, yet the 'incompleteness' Paz speaks of, besides being no altogether bad thing, is understandable—it has reasons that both the reason and the heart know of.

These days charities are run not by enthusiastic amateurs but by trained professionals—chariteers, you might say. A communication from 'my' old Cambridge college—permanently in need of cash since although it is currently prosperous, prosperity cannot be relied on, and while one in four old members of the college subscribed to the first Appeal, three in four did not—breaks down its recent campaign under various heads, including one called 'The nostalgia factor', measured in decades. According to the figures appertaining thereto, the highest response to the first Appeal came from people who matriculated during 1920–1929; this decade fell to third place on the occasion of the second Appeal, possibly for reasons known to actuaries, and top of the league came the grouping of 1930–1939, which may well fall when the third Appeal comes along.

But 'nostalgia factor'? This from the college where Leavis used to teach.

Sure sign of a declining reputation: charities cease to ask for signed copies of your books or manuscripts to be auctioned. But now a request for a donation of £5000: sign of an inflated reputation.

The Salvation Army Tiny Tim Christmas Appeal asks for £9 to buy a child its own Christmas present

Dear Tim,

That you are tiny is neither here nor there. Most children are on the small side. But you are not too young to appreciate that the country's finances are in a shaky condition. Indeed we are currently in debt to the extent of £50 billion—no tiny sum, eh Tim? Consequently not every child can expect its own Christmas present, as your father will confirm. In case you have been reading the papers and the thought has occurred to you—a free education has enabled you to read if not to think—let me say that the award of bonuses to business executives by other business executives is an altogether different matter. These are rare persons who by dint of devotion and force of intellect are pulling the country out of recession. Without them, who knows what the national debt might be!

Christmas, as someone has remarked, is a time for balancing the books.

With seasonal greetings,

p.p. S. Claus MBA

PS   It has to be said that in view of its menacing connotations 'Salvation Army' is a totally unacceptable epithet.

PPS   I trust your leg is getting better.

More season's greetings. The Bishop voices doubts about that inn and there being no room at it. Granted, it may have been a rather poor room, in a one-star hotel (and that the only star in evidence). Possibly the story only means there wasn't any room service. The virgin birth is, well, 'splendidly symbolic', though of what is not vouchsafed. And as for hell-fire, that remains to be seen.

The 'Roman option'. Comical, pathetic rather, the prospective rush and the current trickle of wounded Anglican clergy to the Roman Catholic Church on the conscientious grounds that they cannot accept women priests. A nice instance, I would think, of choking on gnats after having swallowed camels. What future can there be for married priests within the Catholic Church? They can't well resort to divorce. Taking the collection plate round, perhaps, or changing the flowers. The Catholics can hardly be hugging themselves at this sudden addition (of spoils of war, or spoilt children) to their ranks.

The group of rebel clerics known oddly as the Church Society contend that the ordination of women represents a fundamental change of doctrine requiring a full Act of Parliament. In this unlike other shifts in belief which some of us outsiders might have supposed rather more fundamental, and demanding an Act of God.

If not more uplifting, at least more human, all too human, is the story of the Blackpool vicar who asked forgiveness for patronizing sex shops in pursuit of pornographic films — and in the same breath complained about the quality of the tapes, for which he paid £70, and one of which was completely blank. He sinned, but 'I have also been ripped off'. Less prepossessing was the Catholic priest who admitted to an apparently lengthy affair, followed by blackmail on the part of his lover. What he had done, he acknowledged, was wrong, but it was only human, so 'Let he who has never sinned cast the first stone.' Those words, more grammatically phrased, are usually left to someone else to utter. (The layman who was accused of rape after a birthday party and pleaded that he didn't know who the girl was because his contact lenses had misted over . . . At least he didn't appeal to some higher authority.)

Four reasons for the ordination of women: (a) they are human, (b) they are Christians, (c) their natural gifts will stand them in good stead, (d) they actively want to be priests.

God or man? Matthew and Mark agree that Jesus's last words were: 'My God, my God, why hast thou forsaken me?' Robert Graves sees here an acknowledgement, or a salutary reminder to us all, that God's hand cannot be forced (that is, forced to take immediate action: once again, he moves in a mysterious way). Noting that the words are a quotation from Psalm 22 (verse 1), Frank Kermode perceives the latter as 'a source' or 'a prophecy or promise' of what is to come. In reviewing Kermode's *The Genesis of Secrecy*, William Empson wrote: 'It may seem improbable that anyone would make a literary quotation at such a moment, but it is believable in so strange a case, whereas the Gospel-writers were very unlikely to invent it, as two of them found it embarrassing.' (Did they?) Psalm 22 begins in despair which by the end has turned into praise and acceptance, 'For the kingdom is the Lord's . . .' Did the two evangelists expect their readers to grasp this? Or indeed did Jesus have it in mind?

God or man? Luke's account of the last words is pious: 'Father, into thy hands I commend my spirit' (also a quotation or echo, from Psalm 31, verse 5). John's is matter-of-fact: 'It is finished.' But 'My God, my God, why hast thou forsaken me?'—this is spoken like a man. A man who is being crucified. Can there be a rift in the Trinity here?

'The Bishop of Durham celebrated his retirement at a party with parishioners by launching 2,000 purple balloons bearing the message: "You can't keep a good God down".' (News item, 3 July 1994)

Decline of theodicy

A God supreme and immanent
Flickers feebly among the leaves.

A God whom we cannot blame
Because he left it all to us.

A God whom we cannot praise
Since he left it to us to do.

A God who spoke through his vicars
Whose vicars speak of other things.

A God who appointed our rulers
The rulers who disappoint us.

A God whom we cannot fear
Now hell has been annulled.

A God whom we cannot love
Since heaven has been shut down.

A God whose name was not taken in vain
A God whose name is not taken.

A God who was a jealous God
Sees nothing to be jealous of.

A God who gave us life
Who now only buries us.

THEY read between the lines; they don't read the lines. There have long been students of literature, and professors of it, who yield wholeheartedly to the siren song of ambiguity (known to a more chosen few as 'plurisignation'). Caught in the lures of Innumerable Types, they fire off ten or twenty interpretations of a line, a phrase, among them one or two feasible readings, the rest ludicrous, banal, pointless, or labouredly obscene—and rate them all equally. (The long beginning of what Gilbert Adair calls the Theory of Either/ Either.) Useless to protest that the author was an intelligent person, or a believing Christian, or a stern moralist, and couldn't possibly have meant such a thing . . . They only grin slyly at your simplicity, your fallacious intentionalism, your failure to grasp even one type of ambiguity.

That we carry ourselves and our experience into the processes of reading a poem, say, is undeniable. There's no question of going naked into the library or the seminar room. What a vast disrobing that would entail! Even GCSE pupils will have acquired *some* vestments. And what a disappointment, when the poem finds nothing to interact with, to strike and ignite against. If you bring nothing, you take nothing.

It has been claimed that we are better placed to understand the literature of an earlier period since we can view it objectively, from a distance, in perspective, whereas we approach contemporary writing with personal prejudices and presuppositions. (Thoreau had the interesting thought that it was hard for us to be properly critical of a contemporary poet because, shallow though the verse might be, we 'inform it with all the life and promise of this day'; in fact, 'We are such a near and kind and knowing audience as he will never have again.') The opposite case has it that the contemporary is directly relevant to our experience and interests whereas the past is a foreign country in which we wander as bemused as a tourist from Mars. An Australian academic lamented that he couldn't teach his favourite Pope because none of his students had visited Twickenham or seen Hampton Court or knew how to play ombre. (I didn't admit to a like ignorance; or submit that our Singapore students—racially Chinese, Indian, Malay, and Eurasian—seemed immune to this exotic embarrassment.) That's asking for a lot to be brought with one, excess baggage: the reader wrapped in layer upon layer of heavy garments. I suspect such arguments are built on a degree of ill will towards literature, or towards students of it—and may include an element of self-gratification since one is so often the exception to one's own devastating rules.

No two readers experience the very same text. (No two fruit-lovers taste the very same apple.) But much more is common in their experiences than is diverse; they may each have their personal ambiguity or two, but they share one predominant body of meaning. The phenomenon is a central fact of human nature, which I take it preceded the arts: a divine dispensation, one is tempted to say. If humans were totally different one from another, they couldn't begin to live together; if they were identical, they would never want to.

In this connection it is worth noting Lionel Trilling's comment that he had never met a politically idealistic student who was estranged from Stephen Dedalus by the latter's contempt for political idealism, nor a student from a disadvantaged background who felt 'debarred from what Yeats can give him by the poet's slurs upon shopkeepers or by anything else in his inexhaustible fund of snobbery'. Students generally take the point, if they're not discouraged.

Yet someone else has written an attack on Shakespeare, reducing this erstwhile star to a black hole—his works essentially meaningless, or make what you will of them, preferably something shabbily tool-of-the-stateish. Another professor of English, needless to say. When your nest is secure, you can afford to foul it.

Beware the common touch! In a rather earnest book on Shake-speare, based on years of teaching him to honours students in Sin-gapore—quoting a proleptic and idiomatic though not wholly tasteful comment in a student's essay, apropos of Gloucester smirking over his bastard son in the opening scene of *Lear*, that the Earl was 'due for an eye-opener before long' . . .

The book was reviewed by an eminent Shakespearian: 'I do not care to hear that Gloucester was in for an eye-opener . . .' Beg your pardon, madam, only wanted to show how . . .

Over twenty years have passed since I left Singapore, and I see I'm still wheeled out on occasion as an example, presumably ripe, of a 'cultural imperialist', as one carrying that social disease, a 'colonial mentality'.

Not that I noticed any resentment or anguishing on the part of the students at the time. (They were intimidated, I shall be told.) What they wanted was literature, the thing that tells you about life, and in effect English literature was the only possible one around. Politicians—that's different; if you are engaged in welding a nation together, a mixture of races, you are going to need a Common Enemy, preferably one connected however equivocally with the imperial power from which you have lately liberated yourself.

Twenty-four years later, and great changes have taken place. The nation, fortunately a small one, is as welded together as it ever will be, and the industriousness of all concerned has produced a material prosperity enviable in that part of the world, in any part of the world. In the old days they used to send their teachers and a picked handful of students overseas to improve themselves. Now they invite teachers and critics from overseas to attend well-ordered conferences. The first thing is to make clear to these foreign intellectuals that they aren't here to enlighten you so much as to be enlightened by you. Most of those involved are polite, but there's usually somebody who, by way of administering a caution and putting the jet-set visitors in their place, will conjure up that ogre, that ancient and one would have thought long-forgotten Professor of English.

All teachers of literature worth their salt and salary, whatever the literature and wherever they teach, are leading their students into an empire of art, colonizing their minds with the achievements of past and present, opening them to invasion by foreign forces—and helping them to take over, to assimilate, to do their own colonizing on their own terms. That's education.

Reading and Writing: A Free Verse (or a Teacher's Farewell to his Students)

Let a hundred flowers blossom!—or more
Depending on the size of your garden—
And nothing human be alien to you,
Excepting certain savants and self-servers
Who are doubtfully human.
But try to know one literature in some depth:
It will help you with the others.
If it should be English literature,
Don't feel obliged to apologize;
The daffodil is not really a poisonous plant.
Or if it's Other Literatures in English,
Fine, just make sure it's literature.
(Who is it invents these famous difficulties?
Not students.
Who keep warm inside their vested interests?
Not far to look.
What shall we say when the extraterrestrials
Bring us their epics?)
You can get through a lot of reading in a lifetime,
Even without spending much of it in gaol.
Remember, the smallest of literatures
Is bigger than you are;
Modesty in persons is rarely misplaced.
Art attracts theories and then spurns them;
It creates trends, but is not itself trendy,
Too wayward to serve as a safe bandwagon.

Do not complain too bitterly of tyrannies—
Without them you would never know freedom.
Recognize good form before you commit
Your exquisite solecisms.
'Not all things at once does the Highest require':
Verse may not make the buses run on time,
Its relevance to the economy is imponderable;
Relevance itself is often imponderable.
Literature can almost be taught;
It is tolerant of life
(Which gave it life), but has its peculiar pride.
It makes friends, it makes enemies,
It cannot be rendered entirely amenable.
If you cease to believe in what you are doing,
Cease to do it; teaching, for instance.
Poetry is not moral rearmament; or if it is,
Don't await a salvation army.
For 'paving the way' a steamroller is handier,
Walls are built with bricks, not books.
If politicians ask for literature, let them write it,
Then they have only themselves to blame.
By all means disgrace yourself,
But never your art.
Naturally you will take note of 'alterity'
(There's a scholar's word!):
Vive la différence between cultures,
But don't create differences;
Consider also what is common to us
By imagination's grace.
And think twice before using the word 'culture'.
Poetry was never written by a passport,
Though passports sometimes tell sad stories.
As for Comparative Literature,
While comparisons are not invariably odious
(Our heads swarm with them),

To say there are homosexuals in both
Tells us little about Gide and Mishima.
In some countries you need to carry *Playboy*
Wrapped inside the cover of *Das Kapital*,
In others, *Das Kapital* inside *Playboy*;
The best preservative is *Elementary Calculus*,
Elemental, value-free, pure aestheticism.
Read in every language you know,
Tasting its centuries;
Read in translations,
The fleur-de-lis, the hibiscus, the chrysanthemum . . .
Write in whatever language you can,
'That the existing may be well interpreted'.
Do not provoke gratuitously, but
Neither play for safety: it can kill you.
And please (look who's talking!)
Not too much talk . . .
True, if you turn into a book
You can be banned, or quite easily burned.
But something of you remains:
A hyacinth, anemone, or poppy, or even
(Though self-love isn't very pretty) narcissus—
One of those hundreds of thousands of flowers.

One thing I do resent: some affluent person telling me that I—
and my parents and their parents—shared hugely in the loot. The
Empire made Britain rich and powerful, but the power and the
riches were confined to a small minority. It might seem that the
majority actually paid for 'having' an empire. One thing amuses
me: in India, hearing American officials or visiting professors con-
dole with the locals over the oppression suffered under the Raj—
just as they themselves once suffered—and being told gently, 'But
we do owe the British quite a lot—legal system, government, com-
munications, medicine, and . . .' In some cases adding 'and English
literature'.

The university girls used 'Cad' to mean a good-looking young man, from Cadbury's chocolate: 'Maybe he's a dark Cad, bitter but sustaining.' And 'He's just a glamdip.' 'What is a glamdip, darling?' 'A glamorous diplomat. Very vacant, very charming.' And 'You have a voice like a bulbul.' . . . 'In a china-china-shop'. And 'He is good wedding bell material for our Kuku.' . . . 'Wedding bell? Or bedding well?' (Vikram Seth, *A Suitable Boy*.) People who can come up with such verbal inventions and cross-cultural puns can't have lost too much under the Raj, and even seem to have gained something.

A young, growing nation needs bland food, nourishing but not exciting, and the People's Action Party provided it. You can see why English literature might be deemed a post-colonial conspiracy, a rearguard bid, if not to subvert a newly independent state, then to retain it as a 'client' by weakening the resolve of the citizenry. All those accumulated glooms, hemmings and hawings, doubts and despairs, those sickly pale casts. 'Getting and spending, we lay waste our powers'—nonsense, power lies in getting and prosperity in spending; 'those to whom the miseries of the world are misery, and will not let them rest'—not resting is admirable, but misery is counter-productive; 'that dolphin-torn, that gong-tormented sea'—now listen, this is going to be the world's busiest port! . . .

That was Singapore, famous for its delicious and diverse fare by the way. Also for its success. Don't be too quick to bemoan, however benevolently, the success of others, even if it exacted a price (not from you). Success doesn't inevitably spoil people; failure is more likely to do that.

Japan was another story, it seemed. There they lapped up tragedy and world-weariness (so many translations of *The Waste Land*, of *Hamlet*!) and mournful verse and harrowing prose. And then went off to perform their economic miracle too.

The stitching together of nations. It was decided that we should lay on courses in elementary English for students leaving Chinese-medium schools, so that some of them could then enter the relatively apolitical University of Singapore instead of the Peking-oriented Nanyang University. Strange, you might think, that expatriate teachers warned off interfering in local politics should now be conscripted into them. But then, 'political activities' is what dissidents indulge in, whereas governments engage in government, a different matter. And drawing one's skirts aside would be viewed as interfering in politics. Moreover, the undertaking promised to be of interest in respects purely pedagogic and surely legitimate.

A colleague chose *Animal Farm* as his reading text: provocative, but he was a local citizen and an old friend of the Prime Minister, and wouldn't come to harm. Orwell did: the students dismissed him out of hand. What did this Englishman know of the Soviet Union? For my part, I conceived the more ingratiating notion of using Arthur Waley's translations of Chinese poetry.

These students—perhaps resentful of the move to wean them away from Chinese language and culture, and by implication whatever socialistic ideas they harboured—acted tough and a shade disrespectful, as if to distance themselves from English-educated pushovers. They laughed incredulously at Waley. Chinese poetry? You must be joking! Very well, I said, you go and do better. The best of the homework they turned in read much like Waley. Chinese poetry? I asked. They shrugged: what could you expect from a primitive tongue. As I recall, four or five of these erstwhile lost souls, plucked from the burning, were received into the University of Singapore, to read economics.

Though defunct, the British Empire remains in disgrace, without benefit of *de mortuis* . . . It will go on being castigated, no doubt, by those who didn't live in it, whose parents didn't, whose grandparents didn't. It will be abused chiefly in English because it ruined their mother tongue for them. (Pure accident that English commands a larger and possibly more responsive audience.) And cut them off from their roots, impoverishing their lives, those of their parents, grandparents, back through the generations, and forwards.

The first imperialist, what was he but the serpent who invaded Eden, stole its innocent fruits, and laid it waste? Who but the first imperialist, the serpent, brought into the world, if not death itself, then civil war, corrupt dictators, execution squads, famine, plague— and oh, all sorts of woes? Not all of these are conspicuous features of British life, but let's throw in self-righteousness, arrogance, recrimination, attack as the handiest form of defence.

In his *Recollections of the Lake Poets*, De Quincey marvels over the speed with which—thanks to 'the dreadful Republic' and the African, Canadian, Indian, and Australian colonies—the English language is speeding towards 'its ultimate mission of eating up all other languages'. Hence in the future, 'in the recesses of California' and 'the vast solitudes of Australia', Wordsworth's poems will be read even as now Shakespeare is read 'amongst the forests of Canada'. And then every account of Wordsworth will bear the same kind of value as that attaching to personal memorials ('unhappily so slender') of Shakespeare. He himself, we note, is engaged on one such personal memorial.

Concerning 'the dreadful Republic' De Quincey appends this diverting footnote: 'Not many months ago, the blind hostility of the Irish newspaper editors in America forged a ludicrous estimate of the Irish numerical preponderance in the United States, from which it was inferred, as at least a possibility, that the Irish Celtic language might come to dispute the pre-eminence with the English.' Others, it seems, anticipated the same destiny for the German. In the meantime, however, the unceasing activities of the lawcourts, of commerce, and of the Senate, brought about a dilemma. 'If the Irish and the Germans in the United States adapt their general schemes of education to the service of their public ambitions, they must begin by training themselves to the use of the language now prevailing on all the available stages of ambition. On the other hand, by refusing to do this, they lose in the very outset every point of advantage. In other words, adopting the English, they renounce the contest—*not* adopting it, they disqualify themselves for the contest.'

For China (i.e. the current Chinese leaders) to parry Tiananmen Square by adducing the Summer Palace and its burning in 1860 by British and French troops as evidence of Western barbarism is no better than the tit for tat of squabbling schoolboys. We are all barbarians at times; we try to cut down those times. '. . . that what civilization consists in is the diminution of human tears . . .' (a scrap of paper found in a tram).

Watch your tongue

Professors are invited to the Istana—
A red-letter day! For dinner.
We are told to stay put at our tables
And minister by minister
The government will circulate.
We sip at our drinks decorously . . .
Here comes the Party Chairman and Deputy PM,
Chinese by race, scientific by doctorate.
What shall we say to him?
The conversation turns to translation.
One wants to shine slightly:
'Translations, it's said, are like women,
Beautiful or faithful but never both.'
The Deputy PM seems shocked, or possibly anxious,
He looks suspicious, or perhaps inscrutable:
'But a man wants his wife to be faithful.'
One remembers that long a bachelor
He has lately married one of his secretaries.
One remembers he is lacking in humour,
And tries to say something soothing about similes.
One goes from bad to worse.
Once again one commits a bloomer.

Resounding conclusion to 'Teaching Literature', a piece written by Empson for Japanese readers and first published in Japanese in 1934: 'But one cannot set out at the end of an article to show how to stop the Japanese student from feeling embarrassed; if one knew the full answer it would solve many difficulties, both of Japan and of education.' What a pity the article had to end when it did.

In 1967, while I was in Singapore, Q. D. Leavis sent me *Silas Marner* as recently published in the Penguin English Library with her introduction, inscribed: 'A piece of old England to wish you a merry Christmas and a happy New Year'. I hadn't heard from her since leaving Downing and found this very touching, and rather unexpected.

By and large, those of us who worked overseas were regarded with favour, if only because we were remote from the corrupt metropolitan scene. (I think Leavis was pleased, too, that seeds of his teaching should be scattered abroad.) Other corruptions were possible of course. Earlier, after I had left Japan, Leavis asked me whether it was true that Britishers there were given to adulterous affairs. I said that there weren't so many of us in that country, and such behaviour was likelier in former colonies such as Malaya, and even more so in the fictions of Somerset Maugham.

Not that he was as relentlessly censorious as is often represented. At a time when I was reviewing fairly regularly for weekly magazines, it seems he remarked to a third person, 'Well, he has to make his way.' Literary allowances, no, but human ones were possible.

During the weekly afternoon teas the Leavises gave for 'the men', FR would come round with a handsome blue box of Players Navy Cut cigarettes, followed by QD uttering dire words on the effects of smoking. (It could prevent us from ever having children: a warning which left us men baffled.) A tricky decision for unsophisticated undergrads, whether to refuse FR's offered cigarettes or brave QD's disapprobation. Good practice for later life, perhaps.

Leavisian seeds: the richest foreign field was surely India, where William Walsh, visiting from Leeds University, acted as plenipotentiary for many years. In a book published in Mysore in 1963, C. D.

Narasimhaiah, who first heard of Leavis in 1947 when he went to Christ's College on a scholarship ('but my other home was to be Downing'), observed that during the struggle for independence English poets served as 'instruments to plague their own country-men with'. The poets, in particular the Romantics with their love of liberty and the Victorians with their condemnation of material-ism, 'met a vital need of the hour'; and that hour wasn't the time for literary disparagement and revaluation. Later was another mat-ter. When visiting a remote university on the east coast of India, Narasimhaiah was struck by a three-page message from Leavis, framed and treasured on a shelf in the English department. When he asked a young student if he had heard of the man the answer came pat: 'Leavis is the rage here.' The head of the department told Nara-simhaiah afterwards that the boy normally stammered and this was one of the few sentences he could ever get right.

TOWARDS the end of the 1940s the French department at Farouk I University, later renamed more worthily as the University of Alex-andria, was a peculiarly brilliant one. The staff included Jean Grenier, Camus's teacher and said to be the true architect of existentialism; Pierre Souyris, who later published a work called *Désintégration du verbe*; Algirdas Greimas, Lithuanian-born author of *Sémantique structurale*; René Etiemble, novelist, specialist in Rimbaud, and inventor-to-be of the term *franglais*; and (attached to the Lycée) J.-B. Pontalis, who was the grandson of Louis Renault, founder of the car manufacturers, and whose *Frontiers in Psychoanalysis* would be published by the Hogarth Press when I was connected with the imprint.

At one point, when war between Egypt and Israel seemed immi-nent and it was envisaged that foreign Jews would be either interned or expelled, Etiemble, an excitable character, impressed our joint common room by declaring that in this eventuality he would simply drop his trousers and prove he wasn't Jewish. The ploy held little comfort for me, who had been circumcised in infancy for what were seen as hygienic reasons. Also on the strength was a newcomer, one Roland Barthes, perhaps more highly regarded for his good looks than for his mind, though viewed by our French colleagues as a rising star, assuming that he didn't turn out to be an *idiot savant*.

We in the English department were in no position to judge, being underprivileged intellectually as well as financially. (The French government topped up their people's salaries while we lived on Egyptian wages.) There is a grain of truth in the odious insinuation that whereas France sent its leading intellectuals abroad, Britain dispatched its drunks and disorderlies—or, rather, left it to them to go. It should be said, however, that our elderly and gentlemanly head of department had published a book on Donne well before the poet came into fashion.

Our relationship with Egypt was a mixed affair, rarely passionate enough to qualify as *odi et amo*. Some things you liked, others you needed to close your eyes to. There was a degree of violence in the air, which was exciting but alarming; there was a degree of kindliness too, of tolerance which shamed but solaced. For the French, Egypt was more of a symbol, historical and artistic; perhaps symbolic of themselves, at any rate a pleasingly exotic backdrop against which to play out their intellectuality.

There were Down with Britain days; I never heard of a Down with France day. We were doing a humble job made difficult by sudden strikes ('It is Down with Britain day, sir, you must stay at home') and painful by the disappearance every now and then of some indigenous youth, wild-eyed and shabby, into prison or madhouse. The French teachers, so it seemed to us, catered exclusively for luscious Syrian or Greek girls who never agitated on the streets, spoke perfect French, and were *à la page* with the latest Parisian trends. Our colleagues were being fervid about *Les Chemins de la liberté* while we were being pedestrian about

Silas Marner. I can't imagine we were engaged with the same body of students.

In *Mythologies* Barthes gives the impression of knowing what he is talking about; he has seen, heard, or tasted it. Tasted in the case of 'Le bifteck et les frites'. Steak is a 'kind of heavy substance which diminishes under the teeth in such a way as to make one keenly aware at the same time of the strength of its origin and of its plasticity in flowing into the very blood of man'. Soaking up the national glamour of steak, chips are similarly nostalgic and patriotic: returning from Indo-China, General de Castries asked for chips as his first meal, it was part of the ritual celebration of the community regained. He knew that *la frite* was 'the alimentary sign of *francité*'.

The world of *le catch*, all-in wrestling, offers 'the great spectacle of Suffering, Defeat, and Justice', the wrestlers playing roles analogous to the characters of Molière or the verbal portraits of La Bruyère. A bout between goodies, devoid of foul play, treachery or cowardice, moves us momentarily to thoughts of human kindness and decency, Barthes says, but soon bores us. We need baddies, since wrestling is a sort of mythological struggle between Good and Evil. When the gods, whether heroes or villains, leave the amphitheatre, impassive and anonymous, carrying their kit in a bag and arm in arm with their wives, we perceive that wrestling 'holds that power of transmutation which is common to Spectacle and to Worship'.

In pleading the case for neologisms, Barthes remarks that China is one thing and the French petit-bourgeois idea of China is quite another, and for the latter, a *mélange* of tiny bells, rickshaws, and opium dens, the only possible word is *sinité*: sinity or sinocity, or even chinoiserie. The word crops up in a piece on 'Strip-tease', an activity which, at least in its Parisian form, 'is based on a contradiction: the desexualization of the woman at the very moment when she is stripped naked'. I don't know about Paris, but this view would carry weight in Japan, where men and women were used to sharing the same public baths, both sexes desexualized and unperturbed. The truly Japanese, truly teasing striptease, as opposed to the imported variety, would consist in a girl appearing on the stage totally naked and then, very slowly, putting on one garment after another; when she was fully dressed, in a kimono revealing only the nape of the neck and the ankles, there would be a roll of the drums, a brief climactic pause, and the lights in the theatre would go out.

In Western striptease Barthes sees not the dragging to light of some hidden depth but the reduction to a perfectly (and merely) 'chaste state of the flesh'—skin-deep as it were. You begin with the presence of the exotic—fans and furs, a dress with panniers, a Venetian decor with gondola, a Chinese woman furnished with an opium pipe ('the obligatory symbol of *sinité*')—and you end with the absence of the erotic. The contrary of the Japanese ideal proposed above, in fact. If you want eroticism, Barthes suggests, you are more likely to find it in amateur striptease, where 'beginners' more or less awkwardly remove their more or less everyday clothes, unimpeded by opium pipes, gondolas, period costumes, elongated cigarette-holders. You could say it's like spying on the girl next door.

Whether Barthes always arrives at truth is disputable; he certainly achieves beauty of expression, and even clarity, not to mention touches of humour.

According to Betty Friedan, before very long women will be living twelve years longer than men on average. A possible way of redressing the imbalance is indicated in a 1992 prison study which states that on average castrated males live thirteen years longer than their 'intact' fellow inmates.

At least *sex* holds out possible pleasures, but *gender* . . . A *TLS* Special Number is lightened by a misprint: *The Penguin's Book of Women's Lives*. Just picture that pompous, fuddy-duddy bird, unmistakably male, brooding over 'this great doorstep of a book'.

Marina Tsvetaeva, 'Yesterday he still looked in my eyes' (translated by Elaine Feinstein): 'Now for the lament of women in all times'. Oh dear, we know what to expect. What was it I did to you that you should have done this to me? and so forth. All very painful, quite embarrassing. Hardly tolerable, were it not for this stanza halfway through, a poem in itself:

> 'Yesterday he lay at my feet. He even
>   compared me with the Chinese empire! Then
> suddenly he let his hands fall open, and
>   my life fell out like a rusty kopeck.'

The 'Chinese empire': enchanting, magical, opulent, mysterious, benign, sagacious . . . (Not just a solicitous Chinese housewife, a succulent Chinese cook.) But, the 'Chinese empire': capricious, tyrannical, cruel, avaricious, deceitful, paranoid . . . And then, a rusty kopeck: no equivocation there, no *sous-entendu* or second thoughts— not even worth a brass farthing. That was *her* simple simile.

Successful marriage, end of century. The wife is an exhibitionist, she says in the magazine *Marie Claire* (favourite reading in doctors' waiting-rooms), and her husband is a voyeur. As if to remark 'I like cooking and he likes eating.' So 'ours is an ideal union'. They make videos of their marital activities and distribute copies to like-minded couples. (Nothing so crude as selling them in the open market; that would amount to a life of crime.) Should, heaven forbid, the couple ever split up, who would take possession of the video library?

Symposium

During the after-dinner entertainment
Staged by a Syracusan impresario
Most striking was a novelty act,
A girl who juggled with hoops while dancing.
The sage was inspired to remark that
Though lacking in physical strength
And soundness of judgement, women
Had as much natural ability as men,
And any of the husbands present
Could teach their wives whatever skills
They might deem desirable.
Then for heaven's sake, asked a friend,
Why didn't Socrates train his own wife
Who was glaringly difficult to get on with?
The best horsemen, the sage replied,
Didn't concern themselves with docile horses
But with high-spirited beasts.
Hence he had provided himself with Xanthippe
For if he could stomach her, he was sure
He could get along with anyone on earth.
All perceived the justice in this argument,
And to revive the party spirit, Socrates
Asked the Syracusan to teach him how to dance.
Whereupon they laughed and called for more wine.

So Xenophon tells us, who was an expert horseman,
And opined in some other book that should a horse
Behave badly, it said little for the rider.
History has nothing against his wife, Philesia,
It seems she was not especially high-spirited.

One has always admired and respected women, one has even loved
some of them, from the very beginning of one's life.

181

Alas that now, bruised and battered (if only at second hand), one should be provoked, almost, into repeating Tolstoy's remark to Gorky: 'I shall speak the truth about women when I have one foot in the coffin; then I shall quickly pull the other one in and clap down the lid.'

What could that truth have been? There are several classes of people of whom I might be tempted to say, 'I shall speak the truth . . .', but women are not one of them. And I shall be otherwise engaged at the time.

After much bickering and badgering you give in: so OK, they are equal. Till then you had believed they were superior.

'Plymouth Labour councillors have denied that their initial banning of the word "manager" from job descriptions had anything to do with its supposed sexist connotations' (news item).

'Three weeks ago I had a rather troublesome attack . . . Mr Cross has nursed me as if he had been a wife nursing a husband, never leaving me except to get his walk' (George Eliot letting the side down).

'Calling colleagues "love" or "miss" is patronizing. Address them by their National Insurance number' (newspaper advice).

Gingerbread men are in disgrace, and the story of *Romeo and Juliet* is found tendentiously heterosexual. The Water Research Association has disinfected the terminology of plumbing: 'ballcock' and 'nipple' have been filtered out, the former is now to be called a 'float-operated valve' and the latter a 'greasing point', which a journalist has reckoned still a bit dodgy. Once you start looking for smut, there's no end to it. Once you start looking for offence, there's no end to that. Never mind that 'manager' comes from *manus*, an appendage common to men and women—it has a nasty ring about it.

The journalists have had their fun, and now they must find a fresh line. So it becomes deliciously daring to put in a good word for these phenomena. 'After all . . .' etc. Having long derided the popular notion that the moon is made of green cheese, our brightest and best are now suggesting that after all there might be some truth in it.

How demanding correctness is. How enormously complicated. It threatens to make converse impossible. Will it eventually bring about complete silence? Not before there has been a lot more talk about it. A rendering follows, free but by no means licentiously so, of part of a 'dialogue' conducted by a celebrated French intellectual, indicated here as GURU, together with two other men, MALE, and two women, FEMALE.

The question of rape has arisen. What should be said about it? What could be done about it? A terribly tricky question. They have to be extremely careful.

GURU: One might say that sexuality should in no circumstances be subject to punishment. So if one punishes rape it must be physical violence alone one is punishing. It could be said that rape is nothing more than an act of aggression, and, in principle, there is no difference between shoving one's fist into someone's face and shoving one's penis into somebody's sex. But would all women agree?

FEMALE considers that they wouldn't, not really. Not at all.

GURU asks if this means she accepts that there is a 'properly sexual' offence.

FEMALE: Yes, in view of all the little girls who have been attacked in parks or in the underground, which is extremely traumatizing . . .

MALE intervenes to suggest that what she is talking about is 'psychical' rape, not violence.

GURU: She is talking about exhibitionism, isn't she?

FEMALE agrees that she was, but observes that one thing leads to another, and the other thing can be different from getting a smack from an adult.

MALE broaches the Roman Polanski case, involving oral, anal, and vaginal sex with a thirteen-year-old girl, who rang up a friend to tell her all about it; she seemed to have enjoyed the experience.

GURU comments that there are indeed children who throw

themselves at an adult at the age of ten. He is tempted to say that from the moment the child doesn't refuse, there is no reason to punish any act.

FEMALE is willing to shut her eyes to activities between children, but feels that when an adult is involved there is an inequality, an imbalance of discoveries and responsibilities, which is hard to define . . . It's just that she feels the act of violence ought somehow to be *recognized*, so that it doesn't become ordinary.

GURU: Like a street accident.

GURU wonders if rape couldn't be placed outside the criminal law, and simply come under civil law, entailing damages. But women may think otherwise since in this area men—perhaps unfortunately—have less experience.

FEMALE is bothered because she can't think of herself in connection with legislation, and can't go along with the idea of punishment . . .

MALE sees feminism as being on the 'anti-rape' side, but also on the side of 'anti-repression'. Perhaps they should invent a new crime: failure to respect the right of another to say *no*, a crime carrying no punishment but calling for political education . . . That is, assuming no physical injury has been caused.

MALE, desiring to detach rape definitively from sex: Rape is non-orgasmic, a sort of rapid masturbation in someone else's body, not sexual, but a wound.

FEMALE, much relieved: Rape is no longer sexuality, it belongs to a different area, that of physical violence.

GURU politely reminds her that she has said rape was not the same at all as a punch in the face.

FEMALE confesses that it depends on the point of view, it's very difficult to analyse . . .

They go on analysing.

A psychiatrist has announced that there's really no such thing as a maternal instinct. The world is agog with the news, as always happens when someone comes along with a grand generalization which runs counter to an earlier grand generalization. The truth or otherwise doesn't count for much. Most of us have a relish for iconoclasm;

we experience a large sensation of liberation, as if a burden has been lifted from us. For a day or two, and then we find that another burden has been imposed on us, perhaps a more grievous one.

A woman writes to the newspaper that she knew all along that the maternal instinct was a myth, since she never felt it and has never regretted having no children; she advises female readers who are being 'pressurized' into starting a family, 'No, don't do it', adding that she herself is having quite a nice time while most of the mothers she knows are not. Bye-bye, human race. And recently we have heard of modern mothers clearing off to have a nice time on holiday, who leave their young children to cope on their own, possibly to prove that they too refuse to be duped by some disagreeable old myth. (More engaging in an aesthetic sense is the comment of Sarah Dunant's private eye, Hannah Wolfe, concerning the patter of tiny feet: 'The older I get the more I realize I'm too young for it.') If we invoke George Eliot, who spoke of 'the wondrous chemistry of the affections and sentiments' associated with maternity and thus peculiar to women, we shall be reminded that George Eliot bore no children and chose a male pseudonym.

'They fuck you up, your mum and dad,' Larkin wrote in his least appealing poem, so 'Get out as early as you can,/And don't have any kids yourself.' Or, as Sophocles observed, 'Not to be born is best', a rule of thumb confirmed by Ambrose Bierce in defining the word *birth* as 'the first and direst of all disasters'. Funny as Larkin is (and a bit brutish with it), it's pretty feeble to blame things on your parents, but for whom you wouldn't be here writing poetry and dishing out advice.

Johnson said the last word on the subject—given that any word is ever the last—in the preface to his edition of Shakespeare, when alluding to 'those who, being able to add nothing to truth, hope for eminence from the heresies of paradox'. Heresies are exciting things; and—with the rare exception—easy and safe in societies like ours. Shakespeare himself is kicked in the goolies; and then the maternal instinct, in some other region. The silly season passes—exacting its casualties, it may be—and there's Shakespeare back at the top of the tree. And there's the maternal instinct back at work, children are being born, and a lot of them are actually treasured.

A recent publication points out that what we most prize in our own children are the irresistible qualities which appeal irresistibly to the paedophile, and we send videos of our half-naked toddlers to Jeremy Beadle for his television series, *You've Been Framed*, and allow our cute kiddies to be used to advertise washing powder. But which *we* is this we? The impertinent we in 'We are all guilty'. No doubt some of us are guilty of something, but we would rather be left to acknowledge (if only to ourselves) those specific guilts that are truly ours.

That poets were excluded from Plato's ideal society has long been a scandal. (Though some poets have been tickled to think that somebody took them seriously that far back.) Plato knew the natural magic of poetry, its fascination and persuasiveness, but found it too commonly marked by a low degree of truth, even when written by Homer, and hence a fearful power to corrupt. Poetry, when it represented sex or violence, for instance, watered them when they ought to be left to wither on the stalk.

The underlying theory is set out in the history of the bed. God created the first bed, the archetypal form, the only genuine bed-in-itself. The carpenter came along and made the second bed (which at least you could lie in). Then the painter, or poet, or dramatist, took it into his head to portray the third bed—at third remove, represented from some particular angle and therefore a mere appearance, superficial, tendentious, deceptive.

This connects with what was said earlier in *The Republic* regarding the practice of education. You shouldn't tell youngsters stories misrepresenting the nature of gods and heroes, such as the castration of Uranus by his son Cronus, Hephaestus flung out of heaven by his father for coming to his mother's aid when she was getting a beating, Zeus so struck with sudden desire for Hera that he proposed to make love to her on the spot without retiring indoors, or the shameful affair of Ares and Aphrodite caught in the act ('trapped by the knowing net at just the right moment': as retold with relish by Goethe in his *Roman Elegies*) . . . Nor would it do to read gloomy accounts of the afterlife or of women abusing their husbands and blaming everything on heaven. Indeed, 'We shall have to reject the greater part of the stories current today.'

What shall we have to reject nowadays? Not poetry, apart from a naughty poetess or two and an infrequent f-word, and certainly not poetic drama. But a good deal of watering and manuring goes on in fiction. As for biography, much of that amounts to misrepresenting gods and heroes, or—inevitably—portraying a bed superficially, partially, and from some selective angle.

Of course we can tell ourselves that Plato was himself painting at who knows how many removes, postulating an ideal society (let's not say an unattainable one) in which women wouldn't abuse men, husbands wouldn't beat wives, sons didn't castrate fathers, couples didn't couple in public, and we all slept peacefully in our beds.

A conversation between an Englishman and a Punjabi Muslim:

'It is hard to say these things in a language like Malay. But this man Plato believed that all things on earth were a mere copy of a *chontoh dalam shurga*, a heavenly pattern.'

'So there is one motor-engine in the mind of God, and all others on earth try to imitate it.'

'Yes, something like that.'

'And this motor-engine of God's never breaks down?'

'Oh, no, it cannot. It is perfect.'

'I see.' Alladad Khan drove on past another rubber estate. 'But of what use is a motor-engine to God?'

'God knows.'

'That is true. God knoweth best.'

—Anthony Burgess, *Time for a Tiger*

THE JESTER whose heart is heavy with sorrow—we admire him, we are moved, we have heard of a curious link between comedy and tragedy. But the preacher of doom, downfall and universal guilt who goes home and laughs his head off over steak and a good Burgundy—that image disgusts us.

Except that we feel a grudging respect for this fellow, we have to admit. And now you come to think about it—the jokes made by that gloomy clown, were they all that marvellous?

'Your tears come easy, when you're young, and beginning the world. Your tears come easy, when you're old, and leaving it' (Gabriel Betteredge, in *The Moonstone*). So there is hope for a dry middle age?

You have a grim thought, you can't shake it off, it grows more and more plausible. You've lived too long, seen too much, to expect rational, practical intercession, or to look for some felicitous fluke. Quick, touch wood! But where the hell is the wood? It's all imitation, synthetic, anything but the plain, unmistakable, necessary thing.

Would a sheet of paper count? In Nietzsche the question is asked: Why do you write? To which the answer comes: I have so far found no other way of getting rid of my thoughts.

But it's hard to shake off the superstitious feeling that writing about something, something wretched, makes it happen. In the beginning was the word, and in the end the thing. It clips one's wings.

One way of describing this condition: a pitiable loss of control over the imagination. No wonder one used to be ticked off for imagining things. This is not Burke's 'delicate and refined play', not by a long chalk. There was nothing like regular office hours for holding the imagination in check. Short of work, what then? Get lost in a book which will keep the mind quiet, more or less innocuously engaged. (Is that all one asks of reading? It's one thing one asks of it.) Or an occasional literary party, where the imagination is fully occupied in thinking up what to say to whom and remembering what not to say. Or, better, meeting friends, the good, gossipy friends with whom the confiding of direct intimacies would amount to a solecism. Or —expensive in several respects; it isn't exactly the brain one wants to put to sleep—heavy drinking. Or, best of all, but not, it's to be hoped, too constantly available: a minor crisis—provided that present fears are truly less than horrible imaginings.

All of this, it will be objected, doesn't concern imagination, that pre-eminently virtuous faculty, creative and empathetic, but only a *diseased* imagination. (George Eliot observed that too keen a vision of ordinary tragedy would kill us off, adding that 'as it is, the quickest of us walk about well wadded with stupidity'.) Would there were some sort of red light to warn us when health is on the point of sliding into sickness, some certain way of telling whether the bear really is a bush or the bush really a bear.

To make the best use of your mind, you need something to take it off.

A man sits in his den
Frightened by the shadow of his pen—

Who has nothing else to frighten him
Or maybe something truly grim,

And the pen is mightier than the sore.
This has to be the why and wherefore.

Pen, frighten me,
Then I'll snap you across my knee.

WHEN they ate of that tree, our prime parents grew intimate with both the propriety of good and the appeal of evil; they became not 'as gods'—they were hurried away before they could pluck back immortality from the other tree—but as humans.

Brave words uttered in the course of a talk on art and entertainment: 'I have to admit to the belief that nothing has *no* effect at all. If this exposes me as a person with no backbone, no power of resistance—as, in short, a moral weakling—so be it.' What effect could those words have? Apart from exposing the speaker etc.

In her book of 1923, *The Handling of Words*, Vernon Lee (Violet Paget) gives as one of the first precepts of writing that *no adjective is ever without an effect*. Other parts of speech you may waste, 'but you cannot merely waste an adjective or qualifier: an adjective, if it does not help you, goes against you'. We usually imagine, she proceeds, that adjectives add something to nouns. (I would say that we ardently believe so as we search about for the right one, or two.) But 'what they really do is to cut off something, some of the possible meanings of a noun'. When we speak of the stormy sea or the blue sea, we are not adding to the impressions conveyed by the word *sea*, but diminishing them. 'It is probably the increasing richness of connotation of nouns, a richness due to the constant addition made by every human being's experience, which accounts for the increasing use of adjectives.' This explanation—that, consciously or not, we are shutting the doors on unwanted impressions and canalizing those we do want—is perhaps a charitable one; but I shall go back and restore some of the adjectives I expunged.

Vernon Lee insists that 'the reader's mind is the writer's palette', and 'the things which we write in our books, the reader has to read into them'. The writer makes his book not merely out of the contents of his own mind, but out of those of the reader's too. A newborn infant, she reflects, even could he by some miracle see and spell all the words and get the hang of the sentences, would still be blind and deaf to literature, 'because he was newborn, had no life behind him, nothing for literature to evoke, to rearrange, to subdue him with'.

It must be because we neglected it—readers never thought to tell us their side of the experience, or once they started to set it down they became writers—that this truth mutated into a gross, excogitated and despotic untruth. We had best take to heart the dedication of *The Handling of Words*: 'To the many writers I have read and the few readers who have read me'.

Polish your *pensées* with the lightest of hands, or else your fingers will go through them. Remember Wittgenstein: 'A mediocre writer must beware of too quickly replacing a crude, incorrect expression with a correct one. By doing so he kills his original idea, which was at least still a living seedling. Now it is withered and no longer worth *anything*. He may as well throw it on the rubbish heap. Whereas the wretched little seedling was still worth something.' Yes, the better can be the enemy of the good; though the good, as figured here, doesn't sound much of a loss.

In *Metaphysics as a Guide to Morals* Iris Murdoch says that praise for the general usefulness of art might run like this: 'Art is informative and entertaining, it condenses and clarifies the world, directing attention upon particular things . . . Art illuminates accident and contingency and the general muddle of life, the limitations of time and the discursive intellect, so as to enable us to survey complex or horrible things which would otherwise appal us.' Great art, she continues, is 'an image of virtue. Its condensed, clarified, presentation enables us to look without sin upon a sinful world. It renders innocent and transforms into truthful vision our baser energies connected with power, curiosity, envy and sex.'

Horrible things must always appal us; art can't tell lies about them. But yes, great art does enable us to look without sin upon a sinful world, a world we have to look at. Alas that there should be so many books, some of them considered works of art, which encourage us to look *with* sin upon a sinful world. And how readily we enter into complicity with their authors.

If, as a sort of writer, I have no portion in great art, as Iris Murdoch splendidly defines it, it is simply because I cannot attain to it, not because I despise it, or pretend to, or share the feeling she alludes to in passing—that 'traditional Western art is too grand and too out of touch with the awful, and also the banal, details of life' (the which, she adds, 'television can display with such exquisite technical perfection'). My sympathies are with a passage in *Middlemarch* which begins with Dorothea agonizing over art and its 'availability'. She would like to make life beautiful for everybody, and so 'all this immense expense of art, that seems somehow to lie outside life and make it no better for the world, pains me. It spoils my enjoyment of anything when I am made to think that most people are shut out from it.' Will Ladislaw breaks in: 'I call that the fanaticism of art', adding that she might as well be miserable in her own goodness, and turn evil so as to have no advantage over others. 'The best piety,' he tells her, 'is to enjoy—when you can. You are doing the most then to save the earth's character as an agreeable planet. And enjoyment radiates. It is of no use to try and take care of all the world; that is being taken care of when you feel delight—in art or in anything else.'

A certain amount of self-regard or self-protection in both attitudes, I dare say. Scholarship boys, as they used to be called, would need to hold to either Dorothea's view of the matter or Ladislaw's, or else hand back their scholarships. In most cases, I suspect, to Ladislaw's, the more practical, perhaps the less patronizing, albeit the less noble.

A few, very few commercials are good, among the best things on television, inventive, amusing, elegant, apt. Most are pretty awful, variously or in combination pompous, puerile, patronizing, smirking, on occasion absurdly irrelevant or simply incomprehensible.

Downright off-putting, for who on earth—or who with any money to spend—can they impress? Yet presumably they work, the advertisers, not all of them champions of art for art's sake, must be happy with them; they cost money, however worthless they seem.

But it's much the same with books. People feel more comfortable with books they can despise a little, can rise superior to.

It is often claimed that television adaptations of the classics send people to read them: as witness *Middlemarch*. Yet here's Kenneth Baker, a former Secretary of State for Education, saying that he had always intended to get down to reading *Clarissa*, but then the BBC came up with 'a magnificent version' of the novel, 'and so the pressure to read the book has abated'.

This televised version of *Clarissa* struck me as resembling a skilful dramatization of a newly concocted blurb for a hypothetical reissue of the book in mass-market paperback.

'If you don't like what's on the telly, turn it off!' Yes, but it's still going on, you can just about hear it, murmuring away at the back of the set, in the corner of the room. 'Then get rid of the set!' But the people next door have one, so it won't really help . . .

'There can be no sense to a teaching of literature which is not a branch of media studies.'—Colin MacCabe, in 'a justification of the study of film and television'.

That's put literature in its place. Shakespeare a sprig, Dickens a twig, Yeats a leaf . . .

The very best films bear some resemblance to second-rate novels. The poorest novels are akin to tenth-rate films, often aspiring to one of those old X certificates.

By all means let film and television become the objects of study; by no means can it be prohibited. It's not true that the experts can't tell chalk from cheese. They *prefer* to eat chalk.

Richard Hoggart (*Times Literary Supplement*, 9 July 1993) refers to 'the fashionable, the preponderant, view that no fiction, no work of art, no recreation, no judgement is intrinsically superior to any other; and anyone who says otherwise is a bourgeois élitist'. The account is accurate, apart perhaps from the word 'preponderant'. This view is not held by those who on the face of it stand to derive most satisfaction or reassurance from it; people who would *like* to enjoy Beethoven, Mahler, Shakespeare or George Eliot, as they know others do, but, through early or indeed late lack of opportunity, are unable to—people who, despite their manifest intelligence and their maturity in other spheres, are sadly convinced that they are 'not up to it'.

Preponderant? Yes, in a small, noisy clique and its uncertain hangers-on. Fashionable? Yes, for the view has all the tinsel allure of novelty, of 'the heresies of paradox'. In this case a heresy for which, far from being sent to the stake, you are likely to be promoted.

It is the exponents of this view who with more reason could be termed bourgeois élitists: bourgeois in that they tend to be relatively privileged and have had little to do with the working class, and élitist since they commonly occupy or propose to occupy elevated positions in intellectual society (including, alas, education).

Hoggart also observes that popular fiction can offer its readers good attitudes or strengthen the good attitudes they bring to it, and mentions his discovery that to read Catherine Cookson without preplanning one's reactions is 'to recognize considerable perception into moral complexities'. This is not merely the placatory declaration we feel it advisable to make after revealing ourselves as, in the terms of the said view, bourgeois élitists. It is noticeable that the champions of the 'preponderant view' are generally keener on burying art than on praising popular entertainment or recreation.

Jacques Derrida: 'I am very fond of everything that I deconstruct in my own manner; the texts I want to read from the deconstructive point of view are texts I like, with that impulse of identification which is indispensable for reading.' That's OK then. Each man kills the thing he is very fond of.

THE DEVIL has the best tunes? Metaphorically, yes—Milton's Satanic verses, etc. But literally it's requiems that have the loveliest tunes—Fauré, Berlioz, Verdi, Mozart . . . 'All of heaven we have below' (Addison, on St Cecilia's Day). Little sign of the Devil's hand here, unless—'I've waited a long time for this wrathful day!'—as collaborator in the *Dies Irae*.

All of heaven . . . The speech of angels (Carlyle); from heavenly harmony this universal frame began (Dryden); music can improve our joys below while antedating the bliss above (Pope); it was music not fire that Prometheus stole from Olympus for us (Peter Porter); music is the only sensual pleasure unattended by vice (Johnson); it shows the way to heaven's door (George Herbert); more earthily, music is to the soul what a bath is to the body (Oliver Wendell Holmes) . . .

That writers have accorded the rival art such lush tributes may have some connection with the feeling that they can afford to be big-hearted since they won't be believed. Music involves an element (albeit enviable) of cheating, at least evasion, a privileged soaring above the battlefield, whereas writers are the bloody infantry. Men aren't angels, and only in hyperbole do boys sing like them; the universal frame hasn't proved all that steady; not everyone would consider music a more precious gift than fire; sensuality without a touch of vice doesn't make sense. And when you reach it, heaven's door has been closed for some time . . . Still, you've had a glorious journey; and where there's a door, there might just be something the other side of it.

'Extraordinary how potent cheap music is.' If it's potent it can't be altogether cheap.

Why is it that the noise of a party in full flood is dispiriting, and the noise of frogs or crickets or cicadas, no less of a din, is comforting? As if the latter spelt life, the former something nearer death. Although—or because—you, you know, are not an immortal frog, an eternal cricket or cicada, singing the selfsame unending song, but, like parties, you must have an end. Truth is, a glimpse of continuity, however humble, and though you do not share in it personally, is heartening. 'The poetry of earth is never dead,' as a very sick poet told himself.

There may also be a residual respect here for *the other*, for what is *not us*. A feeling which must have grown in recent times as our *self*-respect has taken some hard knocks.

Often heard at parties: 'Nothing shocks me any more.' Who wants to be thought the kind of simpleton who can go on being shocked? But in truth everybody has something—needs something—to be shocked by. Baudelaire tells of taking a 'five-franc whore' to the Louvre, which she had never visited before. As they passed the paintings and statues, she blushed and hid her face in her hands. Tugging at his sleeve, she kept asking how such indecencies could be displayed publicly.

'Nothing shocks me any more': the sort of gesture proper to social gatherings, bold, fearful, and futile.

'But oh the parties were so beautiful . . .' The book, a biography of Stevie Smith, was behind schedule, but the authors, two Americans, had arranged to be in London for its publication, so the launch party went ahead. There were dummies of the book, dressed in jackets, poised here and there. It was something of a dummy party, largely, you might think, the product of a last-minute trawl through

Palmers Green or Parsons Green. An old lady came up as I was pulling out a pipe: 'You'll kill yourself smoking that.' (A bit disconcerting, as old ladies are practically the last remaining admirers of pipes, which remind them of their dear departed husbands. One doesn't ask what caused their husbands to depart.) I was about to say that I would kill her if I didn't smoke this, but instead asked her urbanely if she recalled the old proverb, 'Drink wine, and have the gout; drink none, and have the gout', and removed myself smartly.

I spotted in a corner of the room a furtive, doe-like young man, puffing at a half-hidden cigarette, and slipped over to this miniature ghetto. We were lamenting our criminalized condition when a rosy-cheeked clergyman glided up, one of the species who sent many a youth of my generation fleeing into the arms of Satan. 'Should I enter a public house, I would expect to see people smoking,' he declaimed plummily, 'but I did not expect to at a publisher's party!' As if pubs and publishers occupied opposed extremes of the moral spectrum. To forestall a sermon, I remarked that smokers paid a considerable sum into the national exchequer. Taken aback by this soft answer, the clergyman changed tack: 'Indeed, indeed, I know only too well how high the duty is on sacramental wine!' Making a rudimentary gesture which might be taken as a blessing, he left us.

> '... how the warmth of the parties
> Fascinates me, and the wild laughing eyes
> Of the people hold me.'

One advantage of company, not the only one but considerable . . . It's pleasanter to agree with other people and exchange harmless little lies than to quarrel with oneself and exchange large hurtful truths.

The 'poor benefit of a bewitching minute'; or, as it may be, rather bewildering too. But not poor. For when, abraded by the years, one meets a pretty woman writer or editor and briefly has the benefit of her company, she no doubt tempering the wind to the shorn ram, it seems, if only fleetingly, that there must be some good in the literary world.

Rebuke from the British Haiku Society:

A haiku that rhymes!
It's the acme of bad taste
The lowest of—er, misdemeanours.

Rejoinder:

'Verses to amuse'
Is what the word *haiku* means—
I'll rhyme if I choose.

PROUST'S narrator is obliged to wait in the Prince's library for the music to end before he joins the Guermantes' party. He is about to lose still more time in socializing instead of getting on with his writing. But at least he can take the opportunity to disembarrass himself of a few literary theories—theories to which he reacts like a well-brought-up child who hears strange adults saying 'We admit everything, we are frank', and thinks how inferior the moral quality thus signalled is to 'right conduct pure and simple, which says nothing'.

For one, the notion that the writer, spurning frivolity, should take as his theme great working-class movements or the doings of noble thinkers and patriotic heroes. ('Quality of language is something the theorists think they can do without', being another frivolity since it affords no proof of intellectual merit.) As for popular, easily accessible art: considering where true illiteracy is found, such a thing would better suit the members of the Jockey Club than those of the General Confederation of Labour. The working classes are as bored by novels of popular life as (an up-to-date thought!) children are by the books written specifically for them.

'The artist has to listen to his instinct'—the ancient daemon. We do not choose how we shall fashion a work of art; it pre-exists us, and we are obliged to discover it, not prescribe it. Indeed, 'the function and the task of a writer are those of a translator'. (Translators—that despised breed!)

'A work in which there are theories is like an object which still has its price-tag on it.' Authentic art has no use for proclamations of purpose, 'it accomplishes its work in silence'. In other words, theories are comfy substitutes for the eternal arduousness of liter-ature; perhaps pleasing to one's self-importance, but insubstantial and inconsequent: 'licensed dissipation', to use the expression Leavis was wont to apply to lectures, including his own.

Very soon Marcel will get to grips with his own arduous labours, towards the recovery of lost (but not, it turns out, wasted) time.

Compare what Proust says above with Paul de Man busily decon-structing a lyrical passage from *Swann's Way* (*In Search of Lost Time*, Vol. I, pp. 97–8), on reading in bed on a summer's afternoon with the shutters almost closed:

'The text achieves this synthesis [of inside the room and outside the house] and comments on it in normative terms, comparable to the manner in which treatises of practical rhetorics recommend the use of one figure in preference to another in a given situation: here it is the substitutive totalization by metaphor which is said to be more effective than the mere contiguity of metonymic association. As opposed to the random contingency of metonymy . . . the metaphor is linked to its proper meaning by, says Proust, the "necessary link" that leads to perfect synthesis. In the wake of this synthesis, the entire conceptual vocabulary of metaphysics enters the text: a terminology of generation, of transcendental necessity, of totality, of essence, of permanence, and of unmediated presence. The passage acts out and asserts the priority of metaphor over metonymy in terms of the categories of metaphysics and with reference to the act of reading.'

'Proust se plaît à désidentifier la nation après avoir transsexualisé le sexe': this sentence of Julia Kristeva's, written in a language that doesn't exist, is described by a reviewer as 'subversive'. Poor Proust, a sinuous and sinewy writer, elegant and lucid, who pushed his language to its limits while remaining inside it . . . As for 'subversive', that trendy term, once it had been defined, could be applied with rather more point to Proust himself.

> 'Proceed no further in your Part
> Before you learn the Terms of Art:
> For you can never be too far gone
> In all our modern Critics' Jargon.'
> —Swift, 'On Poetry'

The literary theorist is in demand because he propounds a schematization applicable to all literary works, or the literary works that feature on university syllabuses. When brought to bear on these works, the theory tends to make them all sound much alike. (Cf. 'comparative literature', a process which, if it does anything, fastens on similarities and parallels—'there is salmons in both'—at the expense of distinctions and diversities.) This homogenizing apparently doesn't matter; or, rather, its potency lies exactly there. The fashionable theorist is the opposite of the book reviewer (but keep your fingers crossed), in that the reviewer seeks to evoke the quiddity of the book under review (which won't always amount to much), to describe and to judge it as an individual entity with its own parlous right to exist. This practice is useful to librarians and of interest to lay readers, but not, it would seem, to the specialist readers associated with institutions of higher learning.

'Grey, dear friend, is all theory,/And green the golden tree of life.' But those words, we have to remember, scriptural though they may sound, were spoken by the Devil's right-hand man. Mephistopheles was keeping his hand in, amusing himself with a freshman, already discomposed by the absence of trees on the campus, whom he befuddled further. Elsewhere, however, and in his own person, Goethe—the greediest man for knowledge the world has known—declared that theories are generally the overhastiness of a mind which is impatient to get rid of phenomena and therefore replaces them with concepts, abstractions, often mere words. Life is best instructed, not by the hermetic, but by what is itself alive.

There must be thousands of people who can detail the five hundred various ways in which time is handled in fictional narrative, say, to one who can tell whether a piece of writing is good or bad and give reasons for the opinion. University teachers need their specialities, and there is nothing wrong with specialization so long as it is kept for the weekends, sabbaticals, and scholarly periodicals. Alas, it is too often inflicted on pupils. The student who worries about Milton and the 'reality' of Adam and Eve, or grumbles that Isaac Rosenberg's rats cannot be cosmopolitan because rats have no perception of nationality, is on the right road—there's always a place and a time for ordinary reasonableness—while perhaps needing help in staying on it. He or she is at least searching for *meaning*, in the way one gropes for one's spectacles. On that you can build.

The obvious fact—obvious facts shouldn't be seen as categorical prescriptions or proscriptions, but merely as obvious facts—is that those critics of the past who have talked most cogently of literature, who have most helped us in our effort to understand and our desire to appreciate, are closer to the humble reviewer than to the theorist. The charm of theory resides in its pseudo-scientific air (little arts men would love to be big science men, or even little ones), in its promise of (at last!) authoritativeness and finality, a definitive solution to the mysteries of art, a covenant whereby we are set free from the grind of practice, from having to look conscientiously at every literary work as something possibly new and different, possibly good, possibly not. Theory is a universal key, and what it won't unlock isn't worth opening. Given our present intellectual ethos, and the tendency for offbeat fancies to mutate into established dogmas, it is likely to thrive for some time yet.

Christine Brooke-Rose is . . . *nouveau* or *nouveau nouveau* (or would be were she a masculine *roman*), post- or post-post-. Also very funny, I think; 'ludic' is probably the word, but I can't find it in the dictionary. She is an able writer, she knows a lot, she bandies names about (a little too lavishly), she has, thank heavens, a shady taste for fantasy. She has read all the books that really count—more of them than have been read by the kind of person who says this sort of thing—and quite a few that don't really.

'. . . let the Meta rest': so concludes one chapter, to do with metalinguistics, metastories and metacharacters, in her *Stories, theories and things*; which doesn't discourage metanarrative, metalepsis and metafiction from springing up in succeeding chapters. It's not the end of the Meta by any means.

Concerning co-referential ambiguity and the ever-reverberating Umberto Eco, she notes a curious and possibly wounding imbalance between 'John takes his son to school twice a week, so does Bill' and 'John sleeps with his wife twice a week, so does Bill'. She doesn't want to quibble, but counters with 'Sue sleeps with her husband twice a week, so does Mary'.

She suggests that, far from 'using' psychoanalysis in literary criticism, we should consider it, at its best, as a literary text, 'as Nietzsche's texts are literary texts'. Presumably reading it the way we read the Bible, 'as Literature'. (Much the same could be said of her own writing.) 'Philosophy turns out to be an endless reflection on its own destruction at the hands of literature': this is a seemingly pleasant thought of Paul de Man's, pleasanter at least than the opposite version. Elsewhere Christine Brooke-Rose remarks, perhaps in support of the thought, 'It is as if phiction and filosophy had changed places.'

One chapter, she tells us in its closing sentences, is actually a spoof scholarly essay, intended decently enough to show that she is 'not for the kind of formal analysis that kills the text'. (That grim word 'text': once it used to mean 'Gospel'.) It reminded me of a lecture given many years back by a distinguished professor on research in English departments; he read out a list of foolishly pretentious or plainly idiotic topics, at which we all laughed; then he read out a list of recommended topics, serious and worthy, and we didn't know what to do, they were indistinguishable from the first lot.

She is learned, but can she be wholly serious? She comes out with the forthright declaration, 'I do not myself consider the told orgies of sodomy and shit-swallowing and pee-drinking in Burroughs or certain scenes of *Gravity's Rainbow* to be high literary achievements', but with names such as Kristeva, Sollers and Bataille making a blurry racket in the vicinity, one wonders quite how forthright the declaration is, even whether one has heard it aright. Probably it is, probably one has.

Of her own novel, *Between*, she observes that it was written entirely without the verb *to be*, but she skips 'the writing difficulties of this and the *hors-texte* proleptic analepsis in which after such practice the author went on doing without the verb *to be* for months, out of habit, even anonymously in the *Times Literary Supplement*'. There is, she adds, no reason why anyone except a deconstructionist should notice the lack of something, like the verb *to be*, unless it is announced in the blurb—in which case the book will surely be acclaimed as a *tour de force* or dismissed as one. There follows a reference to Georges Perec's novel, *La Disparition*, in which the letter *e* has disappeared entirely.

It might be said of Christine Brooke-Rose that she contrives to have her custard-pie, and eat it, and throw it.

'A comedy has just been written in Genoa, from which the letter R is throughout excluded...' Stendhal, reporting in the *London Magazine*, January 1826. How modern the past was. How ancient the present is.

Barthes contends, or confesses, that nothing presented in his *Empire of Signs* has anything to do with the real Japan: the latter has merely afforded 'a situation of writing'. There's honesty. At times the 'situations' afforded by reality can leave us a trifle shamefaced. (A fellow I knew used to pin photographs from Vietnam on his walls to ginger up his poems, making small songs out of other people's great sorrows.) Barthes is in the clear; he even offers a foreigner's impressions of a Japan at least recognizable to other foreigners.

Yes, those neon signs in the streets there, ideograms so much more graceful and expressive than our bleak, ungainly alphabetic assertions! And all the more so if, in Barthes's words, we are 'delivered from any fulfilled meaning'. If, for instance, we are unaware that what they express are the merits of corn-plasters or the captivations of girlie shows.

True, a Japanese food-tray is a thing of visual beauty, whereas a Western plateful would best be approached with eyes tightly closed. And Barthes is on to something when he submits that chopsticks transfer harmoniously rather than pierce and pillage; unlike the 'predatory' knife and fork, they do not 'violate' the food. (Squirming prawn please note.) Chopsticks are made for Japanese food, Japanese food is made for chopsticks, and which came first can only be a matter for speculation. (In a Kobe café I once saw an elderly Japanese lady who rejected brutal foreign cutlery and chased her fried egg doggedly with a pair of chopsticks.) Mind you, healthy children attacking a communal dish don't exactly convey the sense of 'caprice' or the 'certain indolence' that Barthes ascribes to the operation of chopsticks.

His definition of the haiku is pretty smart, and recognizable to some other foreigners at least: 'It is the flash of a photograph one takes very carefully (in the Japanese manner) but having neglected to load the camera with film.' (Is there, I wonder, an indignant Société française du haiku?) I would rather think of a Polaroid camera producing instant pictures; anyone can do it. Haiku are the poetic snapshots of the people.

Good clean semiological fun. 'To me,' Barthes declares, 'the Orient is a matter of indifference.' A situation, not geographical, but 'of writing'. Grist to the mill.

Adorno on intellectuals: the fact that they mostly have to do with other intellectuals shouldn't lead them to believe that their own kind is baser than the rest of mankind. 'For they get to know each other in the most shameful and degrading of all situations, that of competing supplicants, and are thus virtually compelled to show each other their most repulsive sides.' The intellectual is eloquent on the sterling qualities of 'the simple folk'. When he encounters them, they too are selling something—their produce, their labour—but they have no fear of the customer setting himself up in competition with them. When pitted against their own kind, these simple folk can be quite as envious and spiteful as the literati.

Moreover, 'glorification of splendid underdogs' is in the end nothing more than 'glorification of the splendid system' that makes them underdogs.

Research topic. The Chinese poet and sage, Tao Tschung Yu, is thought by some to have 'flourished' during the 18th century, but his exact dates are unknown. Allusions to and quotations from him are found in a number of relatively recent publications. The earliest traced so far is an enigmatic reference to his 'Book' in an incomprehensible poem made public in 1965, and the next an irrelevant epigraph to a book of memoirs published in 1969. Thereafter he is cited in a run of anthologies, a popular and much decried genre of the day, ranging from one on the subject of Death in 1983 (a poem including the lines 'All soul!—Now I have time to be./Age suits me best of all my ages', apparently spoken by an old man engaged in a washroom), through Sicknesses of Body and Soul, 1989 (a variation on the old question of whether a man is dreaming he is a butterfly or vice versa, in this instance both human and insect feeling unwell), and Friendship, 1991 (a meditation on the traditional association of friends with mountain walks), to the Supernatural, 1994 (a pathetic or possibly ironic piece on the distress suffered by living scholars when haunted by dead ones).

Strangest of all is a passage on 'the elusive sage', discovered in 1985 and written either by himself or by somebody else, quoting a few typically telling dicta (e.g., 'The secret of an orderly and stable regime: writers should be obscene and not heard'), but casting doubt not only on his dates, in view of an allusion in one of his aphorisms to Fu Manchu, but on his very existence. Elsewhere a text of uncertain provenance ascribes to him the saying, 'If you want my soul you must queue for it', interpreted as a cross-linguistic pun involving the Manchu imposition of pigtails and the subsequent stealing of them, considered tantamount to the stealing of men's souls. This suggests that in the crux mentioned above the anachronistic reference to Fu Manchu could be a transcription error for 'Phew! Manchu!'.

It is astounding that so few sinologists of repute have shown any interest in or even awareness of someone who is clearly a significant figure. Is there a Collected Works lost to sight in the cellars of the Palace Museum in the Forbidden City? Could there even be a biographical study of him buried for safety in the grounds of some temple? A splendid opportunity awaits the enterprising researcher.

The conjecture that Tao Tschung Yu spent some time with Oliver Goldsmith, and was actually the writer of 'Letters from a Chinese Philosopher Resident in London', is ingenious and has a certain superficial charm. Certainly Lien Chi Altangi, as Goldsmith called him, was adept in citing Confucius and Mencius, and expressed horror at the sight of fine English gentlemen wearing pigtails. It would be in Tao Tschung Yu's character to note that in China there were not too many authors for the Emperor to take cognizance of them all, whereas in England every man could be an author since by law they all had the liberty not only of saying what they pleased but of being as dull as they pleased. Likewise one might trace his hand in Lien Chi Altangi's observation that two great rhetorical figures much in fashion in England were *Bawdry* and *Pertness*, and that 'book-answerers', i.e. critics, made a hearty meal when new publications came their way, but, if this failed, 'critics eat up critics, compilers rob from compilations'.

And the story told in these letters, of Muhammad, would have appealed to Tao Tschung Yu's quaint sense of humour. When an old woman importuned the Prophet to know what she should do to gain Paradise, he told her that old women never got there. This distressed her sorely: 'What? Never get to Paradise?' 'Never,' said he, 'for they always grow young on the way there.'

But what surely discredits the identification of the one with the other is the mishap Lien Chi Altangi experienced among the young women he encountered in the streets of London, 'so free, so pressing, so hospitable, and so engaging'. One of them, who had insisted on seeing him back to his lodgings, noticed that his watch was out of order, and kindly offered to take it to be repaired by a relative of hers, who would make no charge. He never saw her or the watch again. We cannot imagine the worldly-wise Tao Tschung Yu succumbing to so blatant a trick. None the less, the theory at least deserves to be taken into account.

Another topic: poetic deaths. It is said that the mother of Li Po bore him after impregnation by the T'ai Sui (literally, Annus Mirabilis, or Ministry of Time). This connection did the poet, prime among the Eight Immortals of the Wine Cup, little good for he was eventually banished from court. He wrote in a poem, 'Drunkenly I staggered along to stalk the moon in the brook'. He died, they say, by falling out of a boat when, in his cups, he sought to grasp the reflection of the moon in the river.

Tu Fu, serious-minded friend of Li Po and celebrator of the

Intoxicated Immortals, also incurred the emperor's disfavour. (Yes, the emperor took cognizance of them all.) Though something of a drinker himself, his trouble lay in eating: having almost starved to death when cut off by a flood, he made up for it by over-eating, which killed him.

'If I say: If there are 4 apples on the table, then there are 2 + 2 on it, that only means that the 4 apples already contain the possibility of being grouped into two and two, and I needn't wait for them actually to be grouped by a concept': *Philosophical Remarks*, translated by Raymond Hargreaves and Roger White. But what endears Wittgenstein to us is this, from his foreword to the same compilation: 'I would like to say "This book is written to the glory of God", but nowadays that would be chicanery, that is, it would not be rightly understood. It means the book is written in good will, and in so far as it is not so written, but out of vanity, etc., the author would wish to see it condemned. He cannot free it of these impurities further than he himself is free of them.'

THAT justified hypochondriac and self-appointed failure, Wilhelm Nero Pilate Barbellion, while suffering from inflammation of the eyes, heard a church choir singing 'God shall wipe away all tears'. 'Hope so, I'm sure,' he remarked to himself.

In another incident from his life-enhancing saga of sickness, he was on a bus, sitting across from a woman who thrust 'a large, red udder' into the face of her fractious infant. The child continuing to bawl uncooperatively, she told it: 'Come on, there's a good boy— if you don't, I shall give it to the gentleman opposite.' This made him realize how miserably ill-nourished he must look.

The man who believed he was so enormous he couldn't pass through the door of his apartment, whose physician ordered him to be led forcibly through it, whereupon he cried out in agony that his limbs were being torn off, and died of that persuasion a few days later . . . And the reports, quite common, of people who were convinced they were made of glass and daren't sit down for fear of breaking . . . Some of these accounts are in an anthology of *Fevers and Frets*, a book which fell mysteriously ill and died young. Had I remembered it, I would have included the story told by Erich Heller, of a distinguished writer who believed that his rear was made of glass and would surely break if it came in contact with a chair. He spent the time walking in the hospital grounds, dictating his distinguished books, or lying cautiously on his stomach in bed. One day the nurse found him seated comfortably in a chair. 'I knew you would be cured!' she cried. 'Such an intelligent man . . .' Yes, he allowed, he had been cured of a slight misapprehension. 'Why did nobody ever tell me that it is unbreakable glass?'

Scenes of medical life

'Sweet little creatures,' said Mary Ann Evans,
Summoning leeches to relieve her headaches—
Provoked on this occasion by a precipitate
And, as was promptly perceived, an unreal
Feeling for a young artist, more exactly a
Picture restorer. She returned to *Das Leben Jesu*.

Sweet little hirudineans, benign vampires
Of the healing art—nothing is known of their fate
But the creatures ate a hearty breakfast.

A student in Bangkok had a slightly deformed ear, a dangling lobe (which surely a little surgery would have put right). This meant he couldn't become a schoolteacher, I was informed, because schoolteachers had to be neat and trim and like everybody else, otherwise pupils would be distracted. Being neat and trim and like everybody else was a general duty, from which peasants, politicians, policemen and plug-uglies alone were excepted. Plainly, he told me, he would have to be a scholar; it was the only course open to him. Once he invited me to accompany him to a place of interest. Could I bring my wife? I asked. He was shocked. 'Oh no, *acharn*, there are ladies there already.' So perhaps the ear was an outward sign of vice, disqualifying him for the teacher's sacred trust? I wonder what happened to him. Unfortunately I was obliged to leave the country in a hurry.

All this health. Packets of food declare the nutritional value, calories count, protein, carbohydrate, total fat (polyunsaturates, saturates), added salt and colouring, and then warn off certain categories of customer.

How did we survive in the old days? When food came naked and speechless from the counter. When we ate what our mothers were able to give us. Stodgy stuff to fill us up, sweet things to keep us happy.

By the way, how do you open these healthful packets? It's like fumbling hungrily at a girl's newfangled fastenings—getting ratty and heading for a stroke.

'Best Before End Of' whenever . . .
And better be a little earlier
With help from scissors, shears or cleaver
Before I grow the worser.

There's something to be said for hardness of hearing . . .
'This is Michelangelo' ('my grandmother', it turns out). 'There's Napoleon' ('the podium'). 'Quasimodo!' ('Austin-Rover'). 'Heroism must not be allowed to prevail' ('Terrorism . . .'). 'A smell of

210

opium in the air' ('of autumn'). 'The book became an article of masturbation' ('of mass production'). 'Prostitutes must be made environment-friendly' ('Phosphates . . .'). 'There's a lot going on in brothels' ('in Brussels'). 'The pension is rising' (alas, only 'the tension').

. . . it brightens up those dull stretches on tv and radio.

Once when I had secured a seat in the underground I scribbled down a poem which ended thus:

> Only the poet
> Peruses his poem among the adverts.
>
> Only the elderly person
> Observes the request that the seat be offered
>   to an elderly person.

Not surprisingly it didn't become a Poem on the Underground. It was the last bit that exercised me most. Those youthful passengers who hurtle past you to flop down, as if parlous health or, since they look abnormally fit, proper pride forbade them to stand . . . Manners have gone sadly downhill. Not that I remember what mine were back then. If I complain that no one ever offers me a seat, I am told that I don't look my age: a soft answer that fails to turn away the aches and pains of arthritis etc. Yet occasionally I see someone offering a seat to an elderly lady. This always cheers me immensely, even though the lady is ten years younger than I. I would have done the same had I been given the chance. I think.

And yet the other day a lollipop lady rushed to hold up the traffic while I crossed the road . . . But then, (a) I was limping slightly owing to a little temporary difficulty with uric acid crystals, (b) the children hadn't begun to come out of school, and she was getting into the swing of it, and (c) quite possibly I reminded her of her dear father who died prematurely in a traffic accident.

The surgeon—he came from a small place in Surrey called Ockham, they said—remarked on his rounds that all superfluities should be trimmed away, whereupon it became easier to understand oneself and be understood by others. I wondered whether his hobby was literary criticism. He seemed taken aback: Heavens, no! His entourage tittered obsequiously. 'The principle of economy,' one of them muttered, and then, in that dog-Latin the profession affects, something like *entia non sunt multiplicanda* . . .

When I woke up, minutes or months later, the operation was over. The last thing I could remember clearly was obliging the trainee nurse ('Mr—— is very particular,' she had warned me) by shaving my groin in a dimly lit shower-room, and forcing the bloodstained hair down the clogged plughole. I took a quick look under my smock to see what else had been trimmed away.

An hour spent under anaesthetic: the best, most complete sleep for a very long time. Maybe death is like that. Except that to appreciate it, it was necessary to wake up. Or was it? Hard to be sure.

Do It Yourself, if you possibly can. There's a machine dispensing coffee, tea, and chocolate along the corridor. If you're peckish, there's a huge institutional toaster behind the desk. 'But I don't have a spoon for my ice-cream.' (Liquid to begin with, and running everywhere.) 'Do you think this is a restaurant? Use your soup spoon.' All this is good for the morale, as long as you have some to start with. As I was leaving, I went over to thank the nurses. They were all busy elsewhere. One flashed past: 'I'm sorry we couldn't look after you better.' Oh, I thought I was looked after well enough. The National Health Service is in tatters—but some of the tatters still shine brightly. The nurses.

'I decided to stand for one hour by Tooting Broadway toilets and see how the public feel about public toilets . . . All were angry at this decision. Several people felt the toilets are part of our heritage and should be protected, not discarded': letter in *Wandsworth & Putney Guardian*.

Well said. Our social comforts drop away fast. The absence of toilets on Putney Embankment, the same paper reports, is 'causing headaches' for the Wandsworth Youth River Club. Those on my local underground station (which used to be cleaned up once a year, in preparation for Wimbledon Tennis) went long ago, on the grounds that they were being misused by winos. No sign of winos for a long time, but the toilets have been converted into staff offices— somewhere to hide when there's trouble on the line?

Let's not talk about rights. But that one of our most elemental needs should be so callously ignored . . .

In the part of town I most frequent, recourse may be had to the National Gallery, where the Gents is well appointed though ill ventilated. Decency requires that one should then spend a few moments in front of some painting in a neighbouring room—just as, if you pop into a pub to use the loo, you feel obliged, with misgivings, to buy a half pint of beer. Generally there is a young man standing in this Gents, not necessarily the same one, but similarly expressionless, motionless, abstracted, whether waiting patiently for a friend or rapt in the remembrance of great art is impossible to tell.

Either way, this puts one off one's stroke.

We laugh at the excogitations and supersubtleties of the Christian schoolmen. The Talmud is even richer in this respect. For example, the question whether a man, wearing his phylacteries, may enter a privy for the purpose of urinating. Some authorities consider it permissible, other prohibit it. One declares: it is forbidden, because the man may relieve himself otherwise (i.e. break wind) while wearing the phylacteries. Further teaching has it that these should be taken off and left, perhaps on a window-sill, at a minimum distance of four cubits from the privy. It once happened, however, that when a pious man left his phylacteries in a hole near the public road, a harlot made off with them, proclaiming: 'Look what so-and-so gave me as my hire.' Whereon the man threw himself off a roof, and died. After that mishap it was ordained that a man might enter a privy holding the phylacteries folded about in his garment.

Laughable? But the number of complications, of do's and don'ts, and the proliferation of doctrine actually strengthens a faith. The mistake of the Anglican Church lies in whittling away, in seeking to make acceptable by simplifying. Getting rid of 'dead wood' can kill the tree.

As one would expect, the sense of decorum is shared by Muslims. In his *Account of the Manners and Customs of the Modern Egyptians*, 1836, Edward William Lane stated that since jinn were believed to inhabit lavatories, the Arabs would politely ask permission of them when entering, and also utter a prayer for divine protection against evil spirits, albeit some would be careful not to mention the name of Allah in such surroundings, and say instead, 'I seek refuge with *Thee* from the devils.'

Yet there was a fearful respect rather than disrespect in the man, mentioned in an essay by Miroslav Holub, who would hear the voice of Justice when he was in the lavatory simply because else-where he felt ashamed, unworthy, to listen to that voice.

'What is there of the divine in a load of bricks? What is there of the divine in a barber's shop or a privy? Much. All.': Emerson. But one can see why Muslims in Blackburn wish to have their east-facing lavatories realigned. The city's housing committee has so far (March 1994) declined to discharge this act of respect at the public expense.

Children in Thomas Mann. Hanno, the too sensitive, music-loving son and heir of the merchant Senator Buddenbrook: who weeps over a line in a poem about a wagoner having to get up at three in the morning, who suffers from *pavor nocturnus* (the only thing the doctor knows about it is the medical name) or night fears. One day he comes across the Buddenbrook family tree among his father's papers. He sees his own name there at the very bottom, and carefully draws a beautiful double line across the page, the upper line heavier than the lower, 'just as he had been taught to embellish the page of his arithmetic book'. When his father asks what possessed him to do such a thing, Hanno stammers, 'I thought—I thought—there was nothing else coming.'

Life flows one way in our veins, death the other. We go on resolutely, obstinately, unthinkingly, we do what is expected of us. At times we are sorely tempted to stop dead, to draw a line: not for the banal fear that things will get worse, nor to ward off the weight of further losses and regrets, but simply out of an impatient impulsion, almost aesthetic, musical, towards an ending. One reached while of sound mind, as they put it.

Hanno dies of typhoid at the age of fifteen. Mann describes the course of the disease thus: 'When the fever is at its height, life calls to the patient . . . as he wanders in his distant dream', summoning him to return. If he recognizes a bond between himself and the existence, 'stirring, colourful, callous', he has left behind, he will turn back, and live. But 'if he shudders when he hears life's voice', if it makes him shake his head and continue onward, then it is clear that he will die.

Of Nepomuk, Echo as he was known in the family, Leverkühn's five-year-old nephew in *Doctor Faustus*, I had not wanted to read again. He is described as a 'fairy princeling' and, by those more austere in their language, as 'sweetly instructive, benignly condescending . . . a friendly ambassador from that other, better clime'. As he is dying of meningitis, crying in torment 'Echo will be good, Echo will be good!', the doctor admits with inadvertent irony, 'I am a simple man. This is a case for a higher authority.' Leverkühn, desolated, curses himself. During the meeting with the Devil (or during the hallucinations attendant on migraine) when he was offered twenty-four years of intense musical creativity, he was warned that love was forbidden him: the fires of hell under the cauldron would liberate his genius, issuing in deeply ambiguous, nihilistic master-pieces, but 'Thy life shall be cold, therefore thou shalt love no human being.' And he had reneged by loving Echo.

Serenus Zeitblom, Leverkühn's humanist friend, though he has sensed in Echo something of the mythical or theological, of the child that had 'come down to us', is appalled by the composer's ravings against an invisible 'hell-hound'—incidentally, on the subject of children dying, Cliff Richard intimates that he is still wonder-ing what God is doing and 'would rather blame Satan'—and by his absurd self-accusations. He is imagining preposterous things, he tells him: the child is being snatched away by 'a blind dispensation', which rends the heart but should not overthrow the reason. It is vain for Leverkühn to submit, mildly enough, 'You must know that children are tender stuff, they are receptive to poisonous influences.'

Often in Mann what you cannot accept is so blended with what you can readily believe that the whole pill goes down before you know it.

Emerson's child, his first-born, named Waldo after him: who died from scarlet fever at the age of five. 'What he looked upon is better, what he looked not upon is insignificant . . . For this boy in whose remembrance I have both slept & awaked so oft, decorated for me the morning star, & the evening cloud, how much more all the particulars of daily economy; for he had touched with his lively curiosity every trivial fact & circumstance in the household, the hard coal & the soft coal which I put into my stove; the wood of which he brought his little quota for grandmother's fire, the hammer, the pincers, & file, he was so eager to use; the microscope, the magnet, the little globe, & every trinket and instrument in the study . . . For every thing he had his own name & way of thinking, his own pronunciation & manner. And every word came mended from that tongue. A boy of early wisdom, of a grave & even majestic deportment, of a perfect gentleness . . . He gave up his little innocent breath like a bird.

'He dictated a letter to his cousin Willie on Monday night to thank him for the Magic Lantern which he had sent him, and said I wish you would tell Cousin Willie that I have so many presents that I do not need that he should send me any more unless he wishes to very much. The boy had his full swing in this world. Never I think did a child enjoy more. He had been thoroughly respected by his parents & those around him & not interfered with; and he had been the most fortunate in respect to the influences near him . . .

'Sorrow makes us all children again, destroys all differences of intellect. The wisest knows nothing. It seems as if I ought to call upon the winds to describe my boy, my fast receding boy, a child of so large & generous a nature that I cannot paint him by specialties, as I might another . . . He named the parts of the toy house he was always building by fancy names which had a good sound as "the Interspeglium" & "the Coridaga", which names he told Margaret [Fuller] "the children could not understand". If I go down to the bottom of the garden it seems as if some one had fallen into the brook . . .' (*Journals*, 30 January 1842.)

This brought to mind John Evelyn's lament for his son, also five years of age, in the *Diary* entry for 27 January 1658. The boy was a prodigy, reading English, French, and Latin perfectly at two and a half, and later forming 'a strange passion for Greek'. 'When seeing a Plautus in one's hand, he asked what book it was, & being told it was Comedy &c, and too difficult for him, he wept for sorrow.' More of our time, in Christopher Leach's *Letter to a Younger Son* (1981), a bereaved father comes on his son's school composition, written a month before, 'The Best Holiday of My Life', about a visit to London, 'a jousting-tournament at the Tower, Regent's Park Zoo, the dinosaurs at the Natural History Museum', and thrusts it to the back of a drawer. Evelyn's boy sounds too good to be true. But what right does one have to say that? And what unholy need?

Of God's warning, 'But of the tree of knowledge of good and evil thou shalt not eat', Kierkegaard observed (*The Concept of Dread*) that Adam clearly couldn't understand what was being said since the distinction between good and evil was consequent on the eating of the fruit. (He would however know the words 'tree' and 'eat', and more doubtfully 'not'.) Nor would he comprehend the warning sentence that followed: 'for in the day that thou eatest thereof thou shalt surely die', since he had no idea of what dying meant. 'But assuming that these words were spoken to him, nothing prevented him from sensing the terrible in them.' Even a beast, as Kierkegaard noted, can interpret the expression in a speaker's voice and his movements. Though it seems risky to ascribe body language to the Lord God.

Innocent or ignorant, the child, one might venture, is in Adam's position. He guesses, he half-knows, under the impression of knowing he makes up or extrapolates, one fancy leading to another, in a form of 'negative capability' *à la* Keats, or 'having no identity'. Children make leaps, which sometimes delight grown-ups, sometimes alarm them. At most you might nudge them into a more useful or more interesting direction. Children who are afraid—that is, made afraid—of 'going too far' in their speculations and deductions will never go very far.

IN AGE your chickens come home to roost, and now they wear spurs. '*My* chickens?' You try to shoo them away. But don't get too involved. Age means being either garrulous or sullen. Hard to find that happy mean: happy without being mean.

The art of living is the most distinguished and rarest of all the arts, said Jung. And 'who ever succeeded in draining the whole cup with grace?'

Death is our common lot. One friend departs, others remain. 'Common is the commonplace,' Tennyson groused when they tried to comfort him in these terms, 'And vacant chaff well meant for grain.' But sometimes comforting is the commonplace.

The nicest commonplace is a sentiment to which practically every breast returns an echo, if a shade reluctantly: one it may be that was often thought but never quite so respectably worded, so that he who meets it persuades himself he has always felt it and probably coined the expression long ago.

It happens in old age that writers shiver at the prospect of yet another long haul. 'We grow tired of seeing our experience choked by the vegetation in our sentences,' V. S. Pritchett says, and 'the moment of the aphorism, the epigram, the clinching quotation has come.'

Mark Twain observed that Adam was on to a good thing—all his utterances (probably quite short ones, outside Milton) were original. Though you could add that even so he possessed the common touch.

In the opinion of the *Jerusalem Post*'s reviewer, gentiles were inexplicably over-represented in *The Oxford Book of Death*: 'The goyim die too, of course, though not nearly as often as Jews.' A Jewish joke? A grim reminder? A reviewer's happy *trouvaille*? Hardly a commonplace, but worth copying into one's book.

One mistake: to suppose you are so different from other people; another: to suppose other people are just like you. Common v. uncommon: lifeblood of many a commonplace.

It seems unlikely for some time to come that our poetry will be one of grand gesture and sonorous voice—like Yeats's, or even Eliot's, grand in its vision of deficiency and disgrace. Nor will it be famously 'obscure'. (By what yardstick of simplicity was modern poetry judged uniformly obscure? By one derived from Shakespeare, Milton, Wordsworth? Randall Jarrell, intelligent reader and writer, misconceived when invited to talk on The Obscurity of the Modern Poet; he was delighted, 'for I have suffered from this obscurity all my life'.) More probably it will be modest, joky, superficial (i.e. concerned with the surface of things: a legitimate subject, God knows), marked by doubts and hesitations yet hinting at small but specific hopes, and above all chastened. Which isn't to be put down to 'gentility' (any fool can avoid that), or nervelessness, or parochiality, but rather to—an elementary form of decency—having one's eyes open. It will take us a while yet to recover from ourselves.

Or, if we see nothing particular to recover from, or we manage to recover fairly expeditiously (and true, we forgive ourselves because we must and not because we will), alternatively . . .

The 'word' is too much with us: another common misprint. O brave new word, that has such purport in it! Typesetters and writers are at one in this. The word's their oyster. All's right with the word. Best of all possible words. Orpheus in the Underword. There is a word elsewhere. God so loved the word. Word without end. Amen.

It can happen that in a writer's age poetry grows dry while prose becomes more liquid. As if poetry was concerned (or thought it was) with immortality, whereas prose, running on from line to line, page to page, has to do (or fancies it does) with prolonging this present life—now the more urgent issue.

Those obituaries: '. . . having shown great fortitude', or 'bravely and with . . .' You don't much care for that sort of talk, you know what it means. All you can do is make feeble jokes.

Fortitude—that's nothing! What about sixtytude, seventytude, eightytude?

Like Odette, Proust's cocotte, now Mme Swann, striving to keep her end up in society, declaring that the burning of the Gioconda would distress her infinitely more than the death by fire of the '*foultitudes*' (*foule*, crowd: a nervous, ingratiating joke) of people she knew. (Hitherto the word was translated as 'millions'; trying to keep the pun, the revised version changes it to 'fulltitudes'.) One has come to sympathize with the anxieties of others and their wretched ramshackle defences.

In Bosnia and Rwanda, on television, reminders of last things. On the streets, in Southfields, reminders of penultimate things: the old laboriously pushing the old in wheelchairs. Did those erstwhile Last Things blot out the penultimate? Did thoughts of heaven, even of hell, palliate earthly pains? Now we have drugs to do that. Which the old need to forswear if they are to go on pushing wheelchairs for a while yet.

Memento mori. A lot of old people live around here. They walk their dogs (often long in the tooth too) or vice versa. Whenever you see a dog alone, you think, Oh God, the poor old boy/girl must have had a heart attack . . . The other evening I passed a little spotty ter-rier of my acquaintance, scurrying along the street, with an agitated air. I hastened round the corner—to find the old man in question resting on a bench. (Presented by a grieving widow in memory of her husband, 'an inspiration and help to all who knew him'; so far it has escaped the attention of vandals.) 'The dog's wanting his supper,' the old man sighed. 'I just can't keep up with him.'

'Rage, rage, against the dying of the light': rather impertinent ad-vice, as if to say, 'Now, father, I want you to pull yourself together and stump around the bed, even if it kills you.' And refusing to mourn the death, by fire, of a child in London, even though some pest has been nagging at you to do so, seems a trifle self-important; while 'After the first death, there is no other' is one of those pious sentiments uttered by jaded clergymen over the coffin of someone they never knew.

What most commonly prepares one not too uncheerfully for removal from the scene are trivialities earnestly pursued, vulgarities that crop up again and again in slightly different guises, when one thought they had been conclusively discredited—the sense of *déjà vu*, *lu*, *entendu*, *connu*, the more it changes the less it alters, and so forth. This tires the spirit, enabling it to keep up conveniently with the tiring flesh. A small mercy? Maybe quite a large one.

Bernard Levin writes: 'I have spent most of my life facing evil, or reading about it, or trying to do something about it, and I am sick of it.' Why, he asks, does he spend more and more of his time with music? Why does he write less and less about the news? 'Because the things *sub specie aeternitatis* are not only the most interesting things, but they are the ones that bring meaning into our lives, or at least mine.' Brave words! To stand by them you need to be young, self-confident and convinced of the value of your activities, or else old and worn and fully occupied with your lack of activities.

I used to think—partly from observing my mother—that Mrs Moore in *A Passage to India* was a pretty accurate account of the apathy or impatience of age, nature's more or less humane way of detaching us from life and its problems. (Though not necessarily diverting us into those eternal things.) 'She had come to that state where the horror of the universe and its smallness are both visible at the same time—the twilight of the double vision in which so many elderly people are involved.' All that wearying commotion over the cave and whether or not something happened there to

Adela Quested! 'Why is everything still my duty? When shall I be free from your fuss? . . . Am I to be bothered for ever?'

But no, it's not the mere stupidities. It's the truly dreadful things that are done. ('If it pleases you to hear the news of the world, you must always suffer disquiet of heart as a result': Thomas à Kempis, anticipating Bernard Levin.) For all that is said about the sourness of old age, the malevolence, you would like the world to be a better place to leave, to leave with some sort of blessing. So, if it seems to be getting worse, you won't want to loiter.

Not quite to the bed's feet has life shrunk. More to the desk-top. And the rest of it? Does all that past living now seem an expense of spirit, a shamefaced waste, so many lost causes? If not outright failures, then undeniable unsuccesses? Perhaps at every stage of life it's necessary to believe that your then existence is *valid* (as British Rail says of its tickets), is right *for you*. Which will seem to rule out earlier stages. Rather as a magnetic tape wipes out what went before as it goes along. Hard to age without rejecting the past. (Except in as far as it fuels the desk-top.) Ah well, there's a lot you have for-gotten, or simply can't imagine—which doesn't mean it's not active in you, in your spiritual veins, invisible. So just forget what you can't remember—and change the subject.

There was a line, wasn't there, in an old poem about an elderly Chinese gentleman? 'He is content with his age, which has always suited him.'

—'To the bed's-foot life is shrunk' . . .
—True, in age life is somewhat constricted, seems to be happening at a distance. But one doesn't mind all that much, does one?
—No, but actually I was thinking of the cat, who habitually sleeps at the foot of the bed.
—Habit, that's another feature of age. Not too unwelcome, though once it was a grim word . . .

—And nothing moves one very much any more. To be honest, can't say I feel acutely for anyone or anything. Just don't care, or only—
—Only for a cat? That's sentimentality—
—Oh no, sentimentality comes earlier in life, when one can afford it, or enjoy it. Age is tougher, more—what's the word?—realistic.
—Yes, you're right, not sentimental. It's plain bad. Sad. Shocking. And cats are notoriously ungrateful creatures.
—But who wants gratitude? Gives me the shivers. Makes me wonder what more I'll have to do to deserve it. Now a cat, when you feed it or pet it, is grateful for a few seconds, exactly in proportion to benefits received, no strings, no balance of expectation carried forward.
—You talk like an accountant! No, like a miser turning over your feelings as if they were pennies and ha'pennies. What a miserable wretch you are!
—That's what I get for trying to be honest . . . I can't help my feelings, or lack of them. With so many feelings around, there's no room for one's own, they get suffocated at birth. Maybe it simply means I'm ripe—
—Ripe, overripe I'd say, for the big sleep . . .
—Fair enough. Except who'd look after the cat?

Zbigniew Herbert, in 'Mr Cogito and a Poet of a Certain Age': 'a poet at an unclear time of life/between departing Eros/and Thanatos who has not yet risen from his stone . . .' Goethe is reported to have said, apropos of the ending of *Faust*, that in old age we become mystics. 'Thou thy wordy task hast done', as I read somewhere. Fair enough, whether mystic or not: 'Warte nur, balde/Ruhest du auch.' Just hang on, soon you'll be at rest too.

True, one can go on working for hours on end . . . But as soon as one stops, the awful weariness that sets in! A sinister codicil to the theme, 'the night cometh . . .', occurs in a poem of Marin Sorescu's:

'When I want to take a rest
I am ill.
Just imagine how ill
I shall be when
Dead.'

Was Ovid's story true? Shall we go on gazing narcissistically at ourselves in the waters of the Styx, in whatever pools and puddles are found in the next world? Shall we preen our feathers, quietly admire our harp-playing, our celestial singing? Shall we continue, even there, to be not as others are, albeit all are equally blessed? Alternatively, in the other place, shall we observe how beautifully we burn, how lovely our limbs shine through blocks of ice, how sonorous our shrieks? Are we still unlike others, although all are equally damned?

If not, then oblivion seems the better fate.

In *The Impressions of Theophrastus Such*, and regarding our dreams of old England, George Eliot observed that nostalgia, however unreal, shouldn't be too readily dismissed, for even perceived illusions 'feed the ideal Better' and strengthen the precious habit of loving something invisible and intangible which is yet 'a spiritual product of our visible tangible selves'.

So our conceptions of heaven ought to tell us a lot about our visible selves. And Neville Randall's *Life After Death*, a book frequently reprinted since its first publication in 1975, does that. Here the word is 'experiences' rather than mere 'conceptions', since what we have is a compilation of reports from 'those who have passed on' as communicated to a medium.

It appears that incompatibility remains a grounds for divorce in heaven; Amy Johnson and Jim Mollison, the two famous aviators, were divorced on earth and remain so in heaven: they meet from time to time, Amy says, but 'we're not together'. Conversely, those whom cruel circumstance kept apart on earth now find themselves united. As we have already been informed, there is no giving or taking in marriage; and no children are born. (Thus averting a theological crisis.) However, the loquacious Rose, erstwhile a cockney flower-seller outside Charing Cross Station, has acquired a gentleman friend, 'a bit highly placed', who brings her presents and calls her 'Ma'.

There are resident architects who will design whatever kind of dwelling you desire, and builders who will build it for you, all free of charge: they do the work because they love doing it. (A higher form of market forces. What occupation a former trade unionist can take up is not mentioned.) Travel too is free, and instantaneous, though there is no indication of where you might travel to. Sleep is unnecessary, but if you like sleeping you can sleep; and you can choose whatever style of clothing you prefer. There is no dirt or dust about. Animals are all tame, and don't kill one another; nor are they slaughtered: one's desire for food fades away soon after admittance. Racial prejudices persist, but only for a while. Not surprisingly, religion doesn't play much part in heaven, as even Cosmo Lang, once Archbishop of Canterbury, Dean Inge of St Paul's and Mahatma Gandhi admit: it entails so many superfluous complications and restrictions.

Naturally there are museums in heaven, art galleries, libraries and schools, and also cinemas (many of the films shown 'have a sort of moral, I suppose you'd call it,' says Rose), and concerts of beautiful music ('not highbrow, but nice, you know', none of that 'jazzy muck'). Shakespeare is still writing—'There is no doubt about it,' Lionel Barrymore assures us, 'he wrote his own plays' —and so is someone perhaps wrongly transcribed by the medium as 'Spencer'.

Rose is happy, Mr Randall comments, but what constitutes heaven in the eyes of an illiterate flower-seller won't do for an actor, a writer or a politician. Unlike Rose, however, 'the educated spirits are sadly short on detail', still too preoccupied with earthly problems to convey much information about their present life. Rupert Brooke manifests himself, favouring an approximation to ancient Greek costume, and launches into a monologue on the difficulties he faces in writing poetry in modern English, which the medium can't be bothered to take down. A 'rich and fruity' voice signals the arrival of Oscar Wilde who, in view of his notoriety, initially passes himself off as Colonel Bogey. He attempts to be witty: complaining that he's not receiving any royalties, and naughty: he lives 'a life of delicious sin', except that in heaven it isn't sinful to be human and natural. But his heart isn't in it. He confides that he has a very beautiful house, and a garden, not too large since 'I was never one for outdoor life'. (Hadn't he earlier said that his favourite outdoor occupation was sitting on the pavement outside a French café?) And in signing off he explains that if he has seemed 'a little acid' in his remarks, it is purely because otherwise people would never believe he was he.

While there is no hell, heaven does provide lower spheres for undeveloped souls. The Wittgensteinian escape clause crops up when Ellen Terry asserts that the higher spheres, abode of the most advanced, simply can't be described, and Holman Hunt agrees: 'You cannot depict something for which there is no language.' Every heavenologist will have to call on some such argument. Indeed— and perhaps this is the chief thing we have learnt about ourselves here—we all need loopholes.

Not all night visitors are succubi, to be feared or deplored. Think of those charming, delicate women, quietly reclining there, seeming to understand you so intimately. At once tender and intelligent, they almost make you feel young again. There is a sad air about them, they have suffered mysteriously. From what? Perhaps from ruder dreamers.

Or, in Roy Fuller's words, comparing first and last loves,

> 'In old age come again
> Those fleeting amours; but now
> Neither time nor flesh allow
> A future of lasting pain.'

A cantankerous thought of some old fellow, best omitted from his published books. 'It' he calls it:

People can't 'handle it', whatever it is. Every calamity, every complaint, has its support group or society or association. Did we 'handle it' in my day? Can't remember. Suppose we must have, or else failed to. Were there any support groups? (There were families.) There wasn't any television . . .

> Watch television
> And all your anxieties
> Will intensify.

So there wasn't much talk . . .

> The more they talk about it
> The worse it gets
> The worse it gets
> The more they talk about it.

Perhaps God was a little more visible then; but not much. Crime a little less. Sickness and death were around. (Especially in families.) Don't remember much fuss about rights. (More interest in dodging wrongs.) We didn't expect so much, we weren't given so much, so there wasn't so much to handle. Guess we were lucky.

To which comes the response, whether from himself in calmer mood or a well-wisher is not indicated:

Do shut up. No use talking about your day, how it was or wasn't, whatever it was. But then, can you handle silence?

'Cleanliness is next to godliness': a popular saying when I was a child, though in fact we had no bath and godliness was in rather short supply. The old fellow comes up with an unseemly reflection:

When I was growing up I gathered it was proper to wash one's hands. Before or after? I wasn't sure, so I washed before and after. In the middle years I knew, I had worked it out. Late in life I grow uncertain again. I can't really be bothered. My hands are wearing out, spotted with brown, swollen with blue. But some anxiety persists. So I turn on the tap and let the water run briefly while I zip up.

The musings of the old can lack dignity, even decency. In addition of course to relevance. Funny, though, what you can't get away with, when you think of what others more enormously do. (One is supposed to be wise?) You can indeed shut up—if you don't mind silence being confused with senility.

> Pills mess up the morning after
> So let's count sheep instead—
> Floundering over fences
> So sluggish you could gather wool.
> Now they're speeding up, now
> They show conviction! But
> These are not sheep, they're wolves.

Thanks to Solzenitsyn—so Milan Kundera says—the concept of human rights reached its greatest glory in the second half of the 1970s. Now there is hardly a politician who doesn't mention ten times a day 'the fight for human rights' or 'violations of human rights'.

Since by and large people in the West don't face prison camps and are tolerably free to say or write what they like, the more the fight for human rights gains in popularity, the more it loses in real content, evolving into 'a kind of universal stance of everyone towards everything.'

'The world has become man's right and everything in it has become a right: the desire for love the right to love, the desire for rest the right to rest . . . the desire to exceed the speed limit the right to exceed the speed limit, the desire for happiness the right to happiness, the desire to publish a book the right to publish a book, the desire to shout in the street in the middle of the night the right to shout in the street.'

That's the way the world has gone. Whenever I hear the word 'rights', I reach for my Browning. 'I found a thing to do . . .' The man had a perfect right to strangle Porphyria. Just as Porphyria—'No pain felt she; I am quite sure she felt no pain'—had a perfect right not to feel any pain. And God of course had a right not to say a word, the right to remain silent.

The best sentence Norman Mailer ever wrote: 'There was probably no impotence in all the world like knowing you were right and the wave of the world was wrong, and yet the wave came on' (*The Armies of the Night*). Aporia hasn't yet carried the day. All you can do is go on being right and impotent. And, to help yourself along, remember Henry James writing to his brother William after the fearful flop of his play, *Guy Domville*: 'You can't make a sow's ear out of a silk purse.'

Things you can only half-remember—things you are only half-proud of. Which don't include monstrosities, delectations, extravagances and consummations devoutly to be deprecated.

'It is all very strange. We see love everywhere, in books, on the stage, in other people's lives. Everybody talks about it all the time. It is something which seems to be extremely important and extremely absorbing. Yet here we are, both of us perfectly healthy, fit for service in affairs of the heart, rich enough to wear clean socks and buy a bouquet of flowers, and with our noses more or less in the middle of our faces—and hanged if we can remember ever having been in love for more than a week at a time.' (*Pages from the Goncourt Journal*, translated by Robert Baldick.)

—But why do you never write about love?
—That's what a stern young woman once asked after a reading.
—I'm asking now.
—Well, so many other people have, and there's no law I know of that obliges one to. I leave it to the experts. 'Not all things at once . . .'
—You're being flippant, your besetting sin . . .
—'does the Highest require' . . . flippant, just as I was quoting Hölderlin?
—Oh, quoting, you're good at that . . .
—'One word is too often profaned . . .'
—For you ever to use it?
—From a poem entitled 'To——dash'. Lots of Shelley's poems are addressed to Dash.
—He had a big heart.
—Very well. Let's see. In the beginning love was imperative for the propagation of the species, and for the care and nurture of the consequent young—which used to mean that the father too hung around for a while. As life grew easier, they invented fire, cudgels, and compound sentences, and this 'love', created so powerful in us, proliferated and diversified . . .
—I see you coming with your heavy sabots. But I was hoping we wouldn't have to go back so far.
—Apropos of which, the Japanese have two words where we have only one. *Ai*, love of a mother for her child, a brother for a sister, a child for a parent, and *koi*, love between a man and a woman, or, to put a finer point on it, sexual love. That's a good start.
—A good start? But we have lots of words! Tenderness, affection, friendship, admiration, gratitude, loyalty . . .
—Don't forget lust . . .
—All of them signifying different but overlapping states of mind, or heart . . . or body.
—Ah, you're beginning to answer the question you kicked off with!
—And all you've done so far is haul in an oriental red herring. What a slippery customer you are! Will you never speak in your own voice?
—Only if it's strictly necessary.

—If everyone followed that principle there wouldn't be much writing around.

—The generalities are easy, they trip off the tongue. 'God so loved the world' . . . but we aren't God. 'We must love one another or die' . . . then we shall die. 'Love casts out fear' . . . but it throws in terror . . .

—I can see the terror!

—And 'What will survive of us is love' . . . yet it seems likelier that what will survive is hate, or the consequences of it . . . Oh, pardon me for quoting! Pardon me for breathing.

—Do continue to breathe.

—And as you'd expect, Larkin hedged that remark about. He was talking of stone effigies, which do tend to survive, and our 'almost-instinct' being 'almost true'.

—At least he said something. And as you'd expect, said it very well.

—But the particularities, the niceties and nastinesses, you won't get them into a line or two of verse, however well said. You won't get them into huge tomes. As Voltaire observed, 'Love has various lodgings.'

—Including a 'mansion in the place of excrement' . . . I can quote too. But I give up. It's plain I'm not going to get anything out of you.

—Come to think of it, I fancy I have written about love, a bit, somewhere. But yes, there must be something wrong with me . . .

—For that admission I'll stand you a drink. Let's go. A pub's the place to talk smut.

—I can only quote other people's, I'm afraid. But I'd *love* a drink.

Through the window

Old nests in winter
Suddenly reveal themselves
In leafless branches—

In old age likewise
Abandoned relationships
And nesting places.

Peter Duval-Smith, variously a BBC producer, a teacher in Cairo and Hong Kong, and a journalist, was said, seemingly with some reason, to be a difficult customer. We found him amenable, not to say amiable. In a den one does as the denizens do, yet it was perhaps a little extreme in him to strip down to his underpants in a Bangkok opium house and swill himself in a barrel of murky water; but he wasn't one for half measures.

Later, passing through Singapore, he gave me his review copy of Naipaul's *An Area of Darkness*—I was to review the book but it had gone astray in the post—with the sage advice: 'When it's a long book, do a long review. You're paid for the words you write, not the words you read.' (In my experience, often for the words they eventually print, not necessarily the same thing.)

He went on to Saigon, where he was found dead in a hotel room. 'The beds i' th' East are soft', but the hotel bedrooms can be fatal for Westerners.

And now Anthony Burgess is dead. A man I much admired—and begrudged in the way one resents those whose temperament is in some respect akin to one's own, but who make much richer use of it. As one envies (up to a point) those who are less cautious than one is, more prepared (and unremittingly) to face violence, more prepared to be violent. And in Burgess's case readier to embrace what looks like a prefiguration of hell.

'So far as we are human, what we do must be either evil or good; so far as we do evil or good, we are human; and it is better, in a paradoxical way, to do evil than to do nothing: at least, we exist.' A pretty dreadful proposition; or else a rash act of theological coat-trailing on Eliot's part. But what he says of Baudelaire—'He could not escape suffering and could not transcend it, so he *attracted* pain to himself'—might be said of Burgess, I think.

Quite a number of King Charles's heads in evidence, I fear. But as the father of the phrase said, 'It's a mad world, mad as Bedlam!' He was persuaded that when Charles the First's head was cut off, somehow or other—Mr Dick could never get it perfectly clear—some of the trouble in it was removed into *his* head. This, Miss Trotwood perceived, was an allegorical way of accounting for disturbance and agitation. Perfectly understandable. We do suffer from what's in other people's heads but won't stay there.

It is indeed difficult not to write satire. But a word of warning comes from Trollope: 'The satirist who writes nothing but satire should write but little—or it will seem that his satire springs rather from his own caustic nature than from the sins of the world in which he lives.'

All very well, these fulminations. And maybe very well founded. But *facile est saturam scribere*, and no doubt one ought to remember Cicero's address to the people after his return from exile: 'There is less labour involved in rising superior to the wicked than in attaining to the level of the good.'

'It seems to have something for everybody, but ends up appealing to nobody.' As much could be said of many a commonplace book or assemblage of *obiter dicta*. Actually the judgement occurs in Eco's *Misreadings*, in a reader's report on a manuscript, submitted for publication, entitled *The Bible*.

Undeniably a hotchpotch. Which word in its more formal usage means the collecting and blending of properties with a view to redistributing them in equal shares.

A great leap in the dark (Hobbes). Or a stumble. Or drift. In John Earle's character of a good old man: 'The next door of death sads him not, but he expects it calmly as his turn in nature; and fears more his recoiling back to childishness than dust.'

Inscription on Winifred Holtby's gravestone, a perfect programme:

> 'God give me work
>   Till my life shall end
> And life
>   Till my work is done.'

The neuroses that beset writers—not that they have a monopoly of them, in fact you would think they were well placed to avoid the worst—seem to increase with age. I don't want to finish this book, I want it to last me till I'm on the point of death. At the same time, I don't want to leave this book unfinished. So what pace shall I set? Shall I dole out a couple of hours a day to it? Then let me know the number of my days. (Perhaps not.) Or shall I work flat out on it? *Flat out*—I don't like the sound of that, either.

Epigraph to Ovid's *Amores*:

> 'I am the author's book. Much fatter
> I was at first. He made me slighter.
> Scant joy you may get from my chatter,
> But think how your labours are lighter.'

Acknowledgements

Grateful acknowledgements are made to a number of writers, living or dead, and to the following authors and publishers for permission to quote from copyright material: Anvil Press Poetry for Vasko Popa's 'He', *Vasko Popa: Complete Poems 1953–1987*, translated by Anne Pennington and Francis R. Jones (1995); Bloodaxe Books for Piotr Sommer's 'A song', *Things to Translate* (1991), and Marin Sorescu's 'When I want to take a rest', translated by Joana Russell-Gebbett and D. J. Enright, *The Biggest Egg in the World* (1987); Jonathan Cape for Umberto Eco's *Misreadings*, translated by William Weaver (1993); Carcanet Press for Clarice Lispector's *Discovering the World*, translated by Giovanni Pontiero (1992), Octavio Paz's *On Poets and Others*, translated by Michael Schmidt (1987), and C. H. Sisson's *On the Look-Out: A Partial Autobiography* (1989); Faber & Faber for lines from W. H. Auden's 'Marginalia', 1965–8, *Collected Poems* (1976); Oxford University Press for *Pages from the Goncourt Journal*, translated by Robert Baldick (1962), and *The Pillow Book of Sei Shōnagon*, translated by Ivan Morris (1967); Penguin Books for *Georg Christoph Lichtenberg: Aphorisms* (1990), *Friedrich Nietzsche: Human, All Too Human* (1986), and *Arthur Schopenhauer: Essays and Aphorisms* (1970), all translated by R. J. Hollingdale; Sheil Land Associates for Anthony Burgess's *Time for a Tiger* (Heinemann, 1956); Sinclair-Stevenson for Roy Fuller's 'First and Last Loves', *Last Poems* (1993). Also to Michael Frayn for *Constructions* (Wildwood House, 1974); Christopher Reid for 'By the By', *Universes* (Ondt & Gracehoper, 1994); and Anthony Thwaite for 'At the International Poetry Festival', *The Dust of the World* (Sinclair-Stevenson, 1994). And to Jacqueline Simms at Oxford University Press for aid and advice at various stages.